Gregor Paul is the *New Zealand*  columnist and is a regular contri the world. He has won multiple journalism awards for news, features and opinion writing, and is a sought-after guest on radio and television.

Gregor was born and raised in Scotland, and has lived in Auckland with his wife and three children since 2003.

Also by Gregor Paul

Steve Hansen: The Legacy
The Captain's Run: What it Takes to Lead the All Blacks

BLACK GOLD

GREGOR PAUL

HarperCollins*Publishers*

HarperCollins*Publishers*
Australia • Brazil • Canada • France • Germany • Holland • India
Italy • Japan • Mexico • New Zealand • Poland • Spain • Sweden
Switzerland • United Kingdom • United States of America

First published in 2023
by HarperCollins*Publishers* (New Zealand) Limited
Unit D1, 63 Apollo Drive, Rosedale, Auckland 0632, New Zealand
harpercollins.co.nz

A catalogue record for this book is available from the National Library of New Zealand

ISBN 978 1 7755 4218 6 (pbk)
ISBN 978 1 7754 9249 8 (ebook)

Cover design by HarperCollins Design Studio
Cover image by shutterstock.com
Typeset in Sabon LT Std by Kirby Jones
Printed and bound by CPI Group (UK) Ltd, Croydon, CR0 4YY

Contents

INTRODUCTION

BACK IN 1995, RUGBY was in the unsustainable position of making hundreds of millions of dollars each year, but with most administrators around the world adamant that the game couldn't declare itself professional and share any of its wealth with the players. It was patently farcical that the committeemen could politick their way to positions of power, influence and perks and yet the players were taking weeks away from paid employment to bash themselves senseless, all for the love of the game. Obviously, something had to change and it finally did in late 1995 when, left with the choice of staying amateur and seeing a rebel, professional league take control of the sport, rugby's global governing body somewhat pompously declared the game 'open'.

This was the world the players had longed for – one where they were finally able to give up their day jobs and be legally paid to play rugby. They were convinced it was going to be a brave new world of untold riches and opportunity. That indeed has proven to be the case, and now the best-paid players earn salaries that are in line with those paid to chief executives of major corporations, and many can retire knowing they will never have to work again.

But the arrival of professionalism has also brought unimaginable new demands, new pressures and new obligations, as those in charge of running the game have had to generate hundreds of millions of dollars to pay for everything.

Many of the challenges brought by professionalism have been universal, but each of the major rugby nations has faced specific issues in their respective battles to generate the sort of wealth required to sustain successful national teams.

New Zealand's journey into professionalism has been the most interesting of all, as this relatively tiny island in the far reaches of the South Pacific, with not quite five million people and an economy dominated by primary industry, is also in possession of the All Blacks, rugby's most marketable and revered asset.

Having covered rugby since 2004, I have seen what I would call an incremental creep of commercial interests into the high-performance realm. It was impossible not to notice how, over time, there appeared to be increasing commercial demands being made of the players. When an end-of-season tour finished in Europe, the players stayed on for a few extra days, visiting sponsors. When they returned home, there was a two-week window in January when they had to be available to make TV adverts and other promotional collateral. On the day before a Test match, they would be off to a bank branch or a retail store or an insurance company's offices to meet and greet and to say kind things about the corporations helping fund their salaries.

Incrementally, too, it was apparent that there were more staff hanging around the team – people were being employed to manage specific sponsorship relationships. There were even times, albeit rarely, when sponsors controlled the media access to the team. No occasion was more overtly corporate than the unveiling of a new All Blacks jersey every few years: at glitzy venues, impossibly young Adidas staff with headsets and iPads would get more than a little sniffy if anyone from the fourth estate spent more than their five allocated minutes interviewing a player.

Where the All Blacks were playing in the world also changed. Once the giant US insurance group AIG became the front-of-jersey sponsor in 2012, the All Blacks were suddenly playing in the United States and Japan every other year. And when they trained, AIG staff would often be watching on, as would clients from All Blacks Tours, the package operator in which New Zealand Rugby (NZR) had bought a stake. At press conferences, the backdrops that displayed the names and logos of All Blacks sponsors carried a greater number of brands from a greater number of different countries. There was no doubting – because there were so many constant reminders – that the All Blacks were a sports brand rather than a rugby team.

Opening the door to professionalism inevitably meant that sponsors, broadcasters, journalists and other stakeholders would want more direct access to the All Blacks, the better to leverage their respective investments, but by 2013 the question that increasingly came up in my interactions with the team's management was: How much is too much? How long would it be before all this commercialisation became damaging to the All Blacks' performance?

It was a question asked with a full understanding of the sport's economics in mind. New Zealand Rugby (NZR) needed to raise money to keep players in New Zealand – many of whom were in global demand. Players were regularly being offered double, if not triple, their current packages to head offshore. Lose the best talent and the All Blacks would be in trouble. If the gloss came off their legacy – if they started to lose more than they won – the sponsorships would dry up, the broadcast deals would shrink and the whole of the New Zealand rugby ecosystem would suffer. It is estimated that as much as 70 per cent of NZR's broadcast income is attributed to All Blacks Tests, almost 90 per cent of sponsorship income is related to the national team and almost all of its match-day income comes from selling Test match tickets. Even in this context, the question remained valid: were the All Blacks being overly commercialised, to the detriment of their ability to perform?

What crystalised this debate was NZR's decision in early 2021 to sell a stake in its commercial assets for $465 million (the currency amounts referenced in this book will be in New Zealand dollars unless otherwise stated) to US private-equity investment firm Silver Lake, which valued the All Blacks at $3.1 billion. It was a plan that effectively put the national union at war with its professional players, who objected to the proposal. It was a landmark moment in the commercialisation of the All Blacks, and sparked my journalistic desire to properly explore the relationship between the national team and big business.

Most New Zealanders believe the biggest threat to the All Blacks' legacy is the rise of the Six Nations countries – England, France, Ireland, Italy, Scotland and Wales – as cohesive, destructive rugby forces, but perhaps it's actually the clear ambition of NZR to monetise the All Blacks' brand in partnership with an investor whose solitary goal is to make returns of 25 per cent. Certainly, the commercial ambitions held by those who have invested in the All Blacks are only going to become more intrusive, and potentially more damaging to the team's high-performance needs.

The narrative draws heavily on interviews with a mix of former NZR executives and directors, former All Blacks coaches and players, and key personnel from major sponsors and stakeholders. Relying on their testimony and my own observations, *Black Gold* is an honest and detailed account to help New Zealanders better understand the pressures of being an All Black, and who really controls the team. It shines a light on just how much influence commercial partners have, and how beholden the players are to the corporate heavyweights who have invested in brand All Blacks.

CHAPTER ONE

WINNING FROM THE END OF THE EARTH

BLACK IS AN UNUSUAL, some might even say odd, choice of colour for a national uniform. It's not even a colour, technically, but a shade – and, in Western societies at least, it was once associated with evil and death. Black is the colour of mourning, of grief and, in Hollywood at least, the obligatory colour in which to clad the bad guys. Over the course of the past 100 years, however, it has also come to be emblematic of all things New Zealand.

No one really knows why New Zealand's earliest rugby teams opted to wear black. It may have been because black fabric was easier to get. There are thoughts, too, that by choosing black, the New Zealand players knew they would not clash with the chosen colours of England, Scotland, Ireland and Wales. Certainly, it's true that the silver fern, the unofficial national emblem that was adopted by the first rugby administrators, had a greater visual impact when placed against a black background. Whatever the basis for the choice, the impact was undeniable.

The black jersey, black shorts and black socks with two white stripes became rugby's most recognisable and revered uniform throughout the course of the 20th century.

There was something total about the package: the way the team played, the success they enjoyed and the simplicity and colour of the jersey they wore worked in unison to deepen the sense of intimidation that New Zealand started to carry. As the legendary Welsh halfback Gareth Edwards once observed: 'There is something about the blackness of their jersey that strikes fear into your heart.' The connotations of black, he was suggesting, were reflected in the team's clinical, ruthless, brutal approach to the game. By the mid-1990s, an image of the black jersey could have been put in front of almost any sports fans in any part of the world and they would have instantly known what it represented.

The decision to wear black in the late 19th century had two distinct unintended consequences. The first was that it spawned a moniker: when the UK press came up with the term 'All Blacks' in 1905, it stuck. The second was that, with the team enjoying great success and playing with a distinctive style, it organically created a holding company in New Zealand Rugby and a brand in the All Blacks. No one set out to deliberately carve off the All Blacks as a distinct asset, but they had a trading name, a logo, values and a global reputation for excellence. All this meant that in 1995, when the game turned professional, there was a ready-made brand that was ripe to be monetised. The decision by World Rugby to allow players to be paid and unions to openly commercialise their assets, was made when it became apparent the sport had effectively outgrown its amateur status. Cash was flooding into the game through the World Cup, sponsorship deals and gate money, and it was no longer feasible to ask players to give as much as they were in terms of training and commitment and retain full-time employment. Changing the sport's status to professional meant there would be an immediate need for national unions to generate significant revenue to pay player salaries.

The jersey, as the embodiment of the All Blacks, was the means to test the market to discover what sort of a goldmine NZR was sitting on. The apparel business was changing, and quickly. The market was coming to be dominated by a smaller number of multinational corporations with global ambitions, and these behemoth organisations – including Nike, Adidas, Puma, Reebok and Umbro – were no longer thinking or talking about 'sponsorships', but were instead viewing their relationships with major clubs and national teams as 'partnerships'.

The difference was more than semantic, and perhaps best symbolised by the US$160-million (NZ$249-million), ten-year deal Nike signed with the Brazilian football team in 1996. While every article of clothing of course bore the famous Nike swoosh, the deal was more than a sponsorship. Brazil had developed a similarly dominant position in world football as the All Blacks had in rugby, and the yellow jersey was just as recognisable and proficient at encapsulating all that the team stood for. But the deal, which was believed to be the largest apparel agreement of any sport anywhere in the world, came with wider obligations for the Brazilian team to play games at Nike's request.

Rugby didn't have anywhere near the global appeal or following of football, but it was a growing sport with hopes of being embraced in a greater number of territories. And with a new, professional mandate, the heavyweight corporations were looking for opportunities to invest. Among them was Nike itself, which, having taken such a strong position in American sports and football, was looking for the next big thing. Two years earlier, in 1994, former New Zealand international cricketer Richard Reid, who headed up Nike's New Zealand operation, had been invited to the company's headquarters in Oregon to present the case for rugby. The company's leaders liked what they heard, and could see the potential of the sport. Nike had empowered Reid to sign off on a handful of sponsorship deals with the North Harbour union, Canterbury and Auckland, as well as with individual players.

These were effectively pre-emptive strikes – strategic ploys to give Nike a presence in the New Zealand rugby market, as well as credibility and relationships with the sport's key figures, which might prove invaluable if and when NZR opened a process to bid for the apparel rights to the famous black jersey.

NZR appointed David Moffett as its first chief executive in 1996, and a tender seemed inevitable when, a few months after taking the job, he realised the All Blacks could almost certainly get a better deal than the existing agreement they had with local firm Canterbury of New Zealand, which was paying $3 million a year to be the official apparel supplier.

'I am not a great one for strategic plans,' says Moffett. 'I listen to my intuition a lot, however, and intuitively I knew we were sitting on much more money than Canterbury was currently paying. Canterbury had been our sponsor forever, and I said to the board one day, "Look, I am going to go to the market because we need to find out what this brand is now worth.'"

The board to which Moffett presented his plan was greatly different to the one that had steered the game into the professional era the previous year. In 1995, the board – or council, as it was then known – had been operating under the amateur setup, where provincial committee representatives made their way onto the NZR board as a reward for long service and, no doubt, sharp politicking. But a bloated committee was not a viable system of governance for the professional age, and a streamlined board was established instead, chaired by prominent Auckland lawyer Rob Fisher and including independent directors.

The first independent appointment was Kevin Roberts, a British-born sports lover who had made waves as an executive at Pepsi in Canada, before coming to New Zealand to work for brewer Lion Nathan as chief operating officer. Roberts had been at the heart of the negotiation in 1986 to secure Lion Nathan's premier beer, Steinlager, as an All Blacks sponsor with naming rights on the front of the jersey. The presence of a beer logo on the iconic black jersey had never sat well with the wider New Zealand populace, who weren't troubled by the morality of having an alcohol sponsor so much as by the disruption it caused to the aesthetics.

NZR wanted to sell whoever ended up securing the apparel rights a 'clean jersey'. And a clean jersey would be entirely black, but for the manufacturer's logo on the right breast, the silver fern on the left and a white trim on the collar. In 1996 the jersey bore Steinlager's logo on the right breast, Canterbury's logo in the centre and the silver fern on the left breast. Lion had indicated it would be willing to move the Steinlager logo from the jersey to the back of the shorts to facilitate any new arrangement. The brewer was more interested in obtaining stadium pouring rights, and sniffed a chance to use the situation with the jersey as leverage.

Roberts, with his decision-making role at Lion, his strong background in sales and marketing and his global network of contacts, was put in charge of NZR's newly formed commercial and marketing subcommittee and empowered to lead the hunt for the All Blacks' new apparel partner. That hunt began in early 1997, when Nike invited him to Oregon.

*

ROBERTS WAS NEVER IN any danger of being branded as a typical executive. He had many conventional qualities – he was smart, erudite, ambitious and ruthless – but he also had a pronounced flair for the dramatic, a love of big gestures and a savant-like ability to see into the future. At Pepsi, he had once machine-gunned a Coca-Cola vending machine. He'd also held a senior management meeting with Lion Nathan staff at Auckland Zoo, famously throwing a box of a rival brewer's product – Foster's Lager – into the lions' enclosure. He joked afterwards that the lions had eaten the box but wouldn't touch the beer. While this deep love of the theatrical jarred a little with rugby's typically staid conservatism, it was in fact precisely what NZR needed if it was to successfully reposition the All Blacks for the professional era.

When the game of rugby union, for all its long history committed to the amateur ethos, turned professional in 1995, the Southern Hemisphere nations had shot out of the blocks, securing an enormous broadcast deal and restructuring their competitions in lightning fashion. The Northern Hemisphere unions had initially been slow to grasp that the movement to professionalism was real and happening. But they were no longer asleep behind the wheel. With vastly bigger populations and infinitely greater corporate horsepower, the UK and France had potential financial clout way beyond New Zealand. In the professional game, money was going to talk: it would buy and retain players and coaches, support high-performance advancement and develop a strong grassroots rugby community.

Says Roberts: 'Unless we got ourselves sorted out, we were going to be fucked, because we couldn't cope with the big money elsewhere. We were making $3 million a year from Canterbury. That is all we made. Three million Kiwi. Fuck me. The world was going to go to England and France and the big TV markets. Whoever had the big TV markets would command the biggest audiences and the big fees, and they both had 50 million people and we only had three. We had to win the world from the edge, is how I put it to our board, otherwise all our players would go to [rugby] league or offshore, and we would be fucked.'

There was a big Nike team waiting to hear what Roberts had to say when he arrived in Portland, Oregon. The group included Nike's founder and chief executive Phil Knight, general manager Mark Parker (who would later become chief executive) and Chris Van Dyk, son of the legendary Dick and the brand director for Nike's Asia-Pacific operations.

'Here's what I said to these guys,' says Roberts. 'After soccer, rugby is the next international sport globally. We are played in 104 markets, we are going to boom in female participation. And we are going to boom across a whole range of countries. Forget rugby league, because it was the fucking north-west of England and Australia. That's it. Forget it. And it was a moronic game – run, run, run, kick. This is going to be the next game.

'Why are we going to grow this game? Because no matter what shape you are, you can play. You can play it with or without contact. You don't have bats, helmets or pads ... you just need a bit of space and you can run. At that time, the rules were easy enough to understand. It's good for TV ... 80 minutes ... in, out and shake it all about.

'I'm also telling all these guys that it is cheap as chips to get in. I know a lot about marketing and advertising, and advertisers would kill to talk to affluent young males – but they can't, because they don't watch shit on telly. But they will watch rugby on TV, and advertisers are going to pour money into this.'

Roberts, passionate and compelling, wasn't telling Nike's executive team anything they didn't already know. He was merely confirming what they had worked out for themselves: that rugby was a growth sport with untapped potential. But now his innate sense of theatre and natural timing paid off.

'And there is only going to be one winner in this,' Roberts announced. He left a suitably dramatic pause – enough time for him to stare across the table and confirm that he had Knight's full attention – and delivered his killer line: 'Whoever controls the All Blacks controls the game.'

Knight, warming to Roberts, asked why.

'Because they are fucking Brazil,' Roberts replied. 'They are to rugby what Brazil are to football. We have tradition, heritage, iconography ... all in black. Are you kidding me? This is to die for. Sex, drugs and rock'n'roll. Heroes, athletes. Everybody wants to be an All Black. The best job in New Zealand is to coach the All Blacks. The highest-profile guy is the captain. Compared with Brazil and Real Madrid, this is going to be unbelievable value. If you get the All Blacks, you fucking win.'

The idea of being the dominant player in global rugby had massive appeal, and the Nike team could see how a partnership with the All Blacks would set it up to fulfil that ambition. They told Roberts they wanted time to digest his presentation.

Two days later he was back at Nike headquarters. He'd talked to Moffett and Fisher after the first meeting, and told them he thought they should be aiming for a three-to-five-year deal worth about US$40 million (NZ$62 million). Roberts wasn't sure if he would be able to negotiate a figure that high, but he'd researched what the likes of Manchester United and Arsenal were getting, and the sort of money that was swirling around track and field, and that was the ballpark.

'I rock up in Portland,' he relates, 'and when I got there, across the entire building was this huge vinyl sign: "Welcome

Kevin Roberts and the All Blacks". I give them the number and they are pissing around, like they do. After about two hours I am really bored of it, and say, "It's simple – it is not going to work if you look at it like a sponsorship. You have to look at it as a total package. You are going to have the All Blacks."

'I ask them about the deal they have done with Brazil, and they say they have to play 14 games in this kind of pro circus. I say, "We will do that. We are going to do a SANZAR [South African, New Zealand and Australian] tournament. Then we are going to be doing a northern tour, and apart from that we will play anyone you fucking like. You can have this big swoosh on the jersey and we will play wherever you fucking want. If you want us in LA, we will be there. If you want us to play in China, we will play, and we will do big dinners, everything you want."

'I agree to five games, and then we got to a number on the cash. They say great. They will talk to their lawyers and I will go to my board to approve it. They say, "We will be in Hong Kong next week, and we want you to present this deal to our operating board. We will do three hours with head of promotions, shoes, rugby ... they will all be there, and they will ask everything about it."'

Roberts, who knew how big corporates worked, was almost certain he'd be closing the deal in Hong Kong.

*

THE NUMBER ROBERTS AND Nike had settled on was US$75 million (NZ$116 million) over five years. It had risen that high because the scope of the deal had changed. Nike had realised how compelling the All Blacks' brand story was, and how it could be leveraged globally – and in the US in particular. If Nike could secure the All Blacks, and possibly the likes of England and South Africa too, it could build what some would cruelly describe as a global rugby circus. This new world order would include sanctioned rugby properties such as the Tri-Nations, the Six Nations and the World Cup, and the unofficial Nike element sitting alongside: exhibition games all over the world, and perhaps even novelty ideas such as the All Blacks playing the Dallas Cowboys in a hybrid version of rugby and American football.

Something else, too, had changed by mid-March 1997: Roberts had stood down from Lion Nathan and had set up his own consultancy business. He was also on the shortlist to become worldwide chief executive of the advertising firm Saatchi & Saatchi. And it was to Saatchi & Saatchi he turned once he was back in New Zealand after his successful meeting in Oregon.

Roberts confided in James Hall, the head of Saatchi's Wellington office, that he was both in line for the global job and on the cusp of securing Nike as the All Blacks' new jersey sponsor. He wanted help with the presentation he would make to the Nike operating board in Hong Kong. And so Hall set Roberts up with his best creative, John Foley.

'Kevin told me he had a big meeting with Nike in Hong Kong, and could I help him with the presentation,' says Foley. 'He said, "I want a big hype video and a strategic plan for Nike to own rugby via the All Blacks." He wanted to get their attention and sell them this five-year plan about becoming the biggest name in the sport. I made this video for a Nike audience, [who] I assumed were largely American and knew bugger-all about rugby. I made it quite aggressive, lots of big hits, and I made it to an epic opera song and wrote this five-year plan: "Here's how you become the biggest brand in rugby …" I go back to Kevin's house a few days later with the video, with the presentation, and Kevin is like, "Fuck, I am taking John with me to Hong Kong."'

The meet was in a suite at the top of a five-star hotel overlooking the harbour. When Roberts and his team got there, an army of Nike executives were waiting.

'I wanted some X-factor,' says Roberts. 'I make this presentation, and I show all this All Blacks footage and it's fucking stirring. The Americans don't really know what's going on, but they are amazed there are no helmets or pads and how physical it is. For a bit of a laugh, I showed some footage of the NFL after the rugby stuff, and I can, in retrospect, see that it was quite provocative.'

Roberts had brought with him All Black legend John Kirwan, who was the first employee of Roberts' Red Rose Consulting. And Nike, he relates, had brought their own former champion, a Detroit Lions linebacker, who did not enjoy Roberts' video.

'He got the right shits,' Roberts recalls, 'and he is huge. He can barely fit under the table, and he starts laying into me verbally, and then he starts getting up. I am engorged now in All Black mythology. I am so deep into the brand, the history, the legacy, the story that I believe every single thing about this, and he came to me, and he was going to fucking belt me and I was going to be sent reeling. Then JK stands up, and he stood up big. People might think JK is a pussy, but he's not, because he's right in front of this guy. Nobody moved. Everyone else is shitting themselves, and then very slowly they calmed down and the tension dripped away.'

Foley sat transfixed by the proceedings, and by Roberts' incredible ability to generate passion and drama. It may have looked like spontaneous theatre, but Foley believes it was a well-calculated ploy by Roberts, who he says knew precisely what he was doing.

'After this guy had gone nuts, Kevin said, "Are you finished?" And it was a brilliant way of saying, "You have asked us to give this presentation, and if you don't want to hear it, maybe go down the back of the room and make yourself a cup of tea." He asked if anyone was interested in hearing the rest of the presentation, and all of a sudden they were laughing at their own guy for overreacting.'

At the end of the meeting, Nike signed a letter of intent to sponsor the All Blacks. It was effectively a done deal, but for the respective boards' approval. It was also agreed in Hong Kong that Saatchi & Saatchi in Wellington would be Nike's agency for the All Blacks and rugby in general. With the deal all but signed, Foley and his team were asked to generate a creative campaign, and were invited to present it in Oregon later in the year.

'Given that Nike was such an irreverent, in-your-face brand, I thought from the get-go that I don't know how that sits with the All Blacks' values,' says Foley. 'If they get too much control over this, they will start to portray the All Blacks in an aggressive, irreverent kind of Nike way, and they are not a good fit. Our whole presentation to Nike was to pull them back. "This is what is at the heart of rugby – camaraderie and humility – and here is how you would align with the All Blacks." We had all this creative ready to go, all these flights booked, and then Kevin calls out of nowhere and says, "Hey, the trip to Portland is off – we are going with Adidas and the deal will be announced next week."'

*

IT HAD, BY THE winter of 1997, become something of an open secret that the All Blacks were close to signing a deal with Nike. And Simon Johnston, Adidas' New Zealand–based sponsorship and rugby operations manager, was unwilling to let the German company's fiercest rival walk off with such a prized asset. If Adidas could become the All Blacks' apparel partner, it would be transformational for the branch office in New Zealand, but of course the local team didn't have the budget or capacity to take on Nike's corporate might. The only way Adidas could compete would be through its German head office. Johnston set out to discover if the All Blacks had already committed to Nike.

Johnston knew Rob Fisher in a personal capacity – the two were tennis partners at the Remuera Racquets club in Auckland – and he rang the NZR chair on the morning of the Bledisloe Cup Test match in Dunedin on 16 August. Fisher happened to be in a car with Moffett, making their way south from Timaru after a dinner the night before.

'I asked "Fish" if it was a done deal, because while it sounded like it was a big-money offer, Nike were going to create a circus using the All Blacks' label,' says Johnston. 'He said no, but it was close, so I rang a guy called Martyn Brewer, who was based in Amsterdam on the sponsorship side, and we had a good discussion about rugby. I did a bit of research for him. He wanted to know the tradition behind the All Blacks, all the good things, their values, et cetera, and where they stood in the world. He liked the tradition of the sport, the growth of the sport right down to grassroots level.'

Brewer was Adidas' head of global sports marketing, and formerly of Nike. He was effectively the right-hand man to chief executive and owner Robert Louis-Dreyfus, an enigmatic and charming Frenchman who had been global chief executive of Saatchi & Saatchi until he bought Adidas in 1994 to try to save it from bankruptcy. Slowly, Adidas had been rebuilding after its previous owner, Bernard Tapie, had flown too close to the sun. The company had listed on the stock exchange in 1995, and earlier in 1997 had made its first big play in professional rugby by sponsoring the British and Irish Lions on their tour to South Africa.

Once word had reached Adidas HQ that the All Blacks apparel sponsorship was still a live prospect, Louis-Dreyfus, a rugby lover, was interested.

'He came to my office,' says Brewer. 'And he said, "What would we do with them – why would we want them?" Not that they are not a great asset. We agreed that it was not just a rugby play. The All Blacks are bigger than that, and when you do a deal of this magnitude you have to think how you are going to separate yourself from Nike. We were never going to go in there and run Nike down, because then you look pathetic. You are never going to outbid them, because if they want something they are just going to write bigger and bigger cheques until they get it. He said, "Spend an hour or two to wrap your head around it."'

Brewer made contact with Adidas' rugby guru in the UK, a Scotsman named Robin Money. They agreed the opportunity was enormous, and a chance for Adidas to be in bed not only with rugby's greatest asset, but with a team that transcended its sport. This was vital, says Brewer. 'Because if we were just signing up for the sake of rugby, there were a lot of other assets we could get. We could sign up individuals – hang your hat on a kicker, or on different positions. But internally there was a lot of excitement about the All Blacks, but also a reality that we all thought they had gone. But we got the apparel guys together, the footwear guys together, and this was all happening within days of my conversation with Dreyfus. We had a list of all the players at NZR, and it was Roberts, Moffett and Fisher. It was decided I should call Roberts and register our interest.'

Despite the lack of chemistry between Brewer and Roberts, it was agreed that NZR should at least hear what Adidas had to offer, and fate had it that Fisher was shortly heading to Amsterdam for a meeting about the women's World Cup. The two men met in what Fisher describes as a 'suitably grotty hotel that World Rugby had put me up in', and immediately forged a connection.

As Brewer remembers it: 'Philosophically, we had the same idea. This was bigger than rugby. If we could build a relationship with this asset and tell a story about the commitment to excellence, this is the one – the All Blacks – that crosses over all country boundaries. In my discussion with Fisher, I got the feeling he didn't want to go with Nike. I got the feeling that he was like, "If we go with Nike, we are selling our soul."'

His intuition was right, because Fisher, Moffett and the rest of the board did indeed have reservations about the Nike deal. The additional games were the biggest problem, but there was also a growing sense that Nike's brand values were not aligned with those of the All Blacks. Having determined that Adidas was seemingly a better cultural fit, Fisher decided to set out NZR's expectations.

'I was pretty smug, because I knew we had the Nike deal in the back pocket,' says Fisher. 'I like to think I was untypically arrogant and said, "You cannot have three stripes all over the All Blacks jersey. You have the silver fern here and the adidas logo here, and it will look fantastic." They seemed to accept that, and then talked through the key elements of the deal, including the money.'

Fisher said what NZR wanted, and no one on the other side of the table flinched. Brewer simply asked what the next step would be, and Fisher said it would be to meet with Moffett and Roberts the following week in San Francisco. What Fisher didn't say, but Brewer suspected, was that Moffett and Roberts would be in San Francisco en route to Oregon, where they were intending to close the deal with Nike. If Adidas was going to stop that from happening, its creative minds had just seven days to put together an incredible pitch and an incredible offer.

The strategy Brewer and his team chose was to sell a vision of modernising the look, feel and thinking of the All Blacks. 'We put together a plan about how we would bring technology into the game of rugby that had not been seen before, because it was a traditional, cotton shirt. Our guys had stats on how many people got horse-collared and how many people got pulled by the shirt. We knew Nike's intent was for the All Blacks to be part of a portfolio, to play friendly rugby within their sports agency. Anyone who knows rugby knows there is no such thing as a friendly rugby game. I thought we did a good job of undercutting the credibility of Nike as the partner for the All Blacks.

'We talked about this not being just rugby and a commitment to excellence, and showed them that this was a tradition on which the Adidas brand had been built, and that they fit what our brand was. Our story was: "We are going to do the right thing for the athletes and the right thing for the All Blacks. We are not going to own you. We are going to be your partner." I think that was the difference. The guy who had been leading the presentation for Nike knew nothing about rugby – I know that, because he had been my boss. He was a schmoozer and a cool-talking guy. We said, "We want to work with you and your players to come up with the best products for the game of rugby," because the All Blacks are bigger than just rugby. They are a nation's symbol and the game's symbol – the team with the greatest winning record in the whole of sport.

'Halfway through the meeting, Roberts said he had to go. He left and Moffett did not say anything detrimental, but you got the feeling that he was awfully excited about the potential of a relationship rather than a sponsorship. We carried on talking about the culture, the product, the brand being owned by a Frenchman who knew rugby, and lo and behold, an hour later and Roberts came back. We knew then that we were in with a chance.'

The deal was sealed a few days later at Adidas's headquarters in Herzogenaurach, Germany. Roberts was there for NZR, and Brewer and Dreyfus for Adidas.

'We made our pitch from a financial perspective, which was a base and bonuses and new technology,' says Brewer. 'What put us over the edge was two things. Kevin wanted exclusivity – for the All Blacks to get those new shirts, new shoes, whatever the hell we were working on. We ended up giving them, I think, six months' exclusivity on new technology. Kevin kept pushing for a little bit more and a little bit more, and eventually Dreyfus gave a marketing spend commitment into the contract that assisted in getting it over the line.'

The deal was US$100 million (NZ$156 million) over five years – US$10 million (NZ$15.5 million) in cash per year and US$10 million in product and marketing per year – with the option to extend for another five. There were no conditions to play additional games, and the jersey would have the desired aesthetic. The deal was also what was known as 'head to toe', as Adidas also wanted the rights to the All Blacks' boots. It was an astonishingly good piece of business for the All Blacks. Brewer says it was one of the biggest deals Adidas had signed – by his estimation, the second-biggest apparel sponsorship agreement in sport, behind Nike's deal with Brazil. It would be transformational in what it would do to NZR's profit-and-loss statement, but also in the profile and reach it would give the All Blacks.

Moffett's instincts had served him well. NZR was indeed sitting on the most valuable goldmine in world rugby: it appeared that the All Blacks had an incredible capacity not only to win rugby matches but to make extraordinary amounts of money. Which was handy, because, as Roberts had so passionately argued, and as Adidas and Nike both demonstrated, money had become the most powerful and influential force rugby had ever known.

CHAPTER TWO

COLLISION PATH

SECURING A US$100-MILLION DEAL with Adidas provided New Zealand Rugby not just with a prolific source of income, but with confirmation that the All Blacks were more than a rugby team. The revenue and the realisation that the All Blacks were a marketable brand, were equally important. Money had been assigned a clandestine role in the late amateur period – or at least it had in New Zealand, where cash was changing hands under the table to protect the All Blacks from the incessant predatory raids by rugby league clubs throughout the 1980s and early 1990s.

What was not appreciated in the gin bars and London clubs frequented by rugby's global administrators was that the game in New Zealand had been facing an existential threat for almost two decades. League clubs had money, and an insatiable appetite for talent. The two codes weren't so different, and converting a quality union player into a league superstar was neither arduous nor expensive, and so throughout the 1980s and early 1990s, the wealthiest clubs in the 13-man code were constantly sniffing around the All Blacks. There were plenty of big fish to be caught, and men such as John Gallagher, Inga Tuigamala, Craig Innes, Frano Botica, John Schuster, John Timu and Matthew Ridge, who had built or would likely build good careers in Test rugby, defected to league.

New Zealand was blessed with a rich supply of quality rugby players, but it could not continue to lose them to league at the rate it was and still see the All Blacks dominate on the world stage. NZR had no choice but to be somewhat innovative and flexible in its interpretation of the word 'amateur'. The prevailing attitude outside New Zealand was that rugby should cling, for as long as it possibly could, to its amateur status, no matter that this might ultimately prove self-destructive, and regardless of the farcical scenarios this approach created. By 1995, rugby wasn't so much amateur as 'shamateur', and New Zealand was pushing the boundaries of credibility the hardest, finding novel ways to skirt the rules around not paying players to play and yet still managing to pay them.

World Rugby, the body governing the global game and known back then as the International Rugby Football Board (the IRFB, but also referred to more simply as the IRB), had archaic views about commercialism of the sport. It believed individuals shouldn't profit from writing biographies; it didn't want the logos of apparel manufacturers to appear on the kit they made; and, somewhat ludicrously, it wanted players to take an increasing volume of time away from paid employment and play for free, despite the enormous wealth that the international game was creating. The 1991 World Cup in the UK and France produced a surplus of $80 million and yet the players, many of whom had either taken unpaid leave or given up their jobs to be there, received paltry daily allowances. The sacrifices the players were having to make to play were extreme and unsustainable, which is why so many jumped at the chance to play league. And it's also why, after becoming All Blacks coach in 1992, Laurie Mains approached NZR board member Rob Fisher to discuss possible ways to raise funds, in an above-board manner, which could then be paid to keep players in rugby.

Their discussion led to the first steps to commercialise the All Blacks and use the team's profile, public standing and brand power to generate income. What they came up with was the formation of the All Blacks Club, and by 1994 they had hit upon the right model.

'We wanted the focus to be something more like the [America's Cup] Team New Zealand family of sponsors,' says Fisher. 'Iain Abercrombie, who worked for Lion, was seconded to the All Blacks Club and individual All Blacks would be assigned to those sponsors, and they would have to undertake promotional work so they were being paid for that rather than being paid for playing.'

These arrangements were not so different to what was happening in Italy and Japan, where major corporations such as Benetton, Toyota and Mitsubishi funded their own rugby teams and employees were granted time off work to train and play. Several big-name players from the Southern Hemisphere had been 'employed' by these companies over the years, earning big money to fulfill nebulous roles. Fisher says World Rugby executives used to tell him that NZR paying players $50,000 a year to be ambassadors for All Blacks Club sponsors was a total sham, but he would argue that he couldn't see the difference between what was happening in New Zealand and the situation in Japan and Italy. 'It was a way that we believed still meant the laws of amateurism were being observed. No one on the IRB was doing anything about Japanese company teams or Italian teams like Benetton. In the lead-up to the World Cup in 1995, most of the players would have received about $50,000, provided they did work. The IRB thought it was a complete sham, but what was the difference between people playing for Benetton or Toyota or whatever?'

The All Blacks Club provided some kind of financial defence against players being poached by league clubs, but paying $50,000 a year for an ambassadorial role with the likes of Philips, Lion or Coca-Cola, who had signed on as sponsors, was really just like putting a finger in the dyke. It was a circuitous way to filter money into the pockets of the best players, but it didn't reward them at their true market value, nor did it enable NZR to exploit the power of the All Blacks brand. This hybrid world of secrecy and subterfuge, where both players and administrators had to pretend no one was being paid, was both farcical and unsustainable, so it was almost a relief in May 1995 when, seemingly out of nowhere, a concept called the World Rugby Corporation emerged as the most direct and potentially destructive threat amateur rugby had ever faced.

WRC was a blueprint for a global, professional competition, bankrolled by Australian media tycoon Kerry Packer, who would use the content for his pay TV station. The plan, led by former Wallaby Ross Turnbull, was to sign the players first and then hope the money followed. It wasn't such a madcap idea, as around the world the best players were at breaking point – unable to keep giving up the increasing volumes of time required to train and play. A compelling offer to become full-time professionals was going to carry enormous appeal, especially when WRC was offering $700,000-plus packages.

The arrival of WRC was both terrifying and galvanising for NZR. For a few months, the possibility of losing the players and control of the game was real, as initially the All Blacks, en masse, as well as the Wallabies and Springboks, signed contracts with WRC. Packer and his rebel competition were going to end 100-plus years of history if the established rugby administration failed to respond.

Despite the mortal threat, in a way the arrival of WRC was the moment NZR and their Southern Hemisphere allies had been waiting for. It effectively created a war to own rugby, and with it a licence to leave the amateur world behind and embrace an open, transparent, fully professional landscape. There was no choice but to tackle WRC head-on and present the players with an alternative offer.

The rugby unions of South Africa, New Zealand and Australia formed an alliance known as SANZAR, and announced a plan to create a new 12-team club competition called Super Rugby, which would feature five sides from New Zealand, four from South Africa and three from Australia. The international programme would be built around the Tri-Nations, where the three countries would play each other annually at home and away. On 23 June 1995, the day before the World Cup final between New Zealand and South Africa in Johannesburg, a broadcast deal worth US$555 million (NZ$840 million) was signed with Rupert Murdoch's News International Corporation.

The players realised that WRC had ambition but no money, and by August the rebel bid had collapsed. World Rugby, in its quaint and slightly pompous way, declared the game 'open', seemingly suggesting it still couldn't bring itself to use the world 'professional'.

This was the new world the players had craved. There was no longer any need to pretend they weren't being paid. There were no unmarked envelopes being handed to them by shady figures after games, no more requirements to hold nebulous ambassadorial roles with All Blacks Club sponsors and no more having to juggle the dual demands of holding down full-time employment while finding the time to complete multiple, arduous training sessions.

It also suited NZR, as now there were incredible commercial possibilities for rugby, as evidenced by the size of the contract signed with News International. In 1995, the total broadcast revenue accumulated by the three SANZAR nations was US$5.7 million (NZ$8.6 million). Under the terms of the ten-year deal they had signed with Murdoch, they would be splitting US$32 million (NZ$48.5 million) between them in 1996, a figure which led to NZR forecasting it would turn over $34 million that year.

That felt like a lot of money, but when faced with the new reality of running a fully professional sport, it wasn't quite the cash mountain it appeared. It was a solid base from which to enter the professional age, but there were two sides to the equation: NZR not only had enormous commercial possibilities, but also massively increased costs. In 1996 there were 130 full-time Super Rugby players in New Zealand who needed to be paid, and their salaries ranged from $50,000 a year to $400,000, with the average sitting at about $100,000. That was $13 million in wages – for players, coaches and support staff – that needed to be found. And then there were the associated costs of running Super Rugby – which wasn't cheap, given teams had to travel regularly to South Africa and Australia – as well as the costs linked to All Blacks Tests and the National Provincial Championship competition.

No one understood the realities of what NZR was facing better than David Moffett, who had come on board as chief executive in early 1996. He'd been working for the New South Wales Rugby Union in 1995 when he was seconded to be part of the SANZAR team negotiating the broadcast contract with News International. Through that process he'd got to know then NZR chair Richie Guy, which led to an offer for him to become the inaugural chief executive of the national body. When Moffett arrived in New Zealand, there were serious problems to be remedied.

'My tasks in the first 100 days? They were to settle it down and to revamp the agreement with the Super Rugby teams otherwise we would have gone broke,' he says. 'The first year I got there NZR had $10 million in the bank, which had been built up over 100 years. That's all. By the end of the first season, it was down to $1 million because they had done this deal with the Super Rugby sides that said we will take all the gate money and we will pay for the players as well. It was obvious we weren't getting the right amount of funds flowing back to us, so I changed it.'

But a distressed set of accounts wasn't going to convince Moffett he'd been wrong to see his appointment as the opportunity of a lifetime. He was aware that big local corporations had lined up to be part of the All Blacks Club. The money had rolled in without many arms being twisted, and he also had seen how eager News International had been to invest in Southern Hemisphere rugby. While it is not easy to guess at the inner workings of the Murdoch empire and its decision-making process, it seems unlikely that News International would have made the monumental investment it did had the All Blacks not been involved.

The All Blacks hadn't won the 1995 World Cup, but they were the team who gave the tournament the mass appeal it needed. They played the sort of rugby that was easy for the uninitiated to understand and for the hardcore followers to admire. They also had, in Jonah Lomu, the most fascinating player the game had seen. The deal with News International was well progressed by the time the World Cup kicked off, but unquestionably it was Lomu – 1.94 metres and 120 kilograms, with the dimensions of a fridge and the acceleration and speed of a sportscar – who had increased the media company's desire to buy in and pay whatever it had to.

The All Blacks were the great entertainers, and they came with a mystique and a legend that was uniquely compelling –

and this was confirmed for Moffett during the bidding war for the apparel rights. He had set out to see how much the fabled black jersey was worth, and ended up with the two biggest apparel manufacturers on the planet fighting over it. If England, Australia or France had tried to entice Nike and Adidas into a bidding war, it never would have happened. Nike honestly believed it could win New Zealand's national team a new and significant audience in the United States, while Adidas had been drawn into the fight by its conviction that the All Blacks were bigger than rugby, a brand that could transcend geographical boundaries and even sporting codes.

Maybe this was the most important thing of all to come out of the hunt for a new apparel partner: the realisation that the All Blacks, in the professional age, would have a dual identity, as both a rugby team and a brand. A brand, after all, is nothing but a story: a journey along which values are consistently displayed, a reputation forged and judgement made. By 1996 and the arrival of professionalism, the All Blacks had displayed such clearly defined characteristics over such a long period that even those who knew nothing about New Zealand had some sense that they did just through observing its rugby team.

For more than a century, the All Blacks had consistently been resilient, ruthless, innovative and resourceful. They were a team that even the most casual follower could see were driven by the need to perform even the basic skills of rugby at the highest standards. They didn't do scandal, off-field dramas, showboating, gloating or hissy-fitting when things didn't go their way. They were collectively calm, focused, clear in thought and precise in deed. The ultimate testament to the strength of their values was their results. The All Blacks came into the professional age with a winning Test record of close to 72 per cent. No other international team came remotely close – and not just in rugby. The All Blacks had no peer in the sporting world; not even the mighty Brazilian football team could compare over the same length of time.

Bolstering the All Blacks' winning brand were unforgettable stories of the sacrifice and commitment individuals had shown along the way. Dick 'Red' Conway told the doctor to chop off his infected finger so he could be passed fit to tour South Africa in 1960; Colin Meads played a Test with a broken arm in 1970; and in 1986, Wayne 'Buck' Shelford continued to throw himself into battle against the French with one of his testicles unravelling down his leg. Folklore enhanced the mystique, while the world-famous picture of Meads carrying a sheep under each arm as a supposed training regime added a strong, quintessentially Kiwi flavour to brand All Blacks. They have always been New Zealand's team, built New Zealand's way.

No other country in the world had a rugby team that had captured the public imagination in the same way, or become so deeply ingrained in the nation's psyche as to be perceived as the near perfect projection of how the people saw themselves. The All Blacks were defined by their humility, their resilience and their commitment to excellence, and their unity in embracing these values gave them higher purpose and a depth of character under pressure.

The battle between Adidas and Nike had illustrated the power of the All Blacks brand story, while NZR's diminishing cash reserves and stubbornly high wages bill demonstrated the changed nature of the business. The arrival of professionalism meant NZR had the dual and often conflicting objectives of operating as a profit-making business to pay for its elite athletes, and keeping enough aside to fund and manage the community game. The economic model it would pursue to achieve its goals was theoretically easy to follow: the All Blacks, sitting at the top of the professional pyramid, would be the cash cow, but it would divide into two distinct units: commercial and high performance. The former would be charged with monetising the All Blacks by selling broadcast rights, sponsorships and match tickets. The latter was the playing side – the athletes and coaches – and they would be responsible for ensuring the All Blacks were successful on the field.

It would be a little like an old-fashioned newspaper setup, with the high-performance side the equivalent of the editorial team and the commercial unit playing the role of the advertising department. Everyone agreed that the business would be most successful if these two divisions were kept as distinct and separate as possible.

But the two units were reliant on one another, of course. The players needed to be paid, and the commercial team needed the players to win Tests to create an asset with a high sales value. The relationship was symbiotic, but just as no editorial operation wants the advertising department to determine what stories it should publish, the high-performance side needed the autonomy to prepare for Tests without the commercial operation making excessive demands on it.

What would become apparent to Moffett and every chief executive who succeeded him is that this model created two perennial challenges for NZR. The first was an endless need to drive revenue. There was a tight global labour market, where demand far outstripped supply, and with rugby league just as hungry for talent as it always had been, wage inflation was going to be a constant problem for NZR. It had to subscribe to the Wallis Simpson mantra that no one could ever be too rich or too thin.

Second, there had to be a non-negotiable acceptance that the rugby ecosystem would only flourish if the All Blacks continued both to win and to uphold the values for which they had become renowned. The brand's value was predicated on the legacy being enhanced, so it was imperative that NZR find ways to monetise the All Blacks without compromising the athletes and coaching staff.

It was that simple: NZR had to exploit its prime rugby asset without destroying the ability of the All Blacks to keep winning. And yet, as clear and defined as this objective was, it had become apparent, on the eve of the All Blacks' first Test in the professional era, that it was going to be much harder to achieve than anyone realised. Ahead of a clash against Samoa, the commercial team was most definitely interfering in both the preparation and the selection of the team. Two worlds that shouldn't have collided did. The difficult lesson learned was that the biggest threat to the All Blacks' legacy in the professional era would come not from the Springboks, the Wallabies or the French, but from commercial imperatives impinging upon high-performance needs.

*

THE SCENARIO THAT UNFOLDED in the days leading up to the All Blacks' first professional outing – in Napier, on 6 June 1996 – was worthy of any Greek comedy. It was never going to be particularly funny, however, as the three main characters were lawyers – David Howman, David Jones and Warren Alcock – who represented three high-profile All Blacks, Jeff Wilson, Ian Jones and Josh Kronfeld. The heavyweight legal trio had been called in to try to resolve a commercial dispute that was threatening to have a profound and detrimental impact upon the All Blacks' team selection.

Jones, Kronfeld and Wilson had all been named in the team earlier that week, but 24 hours before kick-off, their participation was suddenly in doubt. None of them was injured or ill. None had been embroiled in an unsavoury late-night scandal. They hadn't broken any curfews or team rules. What had put their selections in doubt was their intended choice of footwear.

All three players had individual contracts with Nike, and all three were intending to wear boots with the big swoosh. Nike had paid for its association with three of the bigger stars in the All Blacks, and it expected its investment to be honoured. The problem was that NZR, separately, had struck a collective deal with Japanese firm Mizuno to supply the All Blacks with their footwear. In Napier, there would be 12 All Blacks wearing Mizuno boots and three wearing Nike, and that, as far as NZR was concerned, couldn't happen. Notice to that effect was given to the three rogue players' respective lawyers.

In fact, it was more of a threat than a notice: NZR effectively said that if the three players wouldn't agree to wear Mizuno boots, they would not be selected. Which is why the three lawyers found themselves on a conference call with head coach John Hart and All Blacks manager Mike Banks on the Thursday evening before the historic first Test of the professional era.

'We got a notice that John Hart was going to pull all three out of the Test match unless they agreed to wear Mizuno boots,' says Warren Alcock. 'I remember, I got home from rugby training, and I had to go on a phone call with the two Davids, John and the All Blacks manager. We ended up asking John to give us an undertaking that he wouldn't withdraw those players from the Test match team. He couldn't give us that undertaking.'

Without that assurance, the next step was for the three lawyers to write to NZR the following morning with a counter-threat. 'The Test match was that night, and we had letters to the NZR by 9am that morning, stating that if they didn't give us that undertaking by 10am, we would be in front of the High Court asking for an injunction,' says Alcock. 'They gave us that undertaking.'

Jones, Kronfeld and Wilson played against Samoa and wore their Nike boots, and no one was more relieved than Hart. This was his first game as head coach, and the clash over the boots had put him in an uncomfortable position. He was trying to build a culture of trust with the players, but there he was, in the middle of a conflict that had the potential to destroy that plan.

'That was an example of a mess that nearly imploded, and it made my position difficult with Jones, Wilson and Kronfeld because I had to support the union,' says Hart. 'I shouldn't have been involved, but in the end, I didn't want someone to control the destiny of those guys that was not me. That was something NZR should have addressed ... they had a contract with Mizuno and should have been asking what else they had out there. It was ultimately resolved, but it nearly pulled me down in the first game we played.'

The conflicting endorsement deals were a direct consequence of how haphazard the arrival of professionalism had been. The shift had been chaotic and frantic, and NZR's focus during the turbulent WRC period had been to win back the players with counter-offers. While all this contract work was happening at breakneck speed, Nike's head of local operations, Richard Reid, had seen an opportunity. Nike had been looking to strike endorsement deals with New Zealand athletes, particularly in rugby. It had been talking to Jones, Kronfeld and Wilson and when it became apparent that all three were going to sign with NZR, Reid fast-tracked the negotiations so their endorsement contracts pre-dated any subsequent collective deals the national body might agree – such as a collective boot agreement with Mizuno.

None of this had happened with the knowledge of NZR. However, the NZR contracts included a provision for players to detail any existing sponsorships or endorsements they had in place. Having declared their Nike arrangements in their playing contracts, Jones, Kronfeld and Wilson felt they had appropriately notified NZR and had received approval. NZR chair Richie Guy later revealed to the three lawyers that the union had never countersigned the contracts of Jones, Kronfeld and Wilson. In the frantic scramble to secure talent, this fact had been overlooked. No one in the administration had even looked at the returned paperwork, so no one had realised that three first-choice All Blacks had legitimate, declared and NZR-approved agreements to wear Nike boots.

As it turned out, the saga in Napier over the boots proved a catalyst of sorts for the All Blacks apparel war. Jones, Kronfeld and Wilson had worn their Nike boots in Napier with tape over the logo, but NZR wanted a sustainable compromise. Reid and David Howman, who was acting for Nike in New Zealand, met with NZR board member Jock Hobbs shortly after the Test to work on a solution to the problem: a way in which the agreement with the three players could be amended to release them from their obligation to wear Nike boots while playing for the All Blacks.

Reid, sensing an opportunity that would mutually benefit NZR and Nike, told Hobbs that there was a way the situation could be fixed. 'The way we solved this was pretty simple,' Reid recalls. 'We said, "We will make all this go away for exclusive rights to the All Blacks apparel deal." To which they agreed.'

Howman verifies this, and says that Nike believed it had been granted an exclusive opportunity to bid to become the All Blacks apparel partner, in return for agreeing to amend the contracts of Jones, Kronfeld and Wilson so they could wear Mizuno boots in Test matches.

The reason Howman and Reid had met with Hobbs to discuss a solution was simply that they had a relationship with him. Hobbs, a former All Blacks captain and lawyer, had been the NZR board's lead negotiator in the fight to save the game from WRC, but he was also the New Zealand representative for Mizuno. At this time, despite having a full-time chief executive, NZR was an organisation mostly run by its board, with individual members having significant influence on the strength of personal relationships.

It seems that what Howman and Reid agreed with Hobbs was never relayed to CEO David Moffett. This meant that the chief executive opened the tender for the All Blacks apparel contract without knowing that Nike had been granted a memorandum of understanding around exclusivity. It also meant that nothing was ever said to Nike to indicate that the provisional deal it had agreed with NZR at the famously tense meeting in Hong Kong was in jeopardy. In fact, according to Reid, a host of senior Nike executives were booked to fly to New Zealand in October 1997 for a press conference to announce the All Blacks deal. Only the day before that was due to take place was Nike told it had missed out. Reid says that Nike briefly considered taking legal action, but decided that the expense and effort wouldn't be worth it, and that it had no interest in doing business with an organisation that it felt lacked business ethics.

The truth seems to be that NZR lacked good internal communication rather than having a devious bent, but that didn't matter to Nike. Having missed out on securing the greatest asset in the game, it lost interest in rugby. The local offices in England and South Africa did deals with their national teams, but there would be no big money available for rugby out of Oregon.

And perhaps it was just as well that Nike didn't secure an agreement with the All Blacks, because its ambition to showcase the team and build the brand in a manner that would appeal to a US audience would almost certainly have put the team's commercial obligations in direct conflict with its high-performance needs. Adidas had played the smarter hand, selling itself as a partner with a deep respect for the All Blacks' history and a desire to preserve it, promote it and hopefully even enhance it.

The sales pitch had been compelling, but NZR, having signed the contract, became increasingly nervous about whether Adidas was in fact going to treasure the very qualities it had valued at US$100 million (NZ$156 million).

CHAPTER 3

BLACK OUT

THE ADIDAS DEAL WAS announced to the media in October 1997, but the German company would not actually become NZR's apparel partner until July 1999. The long lead-in gave the lawyers ample time to iron out the fine print and, perhaps more importantly, in the context of building the brand, it also gave the company's marketing and advertising teams more than 18 months to strategise how they were going to sell the All Blacks to both the local and international markets. Having an international partner the size of Adidas was new territory for NZR, and the relationship would require the national body to make a significant change to its vision and attitude.

The decision to seek a new apparel manufacturer had been driven by NZR's need for cash. Nike and Adidas were simply the richest and best resourced companies in the apparel sector. But as the process had played out, it had become apparent to NZR that both Nike and Adidas were willing to invest such vast sums in an individual team only because any agreement would come with a detailed marketing and promotional plan. Adidas wasn't about to just sign a whopping cheque and then hope to achieve a return on its investment. As much as it was an apparel company, it was also a marketing maestro with enormous experience and success in brand management.

The fact that the deal specified that Adidas would provide US$10 million in cash and US$10 million in marketing spend annually illustrated just how important it considered brand promotion of the All Blacks. Or, to be blunt, if it was to recoup the US$10 million in cash it was spending on sponsorship, it would have to sell a serious amount of replica shirts and merchandise. Hence, it was imperative that the All Blacks build their profile in international territories, as well as in New Zealand. This was the game Adidas played: think big, spend big, market big and the returns would be big.

But this was a game entirely new to NZR. It had no experience in global marketing campaigns, and it had been locked in a mindset of brand protection for the better part of two decades. The arrival of Adidas as a major sponsor forced NZR, for the first time, to think more seriously about how the All Blacks brand could become more financially lucrative. There would still need to be an element of protectionism applied – careful management to ensure that in chasing brand growth, NZR didn't agree to marketing and advertising campaigns that jarred with or were contrary to the All Blacks' core values. But with Adidas looking to spend so much on marketing, NZR had its eyes opened to the financial possibilities that could result from proactively looking to build the profile and visibility of the All Blacks.

The new apparel deal also forced NZR to think more deeply about what exactly were the All Blacks' brand values, as it would need to guide Adidas in crafting an appropriately themed campaign. Determining who and what the All Blacks were and what sorts of qualities defined them was not a particularly difficult exercise. The team had been built on the same pioneering spirit on which New Zealand had been built.

If there was a single value that best defined the All Blacks, and by extension New Zealanders, it was humility. They were not a team, and New Zealand was not a nation, that had any inclination to brag or talk themselves up. From day one, the All Blacks had stoically reacted to tries being scored without even a hint of joy or celebration. The wildest reaction ever seen from an All Black throughout the amateur era was to look the bloke who had scored the try in the eye and offer a firm handshake.

This lack of emotional exuberance was evidence that the team was a product of its environment: New Zealand in the early 20th century was largely populated by Celtic and English immigrants who were forging a living off the land and operating in tough terrain and amid inclement weather. No one working the land in New Zealand had any sense of comfort, and there was always a reluctance to celebrate victory. These pioneers knew that their fate was at the mercy of the weather gods and other ecological and biological factors, which could wipe out a crop or livestock in an instant.

As well as humility, the All Blacks had a deeply ingrained work ethic that drove them to constantly chase excellence. They famously refused to accept standards they felt were beneath them, or that didn't honour the legacy of those who had played before them. And they were able to demand more of one another because they were a team that was genuinely all about the team. Everything they did was to improve the collective ahead of the individual: players had always accepted that they would have to sacrifice their personal ambition for the greater good.

Just as there was no celebrating of tries among the All Blacks, there was no celebration of the individual, or indeed any desire to denigrate or trash-talk an opponent. Rugby had long had a code of being respectful to one's opponents and to the game, and the All Blacks upheld this tradition. They would never seek controversy. The All Blacks presented as a brilliant, united and innovative rugby side, but one that was also quite cold and clinical, as their humility meant they often didn't say much publicly or appear to take any joy in their achievements. So much so, in fact, that at the 1991 World Cup, when the team arrived in Dublin ahead of their semi-final against Australia, Vincent Hogan of the *Irish Independent* wrote that they 'marched into town with all the gaiety of grave diggers'.[1]

Adidas had a broad sense that the All Blacks had been a hugely successful team for a long period of time. But the German-headquartered group did not have an intricate or nuanced feel for the personality of the All Blacks, so plotting how to spend the US$10-million marketing budget in a way that built the profile of the team without compromising or damaging its integrity was going to be a delicate and diplomatic business.

There had been adverse media and public reaction to the new deal when it was first announced. NZR, in securing the US$100-

million deal with Adidas, had of course axed a long-term apparel relationship with Canterbury, an iconic New Zealand company. But Canterbury simply didn't have the money to compete with multinational conglomerates such as Adidas, and as much as NZR would have liked to continue the relationship, that was no longer feasible in the sport's brave new world. Professionalism brought an insatiable need for cash, and while Canterbury stretched itself to what would likely have been breaking point to make a counter-offer, it was still well short of what Adidas had put on the table.

And so, in 1999, the New Zealand national rugby team had the second-largest kit sponsorship in world sport. New Zealand was a relatively tiny country, with a population of just 3.8 million people and limited economic means, but the All Blacks became a global sporting brand with the same recognition and profile as iconic organisations such as Real Madrid, Manchester United and the Chicago Bulls. The advantage that those clubs had, however, was that they were based in countries with comparatively massive populations, and they played in leagues that had international followings. The English Premier League and the NBA, for instance, had marketed themselves in Asia and Africa as well as in their respective domestic markets of Europe and North America. And because they were club sides, there was no emotional barrier to someone in Thailand, for example, becoming a hardcore Manchester United fan.

Nor would it be right to say that New Zealand were in the same boat as Brazil, who also had a national team with a brand profile that extended beyond their own borders. In 1999, Brazil had a population of 172 million people; in 1995 they had been ranked as the world's seventh-largest economy. Nike had bought into Brazil in 1994 with plans to showcase the team around the world, but the US firm also knew that the local market was enormous and likely to remain the most significant one for it to exploit.

The All Blacks had a unique problem in the world of professional sport: they had effectively outgrown their own country. Arguably, the All Blacks were better known globally than in New Zealand, so the brand's worth was greater than the domestic market's ability to support it. The All Blacks had a profile comparable to Manchester United's, but it was generating nowhere near the same volume of revenue. For the financial year 2000, Manchester United, who were at the time listed on the London Stock Exchange, generated £116 million of revenue, which, on the historical exchange rate, equated to roughly $450 million. In the same year, NZR posted record revenue of $76 million – more than double the revenue collected in 1996, but still tiny in comparison with what the giants of European football were generating.

If NZR was going to realise the All Blacks' brand value in monetary terms, it was going to have to find new fans outside of New Zealand to grow the support base. The cold, hard economics were that there simply weren't enough people in New Zealand to drive sponsorship, broadcast and even gate revenue to the sorts of levels that the All Blacks needed if they were to pay the players competitive salaries and fully invest in their high-performance needs.

This gave the deal with Adidas even greater alignment, because both entities were effectively committed to finding new All Blacks fans.

While the local market wasn't financially powerful, it was still important. Indeed, it was crucial that the emotional bond between New Zealand and the All Blacks remained strong. The All Blacks, after all, were the people's team, and what had interested Adidas was the strength of the connection between the New Zealand public and the players. The love the nation had for its team was a big part of the brand story, and if the nation was going to continue to feel that love, then they needed to continue to relate to the All Blacks. Hence, there was some angst about having signed such a large contract with a German-based organisation that might lack an understanding of the values inherent to the team's culture.

*

THE FIRST POINT OF order, once the heads of agreement had been signed, was to establish that the All Blacks jersey, while it was clearly going to go through a technological revolution and change from being cotton and baggy to skin-tight and dry-fit, would not bear the three stripes for which Adidas was internationally famous. From shoes to shorts to T-shirts, Adidas's kit was instantly recognisable by the three stripes that adorned it. When the company secured the British and Irish Lions contract in 1997, it put three stripes down the arm of that iconic red jersey. For much of the 1980s, the French (as only the French could) had carried three stripes – red, white and blue – with some elegance on their Adidas-made jersey.

NZR was adamant that the All Blacks jersey would remain all black, as would the shorts. Adidas might have paid handsomely for the rights to make the jersey, but that did not mean it could paint white stripes wherever it wanted. Fortunately, it wasn't a challenge to convince Adidas of this.

'It was a discussion that was held early and it was deemed it wasn't right,' says Martyn Brewer. 'You have to make compromises at times if you want to have a relationship and not dilute what it is all about ... It doesn't mean [Adidas] couldn't put [the three stripes] in training wear, or warm-up gear, but when the boys step out to play on game day, they are All Blacks. And we gave them that.'

The only concession NZR made was to adapt the All Blacks' socks from having their traditional two white stripes to three.

The second question to be answered was how Adidas planned to spend its US$10-million-a-year marketing budget. When it had appeared that Nike would likely be the All Blacks' apparel partner, there was some consternation on the NZR board as to whether the US group was the right fit culturally. Nike was brash and irreverent, bold and flashy – qualities that had made it hugely successful in capturing the American sports market, but that would have been at odds with the All Blacks.

The creative that John Foley and his Saatchi & Saatchi team never got to pitch at Nike headquarters had been based on a theme of humility. 'A lot of the work we did for the Nike presentation was pulling them back, getting them to respect the jersey,' says Foley. 'We knew it wasn't going to be as hard a sell to Adidas to pull them back because of their brand values – their whole heritage was a lot more aligned with the All Blacks.'

Foley was right – and when he travelled to Amsterdam in June 1998 to meet Neil Simpson, who was head of global advertising at Adidas, the two men were largely on the same page when it came to the themes they wanted to see in the creative. The only request Foley made was for Adidas to allocate more money to a local campaign to launch the sponsorship, as the new kit was to be revealed in 1999, a World Cup year. The All Blacks were to play home Tests in June against Samoa and France wearing their Canterbury uniforms, before switching to the new Adidas shirts for the Tri-Nations series, which would commence in Dunedin on 10 July against the Springboks. The World Cup would kick off in the United Kingdom in October.

Adidas was focused exclusively on a global launch at the World Cup, but Foley made a strong argument that it should fund a New Zealand-only campaign in the build-up to the Tri-Nations.

'When the deal was announced, there were a lot of people in New Zealand thinking, "Why the hell have we sold our soul to a big German company? They are going to ruin it,"' says Foley. 'There was a bit of "poor little Canterbury, a New Zealand company being shafted", and then everyone was saying [Adidas] were going to put three stripes on the jersey.

'Their agenda when I met them was, "Right we need to talk about the campaign for the World Cup, which will be five months after the first game in Dunedin." I said, "I know you don't have budget for everything, but you have got a whole country that is nervous about you guys stepping in. This team means everything to the country, and we don't want to lose our All Blacks. You have got to understand that jersey is one that the whole country feels it owns. You need to do a campaign specifically for New Zealand, and it won't be about you and what you bring. It is going to be about you, Adidas, being respectful of what you are now partnering with.'"

Simpson took on board's Foley advice and released $900,000 so Saatchi & Saatchi could make a TV ad for the New Zealand market. It was a simple, understated production, in which All Blacks captains of years gone by were filmed putting on the jerseys they had played in, working through the years until the 1999 captain, Taine Randell, donned the new Adidas shirt.

The campaign was a great success. Whether it was the power of advertising, a sense of excitement ahead of the World Cup or the fact that the new jersey was sleek and made by a company whose leisurewear was internationally popular, New Zealanders bought replicas at a volume they never previously had. On the day the new shirt was released, there were queues that went around the Octagon, Dunedin's city centre, with seemingly half the population wanting to get themselves a new All Blacks top. Two weeks later, when the All Blacks played Australia at Eden Park in Auckland, significant numbers of home fans were wearing the black shirts.

This was new, for while New Zealanders loved their team, historically they hadn't worn replica jerseys to Test matches. There had long been a feeling that the only people who should wear an All Blacks shirt were those who had earned the right –

the players who had been selected to represent the nation. But the arrival of Adidas seemed to be changing that mindset. Wallabies coach Rod McQueen noted a few years later that for the Australians, seeing so many fans dressed in black on the streets of Auckland that night had deepened the sense of intimidation.

Further exacerbating the intimidatory environment for the Australians was the intensity with which the All Blacks performed their haka that evening. The Adidas creative for the major World Cup promotional campaign was filmed that night in Auckland. There were 16 cameras placed around the ground and on the field to capture the performance of the haka, with people literally running spools of 35mm film all over Eden Park. Adidas had committed $1.8 million to the campaign, so it was decided that on the Thursday before the Test, the All Blacks should go to the ground to practise their haka.

The haka was a big part of the All Blacks legend – the act in which the team's Indigenous and New World heritages met, and where the uniquely mixed ethnicity of New Zealand's population came together as one. But despite the cultural significance of the haka, and its ingrained importance in the All Blacks story, not everyone in the team understood its meaning and history.

Saatchi & Saatchi had in their midst one of New Zealand's best kapa haka leaders and coaches, Inia Maxwell, the grandson of Sir Howard Morrison, who was concerned that because some of the All Blacks might not know the English meaning of the te reo Māori words, they weren't performing some specific actions as they should. He was given permission to talk to the All Blacks before they went onto the field to begin their practice.

'He walks into the All Blacks changing room at Eden Park,' recalls Foley, 'and he says, "Sometimes I'm embarrassed watching the All Blacks haka because I don't think – no fault of your own – many of you know what it means, and you guys are doing it from the head and not the heart." He said, "You guys think a good haka is all about choreography and being in time. But when you do a haka, it comes from the heart, and I don't care if you are all out of sync if you know what it means and channel the energy and bring it up through the earth."'

He demonstrated what he meant by taking his shirt off and performing a spine-tingling one-man haka, after which captain Taine Randell addressed the team, saying that, as a Māori, it was important to him to get the haka right. The All Blacks agreed.

One recommended change was that when the words *'ka mate, ka mate, ka ora, ka ora'* were spoken – which translated as 'It is death, it is death, it is life, it is life' – the players shouldn't put their hands straight out, but instead they should be palm up, while they looked to the heavens. It was a distinct and powerful change, largely because it forced the players to consider more deeply the words and meaning of the haka, and so forge a stronger connection with it.

If the 1996 shenanigans over the Nike and Mizuno boots was the first example of commercialisation negatively impacting the high performance of the All Blacks, this amendment of the haka was the first positive impact.

*

THERE HAD BEEN LEGITIMATE fears that Adidas would come into the relationship with big and bold ideas that didn't align with who the All Blacks were. But these fears proved unfounded, as Adidas appeared to immediately understand what it was joining. It hadn't bought in to try to reposition the team as something it was not, and it did not make its first promotional campaigns all about Adidas rather than the All Blacks. Those early campaigns accentuated the values of humility, hard work and respect for the heritage of the brand.

'There were five things we wanted to achieve,' says Andrew Gaze, who served as Adidas's marketing manager before becoming its global head of rugby. 'The first was to win the hearts and minds of the owners of the All Blacks, which is the public of New Zealand. It was clear that the way to do that was to show respect to the history of New Zealand rugby and the legacy which Adidas didn't have any rights to. [Second,] the All Blacks gave Adidas an opportunity to move into new sectors and spheres, and it gave them a point of difference because the All Blacks transcended rugby. The third area was we wanted to provide the All Blacks with innovative, market-leading products. [Fourth, we] wanted to build a compelling licensing range. Canterbury had quite a tight range. They had these training jerseys and they called them the uglies. They were great for working on the farm or mowing the lawns, but they weren't aesthetically attractive, either for males or females. The fifth part was to take the brand global.'

There was clearly a sixth, unspoken part of the plan – which was to make money for Adidas. And those first few months surpassed all expectations financially. It took Adidas just three months to make what Canterbury previously had in a whole year.

'In New Zealand we were turning over between $3 million to $7 million a year,' says Simon Johnston. 'When we got the All Blacks, about 18 months later, we were turning over about $45 million.'

And it wasn't just Adidas that felt this positive impact. NZR had negotiated one of the best royalty deals in world sport when it signed with Adidas. Most sports bodies received between 10 and 14 per cent of the sale price for every item sold. But NZR had held out for 18 per cent, and that's partly why its total income in 2000 jumped to $76 million.

All this money flowing into the professional game hadn't come with any excess demands on player time. Adidas hadn't asked for hours and hours with the players to fulfil their commercial ambitions. The only real change was that the team benefited from big-budget, professional advertising campaigns. Adidas effectively showed what could be achieved by spending money, but in doing so it inadvertently lit a fire under the team's local sponsors. Soon every All Blacks sponsor suddenly wanted to get more out of their investment.

CHAPTER FOUR

PLANE SAILING

ON 25 FEBRUARY 1996, All Blacks coach John Hart organised a seminar at the Waipuna Hotel in Auckland, to which he invited 46 players who were either already All Blacks or likely to become so. The seminar was entitled 'Professional Rugby: Opportunities and Responsibilities', and its intent was to give the players insight into how their obligations were going to change. Hart invited speakers with a range of expertise to explain how professionalism would impact the players from a legal, financial and accountancy perspective.

Hart, who had a long background in the corporate world, could see there were obvious dangers in suddenly paying players up to $300,000 a year for something they had previously done for free. The players would be going from a world where they had 'real jobs' that made real demands of their time to being professional athletes, where they would likely have significant parts of each day free after they had trained. It was a risky cocktail of increased income and decreased time commitments. Some players, he innately knew, would invest their new-found wealth wisely, dedicate themselves to training and fill in their spare time appropriately, while others, he feared, would squander their first pay cheques and run into trouble. He suspected, however, that almost everyone he picked in the All Blacks that year would have, at some time or another, difficulty adjusting to the increased demands that were going to come from broadcasters, media, sponsors, NZR and, most importantly, the people of New Zealand.

'I recognised early that the professional game meant a different rule set,' says Hart. 'It meant you had to change a lot of attitudes overnight and put in a new system, and of course some players grappled with that, while some understood and adapted quickly. And the biggest change was that you were owned. You were owned not so much by New Zealand Rugby but by the public, who felt such an affinity to the All Blacks. They felt they owned them anyway, but even more so now that they saw players getting big money. There was a different requirement now. They had to give sponsors their time. They had to give media their time. Accessibility was going to grow. It was a huge transition for the players.'

Hart hoped that by forewarning his players about the likely demands of professional rugby, they would be forearmed when they assembled for Test duty in June. The important thing for him was that they understood the wider responsibilities that would come with their role and the sense of ownership the public would feel. And he wanted his players to arrive in camp with that appreciation, because another key strand to the transition was going to be phasing out some of the older All Blacks traditions that he felt had no place in the professional game.

As amateurs, the All Blacks, like most other rugby teams, had developed an institutional drinking culture. There was also a longstanding ritual built around the back seat of the team bus. The longer a player had been part of the team, the further back in the bus he was allowed to sit, but it created a *Lord of the Flies* mentality, where it was expected that new and emerging players would literally challenge for seats as they built their Test experience. It led to some unsavoury incidents – some straight-out fistfights as young bucks tried to prove their worth. Hart, who had been the team's co-coach in 1991, had seen the worst of it back then and was determined to clean up the team's culture.

The professional game would demand higher standards. There was the obvious physical element – the need for players to realise they were now high-performance athletes, and to regulate and reduce their alcohol intake accordingly. But Hart also knew that his team had to have a more corporate style: that top buttons needed to be done up, ties pulled straight, shirts ironed, shoes shined. He knew that if the commercial team were going to the market to sell the brand to potential sponsors, then the brand had to be living up to the values that were in the prospectus.

Hart, in assessing the professional landscape, had been able to persuade NZR to allow him to hire a team manager, a media manager and a sponsorship manager to work alongside him. He could see, and he was right, that the two facets of All Blacks life that were likely to change the most would be the demands made of players from media and from sponsors. There would be an obvious explosion of media interest given the new Super Rugby and Tri-Nations competitions, and an expectation from the biggest newspaper and TV outlets that the players help them generate content to promote the game. And the family of sponsors that had signed up to be part of the All Blacks Club in the late amateur age – all of which retained their investments once the game went professional – would likely want players to do more to help them leverage their investments.

As Hart recalls, 'I had to ask myself: when the All Blacks are together, what is acceptable and what is not? What are the standards for us? And things like the back of the bus. Things like "court sessions" – a ritual where a senior player was appointed as a mock judge, able to accuse teammates of humorous crimes for which they would be fined with a requirement to drink – you didn't say no, but you controlled the drinking. Some of them I had seen were terrible. I was unpopular with some of the players because they wanted to do a lot of the things they had always done, and I was the fun police. It was a bit lonely. Change wasn't easy.'

*

JUST HOW DIFFERENT LIFE had become is best measured by comparing the All Blacks first big tour of the professional age with the last they had embarked upon in the amateur age. In 1996, the All Blacks toured South Africa, each player earning thousands of dollars in the process: money that was paid, legally, into their bank accounts by their employer. No one was worrying about their 'real job' back home, because playing rugby was now their real job. But on their last amateur tour (excluding the World

Cup in 1995), to England and Scotland in 1993, the players had received a daily allowance that barely covered the cost of a day pass on the London Tube, and had to take holiday time from their employers. They couldn't be legally paid by NZR, and the only way some players could afford to be there was because of the wad of cash they received at the end of the tour from selling match tickets. Back then, players were all allocated two tickets for each Test, and the All Blacks players would appoint a committee to sell the tickets and share the proceeds.

The mindset on that 1993 tour was almost one of financial survival for some players, and while it was stressful at the time, such an attitude had its benefits when the game became professional. Most of the players, by necessity, had developed an acute appreciation for what sponsors could do for them, and so although the transition to professional life in 1996 was indeed hard, the All Blacks mostly managed it well.

In captain Sean Fitzpatrick they had someone who had been professional long before he was ever paid. The same would be true of many of his long-serving teammates, most of whom had come to see engagement with sponsors as an opportunity. There were the immediate in-kind returns sponsors could provide – free kit if they were an apparel sponsor, or, as was often the case, free beer after the game since the major brewers, particularly Lion Nathan, were knee-deep in rugby at the time. Sponsors' events could also provide networking opportunities for players – a chance to connect with a high-net worth, executive fraternity that might lead to job offers or career advancement. While Hart was worried about how his players would make the transition to professional life, many had already developed the skill sets they would need to engage with external stakeholders. More importantly, they understood the value of corporate investors, and came into the All Blacks camp with a healthy respect for the sports' benefactors.

The player with arguably the deepest appreciation for sponsors was Jeff Wilson. Freakishly talented, he had toured the United Kingdom with the All Blacks in 1993, winning his first Test cap at Murrayfield only a few weeks after he'd turned 20. Incredibly, six months earlier, he'd made his debut for the Blacks Caps in a one-day cricket international. It was his potential to star in two major sports that had drawn Nike to him, deepening his awareness of the role sponsors could play in professional sport.

'I was part of a sport that was professional, which was cricket,' says Wilson. 'In 1993, I was in the New Zealand cricket team and I was involved in four one-day internationals of a series of five, and I was away for just over two weeks and got, I think, between $10,000 and $12,000. It was mind-blowing. I was a student in Dunedin and it was a huge amount of money.

'I had a small taste of professionalism, and then six months later I got on a plane to England with the All Blacks, where it was going back to the daily allowance. But the daily allowance was a pittance. We had what was called the "lurks and perks", which was the ticket committee. The perks back then were you used to get these massive suitcases of gear. At the end of the tour the ticket committee had done a great job at selling the tickets and you got a distribution. I got to the end of the tour, and here is an envelope with cash in it and "thanks for everything you have done".

'When I played for Otago, our sponsors would give us certain things. In the old stand at Carisbrook there would be these trays with loaves of bread and bottles of milk, and it was take a handful kind of thing. After the game, Speights was the major sponsor so you would have a few beers. That was the extent of what you received.

'A lot of those senior All Blacks really understood that sponsors were important. Fitzy [Sean Fitzpatrick] was always there with the right bottle in his hand and the right cap on. He got it. The Auckland guys in particular just seemed to be really comfortable around doing commercial activity, and when they transitioned to professionalism they delivered.'

In 1996 the All Blacks had a small group of domestic sponsors – many of which had been part of the All Blacks Club – that included Ford, Lion Nathan, Coca-Cola, Air New Zealand and Philips. There was no detailed legal framework about where and when sponsors could utilise individuals, and players didn't have much, if any, detail written into their contracts that limited the amount of time they were obliged to give. It was more a collaborative, informal, use-your-common-sense setup, where sponsors were asked to be mindful of the players' high-performance needs and to avoid making gratuitous or egregious requests. And it mostly worked well.

'There were some sponsors who I would say I was always available for,' says Wilson. 'There were others that I would be available for some of the time, and then some that needed to be spread out for everybody. If you committed to everyone it would be ridiculous. If Sky asked to do a shoot, it would be, "Sure – what day are we doing it?" Don't get me wrong, there were some days you just didn't want to be there. And if you had a run of them, they could get tiresome. But you always accepted that you had a responsibility to be there.

'It was the same with the media. It is what you were paid for. If I wanted people to watch the game, I had to promote it, tell them about the story behind the game. We still had freedom and time to ourselves, and so when you were asked to do something, it wasn't as if you didn't have any time to yourself.'

While Hart had been concerned about how his players would make the transition to professionalism, many of them actually saw it as an intensification of the All Black life they already knew, rather than a radical revamp. What also helped smooth the transition was that the All Blacks enjoyed two great seasons in 1996 and 1997, losing just once while playing memorably good rugby. A winning team tends to be a happy team, and all the peripheral jobs – the media interviews, the sponsor functions, the photoshoots, the ads – were easier to do with a smile and a sense of gratitude.

But life became harder for the All Blacks in 1998, when they suffered one of their worst years in history. A team under pressure, having their every move considered and reported by the media, is one that doesn't find it so easy to smile for the camera, to talk to the sponsor's clients or give the interview where they must delicately handle discussion of their own poor performance.

The situation by the end of the 1998 season was so intense that NZR chief executive David Moffett says the board met in Sydney after the All Blacks had lost 19–14 to the Wallabies, in what was their fifth consecutive defeat. 'I went for a walk around Sydney Harbour with one of the board members, Tim Grierson,' recalls Moffett. 'John managing the team and everything else had become blurred and he had lost sight of his primary focus, which was to coach a winning All Blacks team. Had we had Graham Henry then as a choice, he would have been appointed to take the team to the 1999 World Cup. But Graham had signed with Wales.'

In late 1998, the impending arrival of Adidas as the All Blacks' lead sponsor was occupying the NZR board's thinking. When Roberts had been in Germany to finalise the deal, he joked as he shook hands with Robert Louis-Dreyfus that now that the deal was sealed, the All Blacks would deliver Adidas two World Cups.

Louis-Dreyfus laughed and took the comment in the lighthearted manner in which it was meant, but his smile couldn't entirely hide the fact that Adidas had high expectations for the All Blacks at the 1999 World Cup. It was rugby's showpiece event – the only time when audiences were truly global – and the All Blacks would be the only Adidas-sponsored team. Nothing had been said directly, but Moffett sensed that Adidas would be disappointed if the All Blacks did not at least make the final. 'They had put so much money into us,' he says. 'It was so important to Adidas to have that logo on the jersey for the World Cup.'

This was new territory for NZR and the All Blacks – the need to consider the commercial ramifications of poor performance. And it wasn't just being felt at board level. The players, or at least some of them, had become conscious of the greater number of stakeholders to whom they were beholden, and sensed a subliminal pressure building when their performances and results weren't what everyone expected. 'Having been great in 1996 and 1997, 1998 was a challenging year,' says Wilson, 'and it was probably the first time that sponsors would have been asking questions. That changed the level of pressure. All these people that had invested in the game would have been asking, "Where is the legacy right now?"'

Adidas had committed for five years on the strength of the All Blacks' legacy, and one poor season was unlikely to spook it. But NZR had to be aware that two bad seasons might damage its commercial relationships and its ability to secure more sponsors and keep the ones it had. As a result, there was serious discussion at board level to determine whether to retain Hart or not. In the end, Hart survived, partly because there was no viable alternative, but mostly because he still had the confidence of the players, and the board felt the coach would be able to learn and grow from the adversity he had faced in 1998.

It proved the right move, as the All Blacks bounced back in 1999, beating Samoa and France, before crunching South Africa 28–0 in the first Tri-Nations Test, held in Dunedin. They would win their next two Tests – at home against Australia and away against South Africa. But while some of the pressure on the field had eased, off it things were more intense than they'd ever been.

Adidas had been respectful of the heritage and purity of the jersey, but it had still raised the bar in how much time it was taking from the players. The hours spent capturing content had increased markedly, and because of the bigger budgets, productions were more professional and took longer to get right. 'You were definitely aware of it,' says Wilson. 'It is a global brand. It's a different mentality. There was more in terms of photoshoots and TV ads. We were a lot more visual, and there was more of a push of the All Blacks' brand and legacy.'

It wasn't just the arrival of the All Blacks' first major international sponsor that was changing the dynamic for the players. Many existing sponsors saw how astutely Adidas was leveraging its association with the All Blacks. Having spent close to $2 million to create its World Cup ad campaign, the company was also investing hugely to show it across the United Kingdom and Europe; the marketing spend even included securing a major billboard in London's Piccadilly Circus. Adidas was making other All Blacks sponsors realise what could be achieved if they invested more in their marketing and advertising. The unwritten rule of sports sponsorships is that the investor should match every dollar it pays to secure the association with one to leverage it. This, of course, was precisely what Adidas was doing.

And it was in the build-up to the 1999 World Cup that life started to change more obviously within the All Blacks. Coming into the professional era, they had definitely operated as a rugby team. But leading into what would be the fourth World Cup – one which was forecast to make gross commercial income of $210 million – they were operating more as a business. They were at the very least a hybrid entity – half sport, half business – and the players were spending increasing volumes of time fulfilling commercial and media obligations.

Hart's concerns about how his players would cope suddenly seemed more valid in 1999 than they had been in 1996. The team had lost a handful of senior players in 1998, and his squad was now younger: more players lacked the maturity and life skills to understand their obligations fully. This at a time when sponsors were asking for more and becoming a greater intrusion, and the media were incessantly looking for content. So there was greater pressure and less ability among the players to cope with it.

One specific campaign clearly illustrated how the new commercialisation of the All Blacks was intensifying in 1999. Air New Zealand, perhaps inspired by the impact Adidas wanted to make in the United Kingdom, decided that it too was going to make a big impression at the World Cup, which was why Hart found himself in a meeting with Moffett not long before the team was due to depart for London. The national carrier had painted a mural of the All Blacks front row on the tail of the plane that would be taking the team to Heathrow. The problem was that no one had consulted the team. Hart was not happy.

'We had a pre–World Cup training camp in Palmerston North, and I used to have a regular meeting with Moffett,' says Hart. 'We had one more day of our camp to go and then we were disbanding for three or four days and off to the UK. He said he wanted three players to come up to Auckland after the camp. I said, "Sure, what for?" He said, "Air New Zealand have got a promotion and we need to have some players at the airport."

"What's the promotion?" He said, "They have got the front row of the All Blacks painted on the plane." I said, "What!" I had some steam up. They were going to uncover this plane, so obviously it had been pre-negotiated months before and the players had no idea.

'I had to go in and tell the players what the promotion was, and they immediately thought I was in on it. I couldn't bag the union because they were my employer too, so I had to be bloody careful. Ian Jones said he would do it, and of course he and the others went up there but refused to be photographed next to the plane. They wouldn't go near it – and that was a good example of a horrible, commercial decision which impinged on the fundamental value of humility, which the All Blacks would say was one of our underpinned values ...

'It was terrible and that put us under all sorts of pressure. Horrific pressure. Internally, that had an impact on the team because they thought I had let them down. That the management had let them down. Mike Banks and I took the crunch, but it was an example where the commercial arm and the rugby arm had no synergy. I reckon they didn't tell us because they knew I would have fought it. And I would have, because I had been taught all my life the value of humility. It is not just a story – humility is a big part of what has made the All Blacks a wonderful team for so long.'

But as much as Hart was incensed by being left in the dark and by the nature of the campaign, this need to bend to commercial interests was now part and parcel of professional life. The All Blacks were becoming corporatised because they had to generate the sort of money they needed to pay their players and meet the running costs of the sport. This, after all, was the very world the players had pushed for in the early to mid-1990s. They had wanted an end to the bad old days of 'shamateurism', they had gladly and willingly turned their backs on the devil they knew, and now it was too late to go back. This was their new reality: a multifaceted world of increased conditioning, training, commercial, media and community demands that could at times, especially in combination, be overwhelming. This was the effect of professionalism, the consequence of creating a money wheel that had to be greased.

This tension between the high-performance and commercial sides of the All Blacks would never go away. There was no way to avoid it, because these two worlds couldn't be kept entirely apart. Most of the time they could live happily alongside each other, but there would be occasions when they would have to meet, and the risk would be that the desires of the commercial team wouldn't sit well with the values of the players. Essentially, the need to commercialise the All Blacks to generate more money to pay the All Blacks had generated what would become a perennial battle of wills between those managing the team and those selling the team, with the chief executive of NZR sitting as referee.

'When John found out that Air New Zealand was going to paint the plane with the All Blacks front row on it to take them to the 1999 World Cup, he hit the roof,' says David Moffett. 'He didn't understand. Air New Zealand was one of our major sponsors and they wanted to do this. It cost us nothing, and John Hart, who is this guy who is supposedly so commercial, basically said he wasn't going to take the All Blacks on that airplane. I told him that, yes, he would be. The saying is that rugby is too much of a sport to be a business, and too much of a business to be a sport in the professional era. But as a chief executive, because I had a business and a rugby background, I was able to understand that and work out how we were going to manage all this stuff. That allowed me to leave after four years thinking we had done a pretty good job.'

Moffett had done a good job. He had been instrumental in securing the broadcast deal in 1995, and then Adidas as the apparel sponsor. He arrived at a time when NZR's annual revenue was about $13 million and he left with it at $76 million, and he'd also put $67 million into cash reserves. That was why he decided, in mid-1999, that the time was right for him to leave. He took up a job as chief executive of Australia's National Rugby League (NRL).

Moffett's replacement at NZR, David Rutherford, would be leading a different organisation to the one Moffett had discovered when he arrived in 1996. The All Blacks had become a bigger brand, and now had a fledgling overseas presence that seemed destined to grow quickly. And given the conflict that had arisen around the plane, it seemed that the new chief executive would need help managing the inevitable tensions between the commercial and high-performance arms of the All Blacks.

In fact, what he needed was an entirely new regulatory framework, through which the players could be better managed. And that was handy, because Rutherford was a highly experienced lawyer, having been a partner at legal firm Bell Gully for much of his career. He was entirely open to an employment revolution.

CHAPTER FIVE

ONE FOR ALL, AND ALL FOR ONE

MOST OF THE WORLD'S best-known brands have a relatively simple relationship with their labour force. That's because most of the world's best-known brands create and sell manufactured products at scale. It is the product for which the brand is famous. If we think of Apple or Nike, for instance, their business, and by extension their profitability, has been built on securing relatively cheap unskilled labour.

The situation with high-profile professional sports teams is vastly different. The players are simultaneously both the labour force and the product. This creates an unusual dynamic, whereby employees' advocates can argue that player wages need to be directly and materially linked to revenue growth. The more successful a sports team becomes, the more the players must be paid, to reflect their contribution as both the labour force and the product.

In the case of the All Blacks, the situation was more

complicated, because unlike Manchester United, Real Madrid and the Chicago Bulls, the All Blacks were a brand within a wider holding organisation, which was New Zealand Rugby. The national body had to manage the All Blacks while also managing the rest of the professional rugby landscape and, just as importantly, the community game too. Commit too much money to growing the All Blacks and there might not be enough to fund the next generation of All Blacks. Fail to put enough money into the All Blacks and they might cease to be successful, which could cause sponsorships and broadcast revenue to drop, and then there is no longer enough money in the NZR pot to fund the community game. Finding the right investment balance occupied much of NZR's time in the early years of professionalism.

There were, however, two critical decisions that had been made in the scramble to save the game from WRC in mid-1995 that had given NZR a high degree of control over its labour force. The first was that it centralised the player contracts. It was the undisputed, 100 per cent shareholder in every professional rugby entity in New Zealand, and the one and only owner of every professional contract. It paid players to be part of the National Provincial Championship, Super Rugby and Test matches. This gave the players certainty and clarity about who their employer was.

This was not the situation in England or France, where the players signed contracts with their clubs, all of which were privately owned and had no connection with or obligation to the national unions. If players were picked to play international rugby, they would then sign a separate contract with the national body. It was a scenario that made for endless conflict between the clubs and the national unions as they battled for access to the players.

The second key decision that NZR made early was to declare that to be eligible for the All Blacks, players had to be playing in New Zealand. This was a simple and non-negotiable condition – if a player didn't have a contract with NZR, they couldn't be picked for the All Blacks. In some ways this was a risky move by the national body, because it was inevitable, given the size and wealth of the major European nations, that the biggest English and French clubs were going to offer players enormous salaries. NZR was never going to be able to compete on monetary terms, so if it had said players could be based in England and play for the All Blacks, an exodus would likely have occurred. But NZR knew the emotional lure of the black jersey was strong, and that many – maybe even most – players would be willing to sacrifice the greater income they could enjoy elsewhere to keep alive that opportunity to play for the All Blacks. What the players gained financially by leaving would have to be weighed against the long-term career benefits that might arise from becoming an All Black.

The black jersey, however, couldn't be asked to do all the heavy lifting. While NZR couldn't match what the European clubs could offer New Zealand's rugby talent financially, it still had to get as close as it could. It had to keep generating revenue to ensure it could put reasonably competitive contracts in front of its best players, so the gap between what they could earn in Europe and New Zealand was not so big that it would convince them to give up their All Blacks aspirations.

In those first years of professionalism, NZR was mostly able to retain its labour force. By 1998, French and English clubs were increasingly looking to New Zealand to buy star quality. But typically the players they were able to entice tended to be older and at the end of their careers. The ones who left were often aware that their days in the black jersey were either over or about to be, and a monumental contract with an overseas club was a way to enjoy an overseas experience and a few additional well-paid years. Those with seemingly achievable All Blacks aspirations mostly stayed in New Zealand.

When the first contracts were offered in mid-1995, most players in New Zealand sought legal advice from one of three lawyers – Warren Alcock, Ian Jones and David Howman. These three shared information about how much their clients were being paid. It created an informal network of intelligence to cross-check that players deemed to be at a similar level of ability and experience were being paid a similar wage. Valuing productivity was not an issue: as a labour force, the players had little to complain about.

But they were, of course, more than just a labour force. They were also the product – the very thing that made brand All Blacks – and this was where tension arose between the players and NZR.

The national body had a decidedly narrow view about what constituted the All Blacks brand. Possibly because it saw everything through a protectionist lens, NZR considered the All Blacks brand to be a tangible entity built around a trademark, a jersey, a logo and properties that could be licensed and sold.

It didn't necessarily recognise that the All Blacks had a human component that shaped and changed the brand.

NZR didn't agree that the intellectual property of the All Blacks was not inherent within the jersey itself, but produced and arguably owned, or at least jointly owned, by those who wore it. The All Blacks had consistent values but regularly changing personnel. The players, especially those who managed to enjoy long careers or capture the nation's admiration and attention, were indistinguishable from the brand. They were the brand, and the brand was the players – and that meant many of the individuals were highly marketable. And one player in particular had more pull than any other. Jonah Lomu, at the peak of his fame in the late 1990s, was arguably a bigger brand than the All Blacks, and in many ways his case reflects the biggest problem with the commercial landscape.

NZR didn't see the players as brands, and it certainly didn't believe they should have any ability to leverage whatever fame they had accumulated from being All Blacks. NZR owned the players' contracts and, by extension, the players – end of story. There was no provision in the employment contracts for players to monetise their image and no framework of regulations to detail the terms on which they could strike individual endorsement deals or conduct promotions separate to their NZR obligations.

'The provisions relating to image back then were pretty brief,' recalls Warren Alcock. 'I am pretty sure the contracts said NZR owned everything, and if you wanted to do something, you had to get their consent, which was never easy. You have to remember that, at the time, the commercial market was pretty immature, and if I look back to that period, we didn't have a huge number of commercial deals for our players. There is no doubt that the commercial aspects of players' rights were not the biggest priority.'

Part of the reason there were so few individual commercial opportunities is that the centralisation model meant NZR was responsible for meeting all the costs of running the game, so it had to control all the means of generating revenue. Sponsorships were all sold around the collective: corporates were buying into the All Blacks, and not into individual players, so NZR had to be militant about ensuring that its investors were protected. Once Adidas came on board as a head-to-toe apparel partner, no individual could have a separate, competing agreement with, for example, Nike. With collective arrangements in place with Air New Zealand, Ford, Coca-Cola and Philips, no player was permitted to sign an endorsement deal with any competing company.

Centralised contracts had their advantages, but this was arguably the one major downside: the players didn't have any contractual freedom to exploit their own fame and profile. Instead, they had to give their time to help promote and market the sponsorships that had been signed by NZR. The benefits of that were indirect: the players had to hope that their servicing of the sponsorship agreements that NZR had made would help to grow the value of the All Blacks brand, and that total revenue coming into the game would therefore grow. And if there was more money, then there was a greater likelihood of the players being able to negotiate higher salaries when their next contract negotiation came around.

But this was risky, because NZR was using the All Blacks to generate income for the whole of the sport, right down to the grassroots. It was entirely feasible that a high-profile All Black might spend hours on photoshoots with Adidas and other sponsors and not receive a cent in return, if his next contract negotiation didn't go well. NZR effectively owned the players' image rights and could use them how they liked – as evidenced by the Air New Zealand promotion ahead of the 1999 World Cup. The three players whose images had been painted across the plane had no right to object once the fuselage was painted, and they could not directly monetise the use of their images. It was never clear what would have happened if, when Moffett requested that a few players attend the unveiling of the plane at Auckland Airport, they had refused. The situation was clearly unsustainable. The contractual engagement between the players and NZR needed to be considerably more detailed, regulated and transparent if it were to lessen the sense of exploitation that was brewing.

*

BY THE TIME THE All Blacks arrived home from the 1999 World Cup, chastened and deflated after their infamous semi-final defeat to France, momentum was building to create a trade union for the players. It was a topic that had been discussed at length during the World Cup, mostly by recent former players who had been invalided out of the game.

The World Cup had highlighted just how much had changed in the four years since rugby had turned professional. The 1999

World Cup had big brands crawling all over it, and TV audiences that it could only previously have dreamed of. Many of the players were now enjoying greater recognition, some even having a profile beyond rugby, and it was apparent that the game's commercial prospects were improving at pace.

But it was also apparent that while change had been rapid in some areas, it had been slow in others. There was no concept of professional development, or any mechanism to aid players who had been injured transition out of the game. There was also limited transparency as to the overall wealth of NZR, or any communication to flag its strategic direction. The players were overly reliant on the intelligence network formed by the small group of lawyers looking after them. The only real leverage anyone had was to threaten to head offshore.

The labour conditions weren't bad as such, but in the aftermath of the 1999 World Cup many became aware that they needed to become more sophisticated, so that those managing provincial, Super Rugby and national teams would be accountable for delivering safe cultures and work environments that enabled players to perform at their best. There had to be more detail built into contracts about medical insurance, employer responsibilities and minimum salary expectations to ensure no one was being exploited. Above all else, the relationship between the players and NZR needed to be better defined so there were fewer grey areas about playing, commercial and community obligations. To achieve this, there had to be greater transparency – a requirement for NZR to reveal the full extent of its accounts so the players and their representatives could understand the totality of the market in which they were operating.

The legal triumvirate of Howman, Jones and Alcock worked with NZR and former All Blacks captain Sean Fitzpatrick to hammer out what a players' association could look like. They also worked with legal firm Bell Gully – specifically Andrew Scott-Howman, David's brother and one of the country's best specialist employment lawyers – to draw up a draft constitution. Within days of the constitution being released, 45 players had signed up and elected a board, with 1987 World Cup–winning captain David Kirk as chair, and former or current players Robin Brooke, Todd Miller, Norm Hewitt, Chris England and Simon Culhane, as well as Sara Tetro (at the time the wife of former All Black Craig Innes), serving as directors. The next step was to look for someone to run the association – to be the hands-on, driving force. NZR took control of that process on the basis it had provided the bulk of the funding to launch the association, and invited a handful of candidates to present their vision and credentials.

One of those invited to interview was a young entrepreneur by the name of Rob Nichol. By early 2000 he was at a crossroads in his career. Having begun his working life as a police officer, he'd left the force to join major accountancy firm Ernst & Young's graduate programme. He knew after a few years there that he didn't want to be an accountant, but he did want to do accountancy work, and he and a senior colleague left to set up their own firm consulting for and investing in emerging businesses. Primarily, Nichol found himself working with Carter

Holt Harvey, a timber and building conglomerate, which had $20 million to invest in startup ideas brought in by its own staff and contractors. Nichol had waded through more than 1600 ideas to choose just six for funding, two of which went on to list on the stock market. It was through this work that his name cropped up on NZR's radar as a potential leader of the association.

Nichol recalls: 'At the interview we said, "We don't want to run this long-term, but it strikes us that you need a business plan. How is it going to be funded long-term? And then you need to recruit the right person to run it. We are happy to do that for you over a three-to-six-month period." That was the pitch. We felt that without a business plan it would be reliant on the NZR for funding, and that didn't seem right. They rang up after the interview and they said, "There was merit in your plan, but we have decided to go with someone else." I didn't think any more about it.'

Three weeks later, Nichol was surprised to receive a call from Sara Tetro. She asked if he would be able to meet in Wellington and talk through his ideas for the players' association with a few of the board members. When he explained that he'd been interviewed and rejected for the role, Tetro said: 'We understand that, and the NZR have sent us across who they want to recruit to run the place, and we have pointed out that they are not the board of the association. We are.'

Nichol duly flew to the capital, met with Hewitt, Tetro and Howman, and a few days later was asked if he would agree to run the new players' association. He asked how much money the new body had available. The answer was $30,000, which had come from NZR. That was all they would have for the first 18 months. But Nichol was sold on the idea, and keen to make a difference, so he said yes, even agreeing to not take a fee until the association had secured a sustainable revenue stream from which he could be paid.

*

HAVING GROWN UP ON Stewart Island, a small island off the south coast of the South Island, Nichol had a pioneering spirit – a capacity to forge through tough conditions – which was going to be handy in his new role. Once he had his feet under the desk, Nichol could see that the player contracting model needed a massive overhaul. The labour market was being controlled by unsophisticated contracts and held together by trust and goodwill. Nichol had no inherent knowledge of high-performance environments as such, but after a few months he understood that New Zealand's players, while they were essentially well enough paid, were not being looked after and protected as they should have been.

'It was very much that top-down control kind of model,' he says. 'The administration were organised and they were making the decisions about the contractual terms and conditions – which were pretty much take it or leave, with the exception of maybe a couple of elite players who could leverage an overseas opportunity. But everyone else was basically handed something and told, "This is what it is." There were a lot of terms and conditions in there that were archaic, such as you had to be fit to be paid. There was no real health and safety purpose – how you create environments that are good for people. The athletes weren't organised, so it was every man for himself. The terms and conditions for the athletes were not that smart, and there was no voice for them around the table, and the collective ability to have hard conversations wasn't there. There was no concept of how much money was coming into the game, no transparency, no information.'

Nichol, having ascertained the state of labour relations, jointly built a strategy with the association's board and then presented it to the players. By early 2000 they had agreed on a long-term vision on where they saw the game going and how they wanted their relationship with NZR to look. There was a sense of new beginnings – not just because the association had been formed and now had a plan, but also because NZR had a new chief executive and a greater sense of how commercialised and popular the game was becoming on the back of the 1999 World Cup.

And so there was an air of optimism, excitement even, when Nichol and Scott-Howman met with NZR chief executive David Rutherford to determine how they were going to forge a new path together. Rutherford, quick-witted and in possession of a brilliant mind, laid out his vision for the game. While Rutherford's background was in law, he'd spent the decade prior to joining the NZR in executive positions in the building and agricultural industries. He'd been a keen rugby player, and when he finished setting out his thoughts on the whiteboard, Nichol flipped it over to set out his.

When they compared the two, they were remarkably similar but for one key aspect. 'At the end of our pitch we said the one thing we need is a partnership,' says Nichol. 'If you haven't got the talent – the athletes – working in partnership with the administration, then what have you got? He [Rutherford] had left that out. The more you have players committed to the vision and the environment, the more likely you are to retain them. If they don't buy in, it is too easy for them to go overseas for money, and they won't feel a sense of responsibility. The athletes wanted to take some responsibility for their environment and wanted to be at the decision-making table, because without it, New Zealand Rugby won't be as strong as it could be.'

Persuading Rutherford to see the importance of building a partnership with the players was one of two major breakthroughs. The second came after Scott-Howman interpreted the new *Employment Relations Act* to deem that the players were not in fact contractors of NZR, as they had until then been considered, but employees. The distinction was critical, because under the act, all employees had the right to bargain with their employer collectively. The labour market would become entirely transparent under a collective agreement, and there would be a guiding document setting out obligations and expectations for every imaginable scenario. That would bring clarity to every aspect of professional rugby players' lives, and there would be no need to rely on goodwill or trust to make sure sponsors and media got what they needed. Those engagements and relationships would be regulated collectively, as long as Rutherford agreed to grant the players the right to enter into collective bargaining.

'We handed him a letter at that same meeting which compelled collective bargaining,' says Nichol. 'He said, "What's this?" We said we wanted to collectively bargain the terms and conditions under which players are employed in New Zealand, and we want to use that as the basis to form this partnership. He said, "You are joking?" We said no, we weren't, and he said, "Give me 30 minutes."

'David is a smart lawyer, and he came back and said, "We have got two choices here: we can fight this and probably lose, which is going to leave us in a horrible position. Or we can embrace it and form the smartest partnership in rugby. We have decided to go with the latter."

'And that's how it started. It wasn't the fight or the fact they would lose, it was the message it would convey to the players that "we don't give a shit about you" ... he'd worked all that out. A different person may have fought it, but he embraced it and we committed to bargaining and it took 18 months.'

The first collective agreement ended up being close to 100 pages, but in essence, Nichol says, it could be boiled down to one key change, which was a reclamation of ownership on the part of the players. In the rush to professionalism, the players had arguably been the big losers, even though, given that they were finally being paid, they had initially believed they'd been the big winners. What they had not realised was that the right to sell their image would be just as important to them as the right to sell their labour.

'Professional rugby really comes down to property – who owns what,' says Nichol. 'And those first contracts were written by NZR's lawyers in a way that gave them everything they wanted ... forever. It was, like, three or four pages around image rights which said the same thing over and over, which was that they owned everything and the player didn't own a single thing. Everything they are and could become belonged to NZR, to do with [as] they wanted. What we managed to establish in that first agreement is that players own their own property rights and the NZR owns their own property rights, and the partnership between the two combined those two rights. Labour is one thing, but the big thing is image rights. Once we established ownership of the players' IP rights, everything could go from there.'

The collective agreement was transformational. Revolutionary, even. It put New Zealand light years ahead of the other major rugby nations, which continued to be ripped apart by the bickering between club and country, with the players sitting between them, very much the victims of the hostilities. New Zealand now not only had a degree of sophistication to its player contracts, but also a partnership. That was critical, as it gave the payers a degree of ownership that drew them closer to the black jersey and made them more inclined to stay in New Zealand even when ludicrous contract offers came in from abroad. They now had a better working environment in which their needs were listened to, and as a result they felt they were at the cutting edge of high performance.

Rutherford, new in the job, had made an inspired decision to grant the players collective bargaining rights. But it might have been beginner's luck, as his tenure would ultimately be defined by two critical mistakes he made in the months that followed.

CHAPTER SIX

CRY FOR HELP

WHEN THE ALL BLACKS lost their 1999 World Cup semi-final to France, head coach John Hart knew his position was untenable. Rather than wait for the sword to take him, he fell on it before the team had even returned to New Zealand. In his place came Wayne Smith, a former All Black recognised as having one of the most astute rugby brains in the country when he'd coached the Crusaders to Super Rugby titles in 1998 and 1999. Smith was not only rugby-smart, however, he was also emotionally intelligent to a rare degree – a coach with deep insight into the human condition and an awareness of how emotions impacted performance. He was business-savvy too. He didn't have the long corporate background of Hart, but he had spent three years as chief executive of the Hawke's Bay Rugby Union before joining the Crusaders.

As a player in the 1970s and 1980s – a time in which he won 17 All Blacks caps and became a household name in Canterbury – Smith generated enduring respect and gratitude for sponsors. It wasn't as if he or any of his teammates were having endless freebies lavished upon them, but he had a relationship with Adidas that provided him with boots and kit.

'As a player for Canterbury, as part of that era, there were a few of us who became Adidas athletes,' he says. 'There was no money, but we had kangaroo hide boots in red and black. I had a huge gratitude for sponsors by the time we came into the professional game. And I have retained that. I have always been grateful that anyone was prepared to give to the game and support us. What it did mean is that I was always happy to go to sponsorship promotions or whatever, and while it may have taken a bit of time, I still maintained that we were bloody lucky to be getting what we were getting. For me it was something you did to pay back.'

When he became chief executive of Hawke's Bay in 1994, Smith says, he had a rudimentary understanding of rugby economics, but his approach to business was unconventional. He relied on the strength of his relationships; he signed one major sponsorship deal on the back of a napkin after a few beers in the office. It was unorthodox but it worked.

While Smith was not a natural chief executive, his stint at Hawke's Bay gave him a greater understanding of how the game's finances operated. Given the corporatisation of the All Blacks that had occurred since 1996, Smith appealed as the right coach: he was clever, compassionate and clued in to the real world of professional sport.

Smith wasn't thinking short-term when he became All Blacks coach. He tried to instil a culture where values and ideas would be enduring. He wanted the players to live up to specific professional and personal standards, and to understand, truly, what it meant to be an All Black.

'I was trying to create a vision-driven, values-based campaign, which the All Blacks had not done before,' he says. 'Start attaching some legacy stuff to it, look at the past. Who are we? Who went before us? Who are we honouring? And how are we going to build that? It was a massive job. It would have been easier just to go in and coach the team, but it wasn't the way I operate, and I wanted to create something special and develop something that was going to last longer than me. That whole concept that when you pass the jersey on it has to be in a better state. It put a lot of pressure on me, or I put a lot of pressure on myself. There was very much an understanding that showing respect to everyone – whether it was a promotion, to the public, a sponsor – you uphold All Blacks standards.'

Smith's vision was perfect for the professional All Blacks. Being a values-based team would suit both their high-performance and commercial needs. The idea of having standards at training and standards off the field was exactly what the professional game demanded, and the sort of vision that would attract commercial interest. But unfortunately, while the theory was perfect, Smith was struggling to get the execution right.

The step up to being coach of the All Blacks was higher than he'd anticipated. The scale of the job was bigger than he appreciated and there simply weren't enough staff and support at the time to enable him to cope with the intensity of the role.

'I had been a professional coach since 1997 without any real commercial pressures compared with the national team, and because I have a big work ethic, and always promise myself I will work harder than anyone else, it put a lot of strain on me,' he reflects. 'I felt that I wanted the job, I got the job and so it was my responsibility to perform. And I spent a good 12 to 14 hours a day trying to do that, and I just assumed I would handle it, but it was difficult.

'I could feel the transition from having been a player with the All Blacks in the '80s to being involved as a coach in the late '90s. There was a whole different level of promotion and recognition around the world of understanding the All Blacks brand. It was just another level to when I played.

'I don't think I did a good job in the commercial space, essentially because I felt a bit overwhelmed coming into the job. I had to get an office in the centre of Christchurch and had a PA to manage my workload. I had to work with sponsors because I had promotional work to do. I had a lot of media stuff, and all I wanted was to be a rugby coach. I left a lot [of commercial activity management] up to the Colonel, Andrew Martin [the All Blacks' team manager], who was good at that and always positive about supporting the union through supporting the sponsors.'

By September 2001, Smith was riddled with self-doubt. The All Blacks had lost three Tests in 2000. They had played good rugby along the way, but the three losses were incurred in a run of four matches, which had given the side an air of vulnerability. In 2001, they looked less fragile, but the concession of a last-minute penalty saw them lose by a point to Australia in Wellington, and then, almost unbelievably, they conceded a last-minute try in the second game in Sydney to lose to the Wallabies for a third consecutive match.

The All Blacks under Smith had won 12 of their 17 Tests, and while this was by no means a disastrous record, it was enough for the coach to publicly express doubt as to whether he was the right man for the job. If it was intended as a cry for reassurance from his employer, it wasn't taken that way at NZR. Rutherford and his board took Smith's comment at face value – as an admission he wasn't up to it – and his job was put on the market. And so a moment of weakness cost Smith his dream role, as after shortlisting four candidates – one of whom was the incumbent, who by all accounts gave a stunning presentation – NZR opted to appoint John Mitchell.

The 37-year-old Mitchell had been a provincial hero for Waikato throughout the late 1980s and early 1990s, earning an All Blacks call-up in 1993 to tour the UK as midweek captain. A qualified quantity surveyor, Mitchell had spent time in Ireland at the end of his playing career, before landing a coaching role with the Manchester-based club Sale, from where he was appointed England's forwards coach under Clive Woodward. He'd come back to New Zealand in 2001 to take up the head role with the Chiefs.

While Mitchell's coaching résumé was impressive, he was inexperienced. What had sold him to the board, however, were his hard edges. Smith's compassion and understanding had been mistaken for weakness. His values-based coaching was ultimately deemed gimmicky and too soft for the All Blacks, who had historically been managed in uncompromising, almost uncaring environments. The board wrongly pegged Smith as a sort of new-age guru, and a desire to move away from that was what largely drew them to Mitchell. He would be a more dictatorial coach, less tolerant of human frailties and less inclined to view his athletes holistically.

In announcing the appointment of Mitchell, NZR chair Murray McCaw said: 'As an All Black, John epitomised many of the qualities that will be required of his players in the next two years if they are to win the Rugby World Cup. John demonstrated to the panel that he has the right combination of old-fashioned All Blacks values and innovation needed to win in the modern game.'

The board's reading of Smith and its appointment of Mitchell were catastrophic misjudgements. It had failed to appreciate the multifaceted demands that came with being All Blacks coach. Smith was on the right track. He was making the All Blacks a genuine high-performance environment where players had an element of self-responsibility and a growing understanding of their wider obligations to sponsors, fans and media. What he needed in September 2001 was more support. He was struggling with the scale of the role at a time when the All Blacks were still operating with a lean, almost skeletal management crew. Rather than oust him, the board should have sat down with Smith and tried to better understand the needs of the team. The All Blacks were no longer a pure rugby entity, and yet, in Mitchell, the board had appointed a coach who was most definitely an old-school rugby man.

Mitchell had been a tough, direct player, qualities that he'd taken into his coaching. He didn't brim with emotion and didn't appear to have much compassion or empathy for his athletes. He had a confrontational style of coaching, but it had proven effective wherever he'd been. Sale had played well under Mitchell, and England had been keen to keep him when the Chiefs offered him the job. His rugby brain was sharp and his tactical appreciation good, and he had no issues telling the players what he thought they needed to hear.

But in convincing themselves that the All Blacks needed a more traditional, hard-nosed coach who was going to bark a few home truths at the players, the NZR board lost sight of the full spectrum of what the head job entailed. Mitchell may have impressed them with his desire to get back to a less collaborative regime, but the All Blacks had moved on enormously since his brief playing stint. While both Hart and Smith had tried to deter and even eradicate some of the older All Blacks traditions – such as excessive drinking and the status of 'the back seat of the bus' – Mitchell saw them as integral to the unity and cohesion of his squad. Hart and Smith had been focused on building cultures where values were universal and applicable in every aspect of All Blacks life. Mitchell didn't share this holistic view, and wound back the clock to some extent on his first tour in charge, to the United Kingdom, Ireland and Argentina in November 2001.

After the team had beaten Scotland in Edinburgh, they held an infamous court session, where team manager Martin was, according to some senior players, bullied into drinking copiously and becoming heavily intoxicated against his will. In his biography, Anton Oliver, who captained the side on that trip, says Mitchell refused to intervene to protect Martin from humiliation, and instead revelled in the manager's embarrassment.

This might be seen to be Machiavellian politics at work. Mitchell had never liked the idea when he took the job that he would be reporting directly to the team manager. In his view, he should have been reporting directly to the chief executive, a point he made clear many years later in his biography, *Mitch: The Real Story.* He revealed in his book that there were two major surprises relating to his contract. He was asked to sign it at the home of manager Andrew Martin when he felt business of this nature should have been conducted in a more formal setting such as an office or hotel. He was more shocked, however, after reading it to see that he would be reporting directly to Martin and not chief executive Rutherford. He says he initially refused to sign, telling Rutherford that he felt as All Blacks coach, he was the leader of the All Blacks.

Mitchell was ultimately given no choice – Martin, a former SAS colonel, came with the job, and the hierarchy was not going to be changed. Mitchell's argument that he needed to be the leader of the All Blacks would have carried greater weight had the All Blacks solely been a rugby team. But of course, by October 2001, when he was appointed, they were so much more than that, and Mitchell, whether he liked the idea or not, could only lay claim to be the head of the All Blacks' high-performance arm. Hence the NZR board wanted Martin, with his broader skill set and appreciation of all the elements required to keep the team functioning and performing in all their key metrics, both on and off the field, to be their direct source of operational updates.

Mitchell had agreed to the structure, but he worked against it once he was in the job. His relationship with Martin was tense and awkward, with the manager hinting in 2003 that he had been undermined and hindered by the coach. 'I wasn't there for the blazer or to just have a good time. It meant a lot to me,' Martin said. 'I was anxious, if not determined, to make it work, even if I was somewhat handicapped by Mitchell. He was not prepared to accept that the manager, as the leader of the organisation, was the person to whom he was answerable. Off the field, John wanted to have the full and final say.'

Mitchell's tactic of ostracising Martin was an unsophisticated and cruel way to try to instigate change. It also had commercial consequences, as Martin remained responsible for ensuring players were fulfilling their sponsor and media obligations. But without any support from his coach, and possibly because he was being undermined by Mitchell, Martin lost traction with the players and standards slipped in 2002.

The Adidas contract included more than just apparel – it extended to balls and other playing equipment too. The June Tests that year saw the All Blacks play with an Adidas ball – one that goalkickers Andrew Mehrtens and Tony Brown voiced their complaints about, with the former referring to it as a 'flying pig'. 'The ball is dead,' Mehrtens told media after the All Blacks had beaten Ireland in Dunedin. 'It doesn't fly and we've told them that till we're blue in the face. I'm not using that as an excuse but the ball's a pig. It's slippery. There should be a standard ball and this one shouldn't be it. Everyone prefers the Gilbert.[2]

To complain about the ball was one thing, but to openly endorse a competitor's product while doing so was another entirely. It indicated an almost cavalier disrespect for a sponsorship that was critical in helping NZR meet its wage bill. The fact that there was no public rebuke for Mehrtens from Mitchell – nor even an attempt to walk back the comments, or apologise for them – spoke volumes. It alluded to the lack of professional maturity within the broader rugby landscape, but specifically within Mitchell's All Blacks. Adidas, as Martyn Brewer admits, did have issues getting the ball right. 'We had problems with the ball,' he says. 'It was not flying right, and biomechanically there were a lot of issues to work out. The team and the players had the right to complain.'

But while the players may have had the right to complain, the process by which they did so was entirely wrong. There were ways to channel feedback – players and All Blacks management could speak directly and privately with the relevant people at Adidas to voice their concerns. To go public and to generate negative headlines for Adidas and have the media sniff tension in the relationship was damaging. It felt needlessly aggressive, almost as if Adidas were being treated with disdain by the players. That sense was intensified when individuals turned up to functions or media engagements in the wrong attire. On one occasion, lock Troy Flavell was pictured wearing Adidas clothing but Puma footwear.

Mitchell had been hired to restore a hard edge to the All Blacks, and he certainly did that. But his desire to toughen the organisation extended too far. The All Blacks could be unforgiving and ruthless on the field, but the modern era demanded something softer and more accommodating in other areas.

Mitchell hadn't fully understood, or had wilfully ignored, the wider world in which the All Blacks were operating. He didn't seem to connect the dots and understand the new ecosystem in which he was living, or to recognise that high performance is not totally detached from commercial realities.

Certainly, the All Blacks regressed culturally under Mitchell, and what it meant to be an All Black was considered through a narrow lens. Mitchell's was not an era of enlightenment, but one where the players were systematically de-corporatised and steadily disconnected from their commercial partners.

The board had to accept culpability for this. They had backed Mitchell on an old-school ticket, hoping his direct approach would instil within the players the mental starch they would need to stop losing games in the last minute, as they had too frequently done under Smith. They had not necessarily misread Mitchell, but they had misread what the All Blacks required. Just as Mitchell didn't appear to appreciate the full range of demands inherent in the professional era, neither did the board. They seemed to have little idea about the commercial realities of running a professional sport – a fact that would be painfully and catastrophically demonstrated in April 2002.

CHAPTER SEVEN

AMATEUR HOUR

THE FIRST WORLD CUP, held in 1987, kicked off on a Tuesday afternoon in Auckland, where a barely half-full Eden Park saw the All Blacks run amok against Italy. The game had begun after what can only be described as a budget opening ceremony, with local kids walking around the edge of the field holding flags, looking a little bemused but also chuffed at having been granted a day off school.

The tournament had a festival vibe, with most of the Northern Hemisphere players – certainly the English team – treating it more as an end-of-season drinking tour with a bit of rugby thrown in. It was all a bit of a laugh – a fun idea dreamed up by a few Southern Hemisphere administrators, who through their perseverance and passion had managed to persuade World Rugby to sanction their concept more out of intrigue than from a genuine belief it had long-term prospects.

That 1987 tournament, jointly hosted by New Zealand and Australia, was put together on the smell of an oily rag. It did, however – thanks to some heavyweight backing from a Japanese telecom giant, KDD – return a relatively impressive $9 million in profit, which alerted World Rugby and the Northern Hemisphere unions to the financial potential of this four-yearly get-together. Having initially been sceptical, the game's global governing body was suddenly a World Cup convert.

The 1991 hosting rights were given to England, Scotland, Ireland, Wales and France. With their bigger stadia and populations, World Rugby was able to find big sponsors, and the second edition of the World Cup returned $57 million in non-ticket income. From being something of an experimental concept, the World Cup quickly became the most significant asset World Rugby owned. Such was the size of its commercial base that the governing body effectively had to set up a separate company dedicated to managing the tournament.

In 1995 World Rugby engaged the International Management Group (IMG) to handle the non-ticket sales component of the tournament – that is, to negotiate broadcast, sponsorship and hospitality contracts. Whatever the 1987 World Cup had started out as, by the time of the third tournament, played in South Africa, it was an entirely different beast.

When in April 1997 World Rugby opened the tender process for the 2003 tournament – the hosting rights to the 1999 tournament had already been won by Wales – New Zealand and Australia agreed in principle to mount a joint bid. They had agreed a barebones outline whereby each country would host two pools, two quarter-finals and one semi-final; the final would be in Australia. Each union would account for and maintain revenue and expenditure relating to the fixtures it managed. In

January 1998, World Rugby announced that the 2003 World Cup would be played in New Zealand and Australia.

While it should have been obvious to NZR and its board of directors that the tournament New Zealand had co-hosted in 1987 would be virtually unrecognisable in scale and legal complexity to the one they would be partly managing in 2003, it wasn't. NZR had won the bid under the stewardship of chief executive David Moffett, but it would be David Rutherford and his chair, Murray McCaw, managing and negotiating the delivery of the tournament. As an official report would later reveal, they were slow to recognise the scale of the commitment they had made.

The global landscape proved more fluid than NZR realised, and the 1999 tournament shifted World Rugby's expectations, attitudes and financial imperatives. The first World Cup of the professional age saw the commercial power of the tournament climb to an entirely new level again. The 1987 event had been televised in 17 countries, whereas the 1999 World Cup was shown in 214. The audience was huge, and as a result the money flowed: some $230 million of revenue was generated over the five weeks. World Rugby – or, rather, Rugby World Cup Limited, which was the subsidiary company set up – enjoyed a profit of $154 million – more than four times the $36 million banked in 1995.

By early 2001, World Rugby began finalising what it expected from its co-hosts, and many of the conditions seem to have taken NZR by surprise. There was a demand for 'clean' stadia – that is, for all venues to have no existing advertising contracts in the grounds or within 500 metres. That extended to corporate boxes, to which World Rugby wanted 100 per cent access. By implication – and supported by explicit reference – this meant NZR would have to consider shifting its National Provincial Championship to ensure it didn't clash with the World Cup – or at least to play it in non–World Cup venues, to ensure they could be kept clean for official tournament sponsors.

All of this should have been relatively easy for New Zealand to achieve. Indeed, given the commercialised nature of the tournament, such requests were hardly unreasonable or unforeseeable. What did genuinely blindside both the New Zealand and Australian unions was World Rugby inflicting them with an unexpected $25 million of costs relating to the accommodation and travel of the visiting teams. When New Zealand ran its forecasts with its share of these new costs, it couldn't find a path to profitability.

In August 2001, Rutherford reported to the board that costs had risen exponentially since the successful bid. Having initially forecast a profit of almost $29 million, NZR was now looking at a loss. If there was no prospect of achieving a significant financial surplus, Rutherford argued, there was little reason for New Zealand to stay involved as a co-host. The tournament, he said, delivered on virtually none of NZR's strategic imperatives, and would hit fans with excessive ticket prices while also impacting the treasured NPC. The options, as he saw them two years out from the tournament kicking off, were to decline the offer to co-host; to try to negotiate from Rugby World Cup Limited a guaranteed minimum financial return; or to hit up the New Zealand government for financial help, since co-hosting the tournament was likely to bring a wider economic benefit of about $100 million to the national economy.

On the playing field, the landscape was changing equally rapidly, and the balance of power in the Southern Hemisphere had shifted since the bid was accepted. Australia had won its second World Cup in 1999, confirming that the Wallabies, who had also won in 1991, were enjoying one of their most successful eras in history. They had taken back the Bledisloe Cup from New Zealand in 1998 and beaten the British and Irish Lions in a three-Test series in 2001. On the back of this success, the sport was making inroads against the other vibrant football codes in Australia.

New Zealand, on the other hand, had crashed out in the semi-final of the 1999 tournament, plunging the nation into an unprecedented introspective mood that fluctuated between disillusionment and anger: students at Massey University were offered grief counselling, while some idiot spat on a racehorse owned by All Blacks coach John Hart. One country was suddenly ultra-ambitious, proactive and eager to drive the profile of rugby higher, while the other was trying to rebuild and reconnect with a disenfranchised fan base that felt the national game had lost its way.

NZR's initial decision to jointly bid with Australia was largely driven by an almost nostalgic desire to have the World Cup in its backyard again. The attraction was emotional, sentimental even. Whether the regime of that period was guilty of not fully understanding the extent of their hosting obligations doesn't necessarily matter, because those demands had changed so greatly in the wake of the 1999 tournament.

World Rugby, from early 2001, recognised a key problem with New Zealand as a co-host: it was simply too small. It had relatively tiny stadia. It was, compared with Australia, that little bit harder hard to get to for the European-based teams. The time zone for broadcasting was that little bit more awkward too. These factors would affect the values of the revenue World Rugby could expect to gain via broadcast and sponsorship sales.

Australia, however, had come of age after Sydney hosted the 2000 Olympics. Rugby Australia (known before 2017 as the Australian Rugby Union) had an executive that was hungry to be involved and to host more games in bigger venues. The best outcome for everyone in mid-2001 – both hosting parties and World Rugby – would have been for NZR to decline its co-hosting rights and transfer them to Australia gracefully and regretfully. Instead, what transpired was a year-long saga in which NZR trashed its reputation on the global stage and seriously damaged its relationships with both Rugby Australia and World Rugby.

Between 9 August 2001 and 18 April 2002, NZR self-destructed. It had no clear strategic direction, seemingly flip-flopping every other week about what it was and wasn't prepared to do to satisfy World Rugby that it could meet its hosting obligations. It made the issue of the provision of clean stadia a needless sticking point, and it seemed to be naively protective of the NPC, at times even appearing to consider it a tournament of equal importance and value to the World Cup. The biggest sin, however, was that Rutherford and McCaw descended into

making public, personal attacks against World Rugby chair
Vernon Pugh.

In March 2002, McCaw told the media that Pugh had
reneged on a verbal agreement he had made about clean stadia.
McCaw then went on to say:

> There's a bit of ... bloody-mindedness from Rugby World
> Cup Ltd and its chairman. The man's a lawyer and he's
> asking us to break legal contracts. Like all consummate
> politicians, they keep their positions by being divisive. It
> consolidates the power in one person, and means he is
> able to control things by his influence. He has too much
> power. I'm not prepared to say it's an abuse of power,
> but it does open up the question.[1]

The combination of NZR's belligerence, its lack of focus and
consistency of argument, and its commercial naivety and descent
into name calling left World Rugby with little choice but to take
away New Zealand's co-hosting rights to the 2003 event. On 18
April 2002, the global governing body's council voted 18–5 in
favour of holding the World Cup solely in Australia.

Shortly after the vote, Pugh said:

> I wanted the tournament to be staged there because New
> Zealand is a country where rugby union is a passion,
> but there comes a time in any major negotiation when
> you have to stick to principles. The Rugby World Cup
> is the third biggest sporting event in the world and it

has to be run properly, which means being commercially hard-nosed and not sentimental. NZR was given every chance to fall into line and it should not blame anyone else for what happened.[2]

Pugh's message obviously got through, because in the wake of the loss, retired judge Sir Thomas Eichelbaum was tasked with investigating the process and events that had led to Australia being granted the sole rights. In July, Eichelbaum produced his report, which was highly critical of Rutherford and McCaw:

> Personal attacks followed by apologies did nothing to advance New Zealand's cause, and severely damaged its reputation and standing in the international rugby community. Not only was it inappropriate behaviour, it was bad tactics. This was not a viable long-term strategy if NZR still wished to pursue a case for retaining the sub-hosting.[3]

The fallout from the report was extreme. New Zealand became a pariah at World Rugby council meetings. Rutherford and McCaw both resigned, and it was then agreed that the NZR board needed to be cleaned out. The only one to remain was Rob Fisher, who was asked to step in as interim chair, with Steve Tew being temporarily promoted from general manager to acting chief executive.

There was one other serious problem that had arisen, but it would only be discovered when Tew and Rutherford – before he resigned – flew to Amsterdam for a meeting with Adidas, where they planned to tell their apparel partner that there was a possibility New Zealand would lose the 2003 World Cup co-hosting rights. By the time they boarded the plane back to Auckland, it was likely that NZR might also, consequently, be about to lose its US$20-million-a-year sponsorship deal with Adidas.

*

FROM BEING CLOSE TO bankruptcy and riddled with inventory, production and organisational issues when Robert Louis-Dreyfus took over in 1994, Adidas was a different beast by the time it signed the All Blacks as its major rugby asset in 1999. Its balance sheet was much improved, and having listed on both the Paris and Frankfurt stock markets in 1995, it had become a more internationally focused company. But while it was in much better shape, it was still a business under pressure as it battled to grow sales in a market that had seen Nike stride ahead and New Balance become a serious competitor. Adidas grew its net global sales by 5 per cent in 2001 – a figure slightly ahead of expectations, and illustrative of the company being in solid, if not spectacular, financial shape.

But what had created a new dynamic for the All Blacks was that in late 2001, Louis-Dreyfus was diagnosed with leukaemia and had to stand down as chief executive and chair. He was replaced at the helm by the German-born and bred Herbert Hainer, who had joined Adidas in 1987 after working his way up the corporate ladder at Procter & Gamble. Hainer was a massive football fan. He loved Bayern Munich, and in 2002 he would approve Adidas buying a 10 per cent stake in the club; the CEO took a place on the supervisory board. But Hainer knew next to nothing about rugby.

Unlike Dreyfus, Hainer had no inherent love for the sport. He understood that the All Blacks transcended rugby, but he had no relationships with any of the key NZR personnel. And, according to Martyn Brewer, Adidas remained a German company at heart, which meant that its first, second and third sports were football, football and football. The All Blacks no longer had a champion at the head of the company, so when Tew and Rutherford revealed to Andrew Gaze, Adidas's head of rugby, that the World Cup hosting rights were all but gone, it was almost a terminal blow for the partnership.

'If you have a home World Cup, whether it is football or the Olympics, and you have the fitting for the home team, licence sales are just incredible, so the fact that the hosting rights were removed was a significant negative and subsequent loss of revenue that Adidas missed out on,' says Gaze. 'The 2003 World Cup was a significant factor [in doing the deal]. A World Cup year and a Lions tour are the only years that you sell enough product to fund the sponsor fee. So those years you want so big that they cover all the others. 1999 had been a huge year [for All Blacks merchandise sales]. It was launch year and we had record sales globally, and it was our second-biggest selling licensed product globally across all sports that year. That was significantly beyond expectation, probably about double. There were 18 months to run on the contract, and my boss said you have until the end of the year to regain the faith of Adidas around the All Blacks contract.'

The odds were against a renewal. Adidas was focused harder on football than it ever had been, the chance of making money out of its All Blacks partnership seemed lower, and concerns had arisen about the ability of the All Blacks and NZR to fully embrace and honour the contract. The episodes where players had worn the wrong gear and criticised the ball had not been well received in Germany. They suggested a lack of maturity about the reality of professional sport, and doubts persisted as to whether the All Blacks really understood how commercial relationships worked. It didn't help either that the All Blacks had crashed out of the 1999 World Cup, had failed to win the Bledisloe Cup back, and couldn't land a Tri-Nations title in either 2000 or 2001. At US$20 million a year, the All Blacks were looking overpriced.

It's possible, too, that Adidas's new executive team considered they had acquired a second, possibly bigger rugby asset once they signed Jonah Lomu to an individual contract. When the game first went professional, Lomu had signed an endorsement agreement with Reebok – one which didn't have a requirement to wear their boots when he played for the All Blacks. But when Adidas became the All Blacks' sponsor, he finished up with Reebok and was signed on a seperate agreement with the German-based group so he could feature individually in adverts and promotions.

And despite enduring serious health issues in 1997 and 1998 – nephrotic syndrome, which would ultimately lead to his premature death in 2015 – Lomu bounced back to top form at the 1999 World Cup. The All Blacks didn't have a brilliant tournament, but he did, again producing his best form on the biggest stage, leaving audiences stunned by his size, speed and athleticism. Brewer says: 'I was at the 2000 Olympics in Sydney and we had Jonah come in and do a clinic with kids. I can tell you, the CEO of Adidas at the time [Hainer] wanted to meet him.' Could Adidas lose the All Blacks but keep Lomu and still effectively 'own' global rugby? That was a thought swirling around among Adidas's top executive team in early 2002.

Conversely, shortly after Tew returned from Amsterdam and took over as acting chief executive, he discovered that conversations had already been had internally at NZR about renewing the Adidas deal early and asking for more money. It transpired that a handful of board members had been unhappy with the way the deal was being executed at Adidas's end, with concerns growing that it wasn't spending the promised US$10 million on marketing, advertising and kit. Tew, barely days into the hot seat, was tasked with delivering an improved agreement two years before the expiry of the existing deal in 2004.

Gaze hadn't revealed that the executive team at Adidas were cool on the idea of an extension, but Tew managed to gather this information through an alternative network. He had a friendship with Chris Liddell, the New Zealand–born executive who ended up as chief financial officer of Microsoft (and as deputy chief of staff for Donald Trump when he was president of the United States). Liddell, in turn, had a friendship with Robin Stalker, another Kiwi, who had risen to be chief financial officer of Adidas in 2000. It was through this link that Tew discovered that Adidas was thinking of not renewing.

'We had some breaches – some untidy stuff, the players wearing the wrong thing,' says Tew. 'And no one had been back up to Germany to see them [since signing the deal], and the relationship was not good. At the same time when I became the acting CEO there was a conversation going on around how we could renew the deal early, and whether we could expect to get more money ... We were never going to use US$10 million of kit, but they could run US$10 million of ad spend. NZR was quite grumpy with [Adidas] – they didn't think they spent it all.'

This was yet more evidence of the NZR board being detached from commercial realities. Just as they had refused to provide clean stadia in the hosting bid, and then appeared to believe that the NPC was on a par with the World Cup in profile and importance, they now wanted to demand more from one of the world's largest sporting corporations, despite the All Blacks having delivered relatively poor on-field results, while appearing to have a touch of disdain for the detail in the contract. It didn't put Tew in an easy place – stuck between a board that had unrealistic expectations and a major partner that was losing confidence in the All Blacks.

Once Tew became aware the contract was in jeopardy, he and Gaze began strategising as to how the new Adidas leadership could be persuaded that the All Blacks were bigger than rugby, mature enough to understand their obligations and worth the investment. The first and most important thing for Tew was to get himself to Germany and meet the executive team – specifically

Hainer and the head of global marketing and sports relations, Michael Riehl.

While there was daily interaction between the All Blacks and the local Adidas representatives, there was no regular dialogue or connection between the respective executive teams. Nearly all the individuals involved in negotiating the initial deal had moved on, so the new leaders on both sides didn't know the background, context and nuances of the contract and the ambitions held for the partnership. There were no personal relationships to lean on to advance the parties' mutual understanding.

'I did two things,' recalls Tew. 'I went to South Africa and we won the Tri-Nations after we beat the Springboks and the following week they beat the Wallabies. I ended up picking up the trophy because the team had come home. I then went up to Germany and met them all. I met the CEO and Mike Riehl, who is no longer with us, and got the conversation back on track. They just liked the fact that someone turned up and we had a very honest conversation. I knew exactly what they were thinking after that meeting.'

Winning the 2002 Tri-Nations was also important, as the All Blacks had not enjoyed a great run of form since Adidas had come on board. When Tew turned up in Germany with a trophy and a desire to reconnect, it felt a little bit like starting the relationship again. Gaze, who had shifted his family to live in Amsterdam earlier that year, realised that he had an internal PR job to do. He needed to bombard his colleagues and executive with tangible evidence of the All Blacks' profile and prominence in their home country. He subscribed to *NZ Rugby World* – the agenda-setting glossy magazine – and left copies lying around the Adidas HQ.

In fact, the most important act in winning over the Adidas executive had already occurred back in November 2001, when Gaze had taken Heiner to watch the All Blacks play Ireland. 'He had never been to a game of rugby,' says Gaze. 'We took him to a game in Dublin in 2001, which happened to be Richie McCaw's debut. Herbert was used to these state-of-the-art football stadiums, and there we are at the rickety old Lansdowne Road. The All Blacks were down at half-time and he asked me if I was worried. I said, "Nah, nah they will come back, they have never lost to Ireland."

'Early in the second half, Ireland were hard on attack and Norm Maxwell slapped the ball down and it should have been a penalty try. The ref, for whatever reason, said knock-on, and the All Blacks shoved Ireland off the scrum and they stormed back to win the game. It was still in the days when there were after-match functions, and McCaw got his cap after the game. Herbert saw the haka, he saw the emotion of the Irish fans and the resilience of the All Blacks coming back, and he saw the emotion of Richie receiving his cap after being player of the day.'

Heiner had seen enough in Dublin that day to be sure he wanted to continue sponsoring the All Blacks, and to know that rugby had something football didn't. Heiner saw a sport with soul that day in Ireland. He saw how the All Blacks players were connected to the jersey, and how they stayed so calm when they were behind and worked so hard and cleverly to force their way back. As he would later tell Gaze: 'Rugby has spirit and soul, and I don't see that anymore in football. We can't afford to lose that.'

All the new executive team at Adidas needed to see from NZR was some willingness to connect. As Woody Allen said once of parenting, 90 per cent of it is just showing up, and that's all the Germans really needed: a sense of who was at the helm of NZR, and that they cared enough about the partnership with Adidas to get on a plane and say hello.

After Tew's visit, a renewed deal accelerated towards a conclusion. The only problem was that the Germans had set a deadline for the deal to be concluded by late 2002, and because of the upheaval in July and August, in which Rutherford, McCaw and the entire board had stepped down, Tew didn't have a higher authority in place to sign off on the proposal. He took a gamble and rang Jock Hobbs, who was rumoured to be in line to become the new chair.

'I knew Jock, but I didn't know him well,' Tew says, 'and I said, "Listen, I hear you are going to be the chair and I need something done at the first board meeting." And he said, "I don't know that I am going to be elected because I fucking wasn't the last time, and I don't know who says I am going to be the chair." And I said, "Everyone but you."

'So we had a meeting in a dark, dingy cafe, because he didn't want to be seen by anyone, and I gave him the rundown. When the board was elected, we ran an induction meeting and we then handed the paper out and said, "You have half an hour to read this and get it done." We dropped the non-cash value down from the US$10 million, so it shrunk to something more sensible. But it remained the most lucrative jersey sponsor. People said we didn't have a jersey sponsor, but we did – it was Adidas, and they paid for that right and the clean jersey.'

Tew had saved the day, won back the hearts and minds of the Adidas executive and put a renewed deal on the table that gave the balance sheet and the All Blacks the security they needed. His reward for all his hard work, however, was to learn that he would not be graduating from acting chief executive to chief executive. The Adidas renewal was made public on 17 December 2002 at a press conference at NZR headquarters in Wellington. But the day before there had also been a press conference, this one announcing that Chris Moller had been appointed chief executive of NZR.

As hard as that was on Tew, the combination of a new deal with Adidas, a new board and a new CEO sent a powerful signal that NZR was resetting. It was modernising itself, shifting the dial more towards business than rugby, and was going to operate with greater financial awareness and better commercial practices.

The only problem was that while NZR was on a new track leading to a more commercialised world, the All Blacks weren't. The newly appointed Moller was starting to think that Mitchell had gone rogue, getting the impression he saw himself as the chief of an autonomous kingdom.

CHAPTER EIGHT

THE GREAT AWAKENING

HAVING ENJOYED A LONG and successful career with Fonterra, where he had risen to the role of deputy chief executive after heading up the dairy giant's commodity products subsidiary, New Zealand Milk Products, Chris Moller was ready to step away from corporate life in October 2002. He was only 48, but having also had roles in investment banking, at Baring Brothers in London as well as at the Broadbank Corporation, Moller was ready to take on a governance career. He fancied using his experience and knowledge to hold a few directorships and enjoy a more sedate pace of professional life. Anyway, that was his plan when he stepped down from Fonterra – until his phone rang one day and the voice at the other end introduced himself as a current board member of New Zealand Rugby.

As Moller remembers it: 'Someone rang me out of the blue and said, "Would you consider being chief executive of the rugby union?" I said, "Pardon? Why me? I'm a great sports follower and have a passion for the game, but ..." The voice at the other end of the phone said: "We have got enough bloody rugby people. We want someone with international business experience."' And just like that, Moller's career was on an entirely different track to the one he had anticipated.

At first he couldn't see why he was being targeted to take the role. He didn't necessarily see his experience and skill set as a natural fit with NZR. But the more he discussed the role with the board and considered where the organisation was at, the more he saw that he could make an impact: that he was better equipped to be at the helm than he'd realised. NZR had been damaged by the fiasco with the World Cup co-hosting rights. Its reputation had been tarnished globally, and its relationships with other national unions had been strained to breaking point. New Zealand had few allies in the global game, and therefore had little to no leverage around the World Rugby table.

The Eichelbaum Report had painted quite the damning picture. NZR didn't appear just to be friendless, it also seemed to be a little clueless. On the surface, the financial picture looked relatively rosy. Revenue was consistently growing, with turnover jumping from $80.2 million in 2001 to $90.1 million in 2002, with net profit also jumping from $3.4 million to $9.8 million in the same period. So the money was coming in, but perhaps not at the volumes it could have been.

When the new board assembled in late 2002 – one that included former All Black captain Graham Mourie, long-term Crusaders chairman Mike Eagle, and of course another former All Blacks captain and skilled litigator and business operator,

Jock Hobbs, as chair – they had a definite sense that the organisation was not fulfilling its commercial potential. The Eichelbaum Report had labelled the former executive and board commercially naive, and that led to the new board wondering whether financial opportunities were being missed as the former board had simply not been aware of the financial opportunities. NZR was turning over $90 million, but should that be closer to $100 million? Would a more corporate-savvy chief executive with real international business experience be able to identify new and more lucrative ways for the organisation to exploit the All Blacks brand?

There was the fundamental issue of trust and confidence to be broached as well. NZR needed to be able to convince current and potential commercial partners that it was a world-class organisation run by skilled and credible people. Its reputation had been dragged through the mud for much of 2001 and the early part of 2002, and big business, players the size of Adidas, seemed unlikely to want to partner with what appeared to be an amateur organisation.

As the mystery board member had made clear to Moller, NZR had not got the balance right under the stewardship of Rutherford and McCaw. It was too rugby-focused, mired perhaps in a forgotten age of patch-protection and small-mindedness. The game had been professional for more than half a decade but between 2000 and 2002 NZR had wound back the clock, to some extent, to the days of amateurism, where administrators worried mostly about how many free Test tickets they would receive and whether they would be able to park at the ground.

The new board felt there had to be a statement appointment made at chief executive level to signal that the organisation recognised that it needed to change, to be more commercially driven and business-focused and to view itself more as a corporation than as a national sports administration.

Some of Moller's concern around the amount of revenue being generated wasn't just being driven by a vague sense of commercial underachievement. There was, to some degree, an element of falsehood about the way the balance sheet was being presented. A total of $17 million of profit was posted between 2000 and 2002, but what the accounts didn't show was how elite players had been lost to offshore markets. By 2000, European clubs were consistently picking off New Zealand talent. Mostly they would come after players who had either been regular All Blacks and were suddenly being left out, or those who were universally deemed to have been unlucky not to have made it.

This was the vulnerable group, because contracts, oddly, were still structured so that players would agree a fee they would be paid for Super Rugby and a fee they would receive should they be selected to play for the All Blacks. They had to be selected to trigger that fee. What this meant for someone like Todd Blackadder, who had captained the All Blacks in 2000 but was dropped the following year, was that his income could fall without warning by $200,000. And so when Edinburgh Rugby offered Blackadder a deal in 2001, he took it. Other headline acts to have succumbed to foreign contracts in the early part of the new millennium included Daryl Gibson, Scott Robertson, Bruce Reihana and Mark Robinson. While the All Blacks were weathering the loss of these and other departures, it wasn't easy. The Test team was going okay, but they weren't dominating the world game, and they were consistently being beaten by Australia. If they could spend a bit more to keep a few more key players, it would make a material difference to the high-performance potential of the All Blacks. There was a sense among the new board that the balance sheet looked as good as it did – that the profit was as high as it was – because not enough was being spent to retain players. Essentially, there was a view that it would be a more sustainable long-term strategy to invest more heavily in the high-performance side of the business. More Test wins – something that may happen if the squad was not losing as many players as it had been – would lead to greater commercial returns. Something had to be done to lose the vulnerability from the labour market, hence the new board's sense that the balance sheet was not illustrative of the organisation's true financial position.

Bringing in a corporate heavyweight such as Moller was the way to start rewriting the narrative and rebuilding the reputation of NZR. This was how the organisation was going to regain the trust of corporate New Zealand, and potentially seek more international partnerships. There was also a time-critical need to rebuild relationships with the SANZAR partners as the original US$555 million (NZ$848 million) broadcast deal was due to expire in late 2004, and negotiations to renew it were likely to begin midway through 2003. Plans were in the pipeline to expand Super Rugby to 14 teams, with one new entrant coming from Australia and one from South Africa. The SANZAR partners needed to be aligned on these expansion plans and their potential value to a broadcast partner, and on how the three unions could fairly split the money, given their respective cost bases and audience value.

The 1995 deal had been agreed through a relatively clean and simple process which the SANZAR partners wanted to repeat. They had sold all the Super Rugby and Tri-Nations rights to just one player, News International. The giant Rupert Murdoch–owned media house had then on-sold the rights to the respective domestic bidders, which in 1995 had been Super Sport (in South Africa), Foxtel (Australia) and Sky TV (New Zealand).

This was the preferred route for the renewal, but to extricate maximum value and generate confidence in the solidity of the partnership, NZR and Rugby Australia had to patch things up. Really, they needed to start over. And while Steve Tew had led the organisation well in his time as interim chief executive, and had certainly saved the Adidas contract, he was linked to the old regime and therefore deemed not the right choice to take the role permanently.

'When they appointed Chris [Moller], I was pretty grumpy,' says Tew. 'I thought I had done a pretty good job in the acting role in difficult circumstances – almost impossible circumstances, in fact. I couldn't fathom the rationale that suggested I just couldn't carry on. But they made that decision, and with the benefit of hindsight it became clear quite quickly that it was going to be a good decision for me longer term. Whether it was fair or not is another matter, but they made it.

'I think I got told on the Friday, and Chris and I met on the Sunday at his house, and he said, "Look, I have been really impressed with what you have been doing, with what I have been seeing from the outside. I need you to stay and have whatever job you like. You can be 2IC if you want and have everyone report to you." And I said, "Well, what the fuck are you going to do, then?" We kind of designed a job for me, and he said, "You can do whatever you want to do, but I don't want any surprises." He never wavered from that. He never interfered and he was bloody supportive, and we had a bloody good relationship that worked well.'

*

AFTER A FEW WEEKS poking around the business, Moller fixed on a three-point plan as his priority. He didn't need to delve into many dark recesses to know that the business was essentially in disarray culturally. He had taken the view that his arrival, as an outsider, was strong evidence that the new board wanted dynamic and bold changes to be made. 'If you are happy with how the organisation is, you normally promote from within,' he explains. 'If your organisation needs a completely new focus and direction, then you bring in someone from outside. It is evolution versus revolution. They didn't necessarily want more of the same, and they took a risk.'

What was harder for Moller to ascertain was the true state of the balance sheet and the economic sustainability of the business. It was profitable and turnover was rising, but he needed to know whether the business was making an operational profit, and what icebergs may be lurking. He discovered that there was an element of illusion to the accounts. The business had benefited enormously from a decision made in early 1996 to take out foreign exchange cover to protect the broadcast income from currency fluctuations. The original deal was paid in US dollars, and when Moller arrived, there was still five years of forward cover left on the contract. The New Zealand dollar had soared to around 70 cents against the US dollar in early 2003, but NZR would be paid out as if it were still at 40 cents. That was effectively worth anything between $5 million and $12 million a year, depending on the exchange rate. New Zealand would also be hosting the British and Irish Lions tour in 2005, and with three Tests to be played, as well as seven other games, the national body was forecasting it would bank an additional $25 million of profit from increased broadcast revenue, gate receipts and short-term sponsorships.

The foreign exchange cover, the Lions tour and the renewal of the Adidas contract were three sturdy pillars on which the balance sheet could rest. But it was imperative that NZR strengthen the fourth, which was the broadcast deal. While sponsorships were a growth category for NZR, broadcast income still accounted for about 60 per cent of all revenue, and the importance of agreeing a deal that was at least comparable to the existing contract, if not better than it, was critical, because Moller was certain that costs were going to rise exponentially.

'Things weren't too bad [financially],' says Moller. 'But like any sports organisation, I often use the phrase, "expenses rise to exceed revenue" because it is a thirsty machine to generate as much revenue as you can to plough that back into the game.'

He could sense that the labour market was more under siege than it appeared. Having worked extensively in the United Kingdom, he was well aware of rugby's private school connections in that part of the world, and that many captains of industry and prominent business figures had a deep connection with the game and a willingness to splash their enormous wealth into vanity projects such as their local rugby club. The 2003 World Cup would inevitably reveal the extent of the All Blacks' playing riches, and predatory clubs with plenty of money would soon be hunting New Zealand talent.

In early 2003, Moller convened a two-day board meeting in Blenheim, where he planned to set out his stall for the year. 'We went through the strategy that we wanted to adopt and the culmination of that was three priorities,' he says. 'The first was to win the World Cup in 2003. The second priority was to undertake a competitions review because there were concerns about what was then called the NPC. And the third one was the renewal of the broadcasting contract. We resourced up. We engaged Sir Brian Roache and Bruce Wattie to undertake the competitions review. Tewy worked with them because he had the rugby knowledge. Greg Peters worked on the broadcasting, and I worked with him because of my business knowledge.'

As far as winning the 2003 World Cup went, Moller's goal was to ensure the All Blacks had all the support and resources they needed. A decision had been made, one that pre-dated Moller, to allow Mitchell to take a relatively young and inexperienced side to play England, France and Wales in November 2002. Mitchell had wanted to keep many of his best players in New

Zealand, so they could enjoy an extended off-season and prepare for the World Cup. It was a smart move in that it would allow battle-weary, seasoned campaigners to rejuvenate and condition properly for the tournament in Australia. But it also came with risks, as it meant the All Blacks would be vulnerable in Europe. The legacy of the brand didn't afford much leeway for defeats and poor performances, and history wouldn't stick an asterisk next to the 2002 touring squad and explain the context. But, on balance, the board felt it was a short-term risk with long-term benefits, so they agreed to what Mitchell had asked for. It was a high-performance win.

But as 2003 played out, it transpired that Mitchell wasn't really looking for support from his chief executive and board. He wasn't really looking for their permission either, whenever he wanted to do anything. As would become clear to Moller, Mitchell felt he was running an autonomous high-performance kingdom with the All Blacks that was detached from any commercial operation. As Moller saw it, 'Under the leadership of John Mitchell, the All Blacks had declared unilateral independence from New Zealand Rugby.'

*

DESPITE THE FACT THAT the All Blacks had clearly become a more commercial entity in the professional age and the most significant driver of NZR's revenue, the primary task of the head coach was still to build and manage a team to win Test matches. The All Blacks' narrative had to have success at its core: the statistics had to continue to be mind-blowing if the team were to have a story that no other nation could match. That's what drove the brand value, and Mitchell, since his appointment in late 2001, was producing results that were on brief.

Nine games into Mitchell's tenure, the All Blacks were undefeated. They suffered their first loss in Sydney, before beating the Boks in Durban to secure the Tri-Nations in 2002. A 90 per cent win ratio was a brilliant start for Mitchell, and while the All Blacks lost their November Test to England at Twickenham, and then drew with France in Paris before beating Wales, they did so, of course, with many of their best players resting back in New Zealand. There was no doubt that the All Blacks, having wobbled a little under Wayne Smith between 2000 and 2001, were back on track. Mitchell was delivering on his core KPI.

But however important it was for the All Blacks to bank the victories, it wasn't true that the coach would be judged by his employer exclusively on wins and losses. There was an expectation for the coach to preside over a side that met all its commercial, stakeholder and media obligations. How this expectation was communicated, or even if it was, is unclear.

When John Hart was appointed coach in 1996 at the dawn of the professional age, he had such a strong grasp of what professional rugby would entail that there was even a sense that he was ahead of his employer in this regard. As he himself says: 'I think in part my selection as All Blacks coach was helped by the professional era coming along. My background was in the corporate world so I understood a lot of the professional responsibilities.'

Hart was perhaps ahead of his time in how he saw the worlds of high performance and commercial splicing together, and his All Blacks – certainly in the first two years of his tenure, at least – understood all their obligations and executed them without incident or fuss. While his successor, Smith, admits he was overwhelmed at times by the scale of the job, he had in Andrew Martin a strong manager with a full appreciation of what the players were expected to do, and he made sure they did it.

But Mitchell, it seemed to Chris Moller, had come to believe that there was no expectation at all to deliver on any other front other than high performance. The new chief executive felt the All Blacks coach had been permitted to free himself and the team from the commercial realities of professional sport, and had somehow been able to operate with not-so-veiled disdain for media and sponsors without fear of recrimination.

Circumstances had no doubt helped Mitchell establish his autonomy. From his earliest days in the role, the NZR executive and board were increasingly embroiled in the hosting rights saga. It was a day-to-day drama, sucking up much of their time and energy, hence the microscope was never really on the All Blacks. Besides, Rutherford and the board were relying on team manager Martin to steer the ship to some extent, and certainly to make sure the team delivered on its commercial, media and community responsibilities. They didn't realise the extent to which Martin was being undermined, and how little Mitchell liked reporting to a manager rather than direct to the chief executive. When Rutherford and McCaw resigned and the board was cleaned out, Mitchell took his opportunity in the leadership vacuum: in September 2001 he persuaded Tew to restructure the reporting lines and effectively disestablish Martin's position.

This was a classic power play by Mitchell, putting him in sole charge of the All Blacks: free to govern the team how he liked, with no one authorised to challenge him. Mitchell's new team manager, Tony Thorpe, was employed as a logistics operator only – an organiser and fixer who would make sure the players and their kit turned up in the right places and the water bottles were all full at training.

Even when Martin had still been there, signs of a lack of respect for commercial partners had been visible. But once he departed, some media and sponsors felt they were treated poorly by the All Blacks.

Press conferences routinely began later than scheduled, and Mitchell became increasingly hard to decipher. Often his answers could be obscure, punctuated with meaningless phrases that failed to convey anything. He became overly fond of saying he 'wasn't ready to share that', and relied on metaphors that made little sense. The strange thing about it was that his All Blacks were playing with enough elan and winning with enough panache as to have the media firmly on his side. Mitchell was young and had built his coaching reputation overseas, which made him faintly exotic but also added to his credibility. If he'd just been himself, spoken in plain English and treated the media less as an adversary and more as a conduit to the fans – who were eager to hear more about how this team was beginning to play some memorably good rugby – then not only would he have won more support from his employer, he would also likely have received more favourable reporting. Instead, the media coverage tended to distinguish Mitchell from his team: this was a good rugby side that was being coached by a cold, disengaged, even slightly weird figure.

The more problematic issue was the team's non-compliance with sponsor obligations. 'There were tensions,' Moller recalls. 'There were reasonably regular complaints about players not turning up. About players not having the right attitude. Players saying they had been told not to do things. Constant friction between the commercial staff and team management.'

According to Simon Johnston, Adidas's New Zealand–based operations manager, who was responsible for kitting out the team, there were occasions when the lack of compliance came with a direct financial cost to NZR.

'As you build into a season, all the planning is done six months before,' he explains. 'We had to have advanced planning to secure the days we would have access to the players, because Adidas would bring 30 people down from Europe for a photoshoot. Everything was put in the calendar, and we worked hard with NZR, and the All Blacks management team were always in the meetings to say, "Yes, these dates work for us, that will be the day for the outfitting," et cetera. We would try to not take too much time, but we did have to get our time with the team. But Mitchell delayed a photoshoot when we had the Naval Base dry dock at Devonport emptied, ready to go for the big photoshoot. He said, "No, I don't like it on those days," and said very late he wanted to change it, which meant airfares were lost and all sorts of things, so it cost NZR a fair bit of money having to reimburse things.

'The same thing happened with Steinlager. They were allowed to have Steinlager on the training gear for public trainings on Tuesdays. That was the only place they could have it and it was a green jersey. John said he didn't like green on Tuesdays when the public were around, so Steinlager got all their money back pretty quickly. Everything was difficult. Even outfitting the team, he got precious about so many things, and he was rude to people too.'

Midway through 2003, Moller was acutely aware of the issues that were mounting. But, despite being chief executive, he felt he was to some degree powerless to intervene. 'As the CEO you have input into the decision of who the coach is – I didn't, because Mitchell was already there – and then it is almost hands off,' he says. 'You can have a relationship with the coach. You can talk to them, you can encourage, but at the end of the day you can't direct. They are the person charged with selecting the players. They are responsible for the on-field, the game activities, et cetera.'

With the World Cup kicking off in October 2003, Moller didn't want to pick a fight with Mitchell and be seen to be micro-managing him. What mattered most was for the All Blacks to get the high-performance side of their preparation spot on – and having ripped through the Tri-Nations undefeated in 2003, there was no doubt the team was building nicely. But Moller's patience was pushed to breaking point a few weeks before the All Blacks left for the tournament.

The team was in camp at the Terrace Downs Resort, on the outskirts of Christchurch, and NZR had invited its sponsors to a function to see the team off. Moller had asked Mitchell if he could drop in to say a few words to the assembled guests, shake a few hands and give a little insight into how the team was feeling. Mitchell said he wasn't able to as he had a critical management meeting. However, when Moller was addressing the guests at a drinks function later that night, and passing on his apologies that the All Blacks coach couldn't make it due to an important meeting, Mitchell was seen through the giant window behind the chief executive going for an early evening run. Moller's embarrassment was acute. While Mitchell didn't know it that night, his decision to snub the sponsors made it more likely he would not be reappointed as All Blacks coach, even had the team won the World Cup.

Whatever small chance Mitchell had of salvaging his job died a few weeks later, during the group stage. Moller and Hobbs had arranged a meeting with Mitchell at the All Blacks base in Melbourne. 'When we got there, a messenger from the team who was not an All Black was sent down to tell us we were not welcome in the team's hotel,' says Moller. 'Because we were still in the World Cup, we left, because that was the sensible thing to do, but it wasn't the right thing.'

That was the final straw. The All Blacks couldn't exist independently of their union. High performance couldn't be divorced from commercial imperatives, and it wasn't possible for the business to run to its full potential – either on the field or off it – if the All Blacks coach wouldn't respect or even acknowledge the authority of the NZR chief executive.

'I remember when I joined, there was always this constant debate in the media and on talkback radio: is it a business or is it a sport?' says Moller. 'And of course, the answer is that it has to be both. It is joined by an umbilical cord. There was a unilateral declaration of independence, and there were issues with sponsors not getting what they perceived they had paid for.

'I suspect Mitchell had declared independence well before me [arriving]. I don't think it was just me coming along, and it was a World Cup year so there was probably more tolerance than there otherwise would have been, had this been the first, second or third year of the cycle. Mitchell reapplied for the job. Graham Henry applied and we appointed Graham.'

When Moller joined NZR in early 2003, it was the commercial side of the business – the executive, administration and governance – that needed a hard reset. But by 2004, with the All Blacks having bombed out of another World Cup and the team's relations with sponsors and the media strained and fractious, fixing the high-performance division became the highest priority.

CHAPTER NINE

NEW RULES OF ENGAGEMENT

A FEW DAYS AFTER Graham Henry had been appointed All Blacks head coach, he was asked by Moller to address the NZR staff, to introduce himself and share his ambitions for the team. A former school principal and long-term educator before becoming a professional coach, Henry was a gifted public speaker: dry, punchy, self-deprecating, often hilarious and, if he wanted to be, genuinely captivating.

That he had landed the head coaching role was due not just to his stellar track record and experience, but also to NZR finally seeing sense and abolishing a rule it had imposed somewhat impetuously and spitefully back in 1998, when Henry took a five-year contract with Wales.

Having coached the Auckland Blues to the first two Super Rugby titles in 1996 and 1997, and then to the final in 1998, Henry lost faith that he was ever going to be promoted to the All Blacks, and so began negotiating a job with the Welsh national team. The timing was unfortunate, as just as negotiations between Henry and the Welsh were concluding, the All Blacks fell to their fifth straight defeat and the NZR board, on the recommendation of David Moffett, would have replaced incumbent coach John Hart with Henry. But Henry was committed to Wales.

Slightly miffed at his decision and at the timing of it all, the board created a new rule that no one who coached a foreign national team would then be able to take charge of the All Blacks. Not only was it an incredible restriction of trade, it was also an ill-conceived measure that, ultimately, was needlessly punitive on the All Blacks. In a highly globalised coaching market, it made no sense to ban those who sought opportunities offshore from bringing their knowledge and experience back to New Zealand. A few years after Henry left, the rule was changed.

In a further sign of how NZR was broadening its view and plugging itself into the real world, Henry and his new All Blacks assistant coaches, Wayne Smith and Steve Hansen, received explicit instructions on how they were to handle media, sponsors, broadcasters, commercial partners and all other stakeholders. Moller had never had the chance to detail his expectations to Mitchell, but it was the first thing he did when Henry was appointed. Moller wanted his coaching team to appreciate the commercial world in which they were operating. He wasn't going to suffer the indignity of having a second All Blacks coach unilaterally declare autonomy and operate beyond the reach of the mothership. 'We had a chat with Graham when he was appointed about the new rules of the game,' says Moller. 'And Graham, to his credit, took it on straightaway.'

And so, when he spoke to the staff at NZR, Henry said, 'We are the little team, you guys are the big team. And we as the little team are part of the big team.' This was Henry acknowledging that he got the modern landscape, and that he understood how the two worlds of high-performance and commercial were connected. Part of his role was to ensure there was a bridge between the two.

The Moller regime would be defined by his attention to detail, his clarity of communication and his efforts to improve NZR's business practices and culture, all with the aim of giving the organisation a sharper, more defined corporate edge. He'd been appointed to reshape NZR from a sporting body to a business entity, to drive revenue growth and to present the All Blacks as a high-performance machine that major corporates could trust to deliver a mutually beneficial relationship. With this goal in mind, Moller and his board agreed that they should return to the previous structure of the head coach reporting to the All Blacks manager.

The manager's role would be to oversee all aspects of the team – to ensure that commercial requests were fulfilled without interfering with high-performance needs. The manager, rather than the coach, would be part of the NZR executive, but Graham Henry would still report directly to the board at times, when they wanted specific high-performance updates. The setup felt more in tune with the modern landscape, as Henry and his coaching team were empowered to drive high performance and focus mostly on that, while the manager – Darren Shand, who had been with the bungy-jumping pioneer AJ Hackett and then the Canterbury Crusaders – would be responsible for ensuring the team met its non-rugby obligations. But Shand would also sit in with Henry and his coaching team to ensure that there was time set aside for everything the team needed to do.

With this robust new structure in place, the early indications were that it was working well. The Henry era began with two solid defeats of the world champions, England. Further home victories came against Argentina, the Pacific Islanders, Australia and South Africa, and confidence soared within the All Blacks and NZR that there was now a harmonious relationship between the two, and that the team had a better attitude towards commercial work and professionalism. Unfortunately, when the All Blacks headed offshore for the first time on Henry's watch – to Australia and South Africa – it became apparent that there were still habits and behaviours that were proving somewhat toxic in the quest to modernise and professionalise the team.

Strangely, it was the first cohort of players – those who had transitioned from the amateur era – who proved the most professional. They had learned the art of self-responsibility and personal accountability by holding down jobs in the amateur era. However sham some of those jobs were, especially in the last few years before the game turned professional, individuals still had to turn up at work, get themselves to training and be responsible for organising their daily lives. Back then rugby was a hobby, albeit a time-consuming one with ever-increasing demands, but real life took precedence, teaching the players vital skills.

But by the early 2000s, that first wave of transition players had mostly retired, and in their place came men who had known no other life but as professional rugby players. Few had been enrolled in tertiary education or apprenticeships, or held down nine-to-five jobs. The majority had been recruited into elite programmes immediately on leaving school, where they were indoctrinated into the high-performance sporting life. They were institutionalised in the sense that they only knew the rhythms of professional rugby teams. As Henry would discover, the modern professional was not worldly, self-reliant or motivated to do much beyond training and playing. Worse was that, despite the efforts of first John Hart and then Wayne Smith to rid the All Backs of their institutionalised drinking culture, by 2004 it was still prevalent.

It was only when the team left New Zealand that it became apparent how insulated many of the players were. When the team played at home, their families were often heavily present at the team hotel. Players typically had friends they would catch up with in the various cities in which the All Blacks played. But once they left New Zealand, everything changed. Few of the players had interests outside of the game. A handful played golf, but most of the team had little desire to explore the cities they visited, preferring to spend their downtime playing video games. There was no balance in their lives, and no worthwhile distractions. It troubled Henry that his All Blacks weren't the rounded, self-motivated, self-reliant men he wanted them to be.

After a loss to Australia in Sydney, in a performance that was vague and disjointed, Henry was starting to wonder if there was a link between the lack of leadership on the field and the lack of interests off it. The first five Tests of the year had been at home, so the psychological cracks had been papered over. In their first away Test, though, the All Blacks had crumbled under pressure. Henry kept coming back to the thought they had done so because they had no culture of self-responsibility. He feared that the high-performance system cosseted the players – everything was done for them from too young an age, and the players who graduated into the All Blacks had virtually no life experience, and no natural leadership qualities as a result. The real world had built All Blacks leaders in the amateur era – men who ran farms or their own businesses, and who held down corporate positions – but the professional system was leaving large gaps in the development of emerging players.

This lack of exposure to adversity and graft was not conducive to building strong leaders on the field, but they were ideal conditions in which to foster unwanted habits. These young men were well paid. They had time on their hands, and because they were operating in a highly pressurised environment, they were enabled in building a reward culture for their hard work. And that reward was being allowed to drink heavily.

This culture materialised when the All Backs followed their loss in Sydney with a more galling one in Johannesburg. The Springboks outclassed them at Ellis Park, but the All Blacks players weren't going to let that stop them having an almighty piss-up. A court session had been locked into the diary almost as soon as the Tri-Nations schedule had been released earlier in the year. Carnage ensued that night, with players passing out all over the hotel grounds, and some having to be put into the recovery position while they waited, comatose, for their slightly more capable teammates to put them to bed. It was a horror show, and NZR's confidence that the All Blacks were building the professionalism both to win games and to appeal to new sponsors was shattered.

'I was there in South Africa at that very time,' says Chris Moller. 'I saw some, but not all, [of]the behaviour, and of course the great thing about "Ted" [Henry] and "Shag" [Hansen] – one was a teacher and the other was a policeman, and they knew how to handle people. They knew what was right and what was wrong.'

On the flight back to New Zealand, Wayne Smith came to see Henry and told him, unequivocally, that things had to change dramatically, and quickly, or he would be quitting. Smith had no interest in being part of a setup where young men were so easily able to waste their potential. He didn't want to be part of an All Blacks side that had such poor personal values, and one that endorsed habits that, in his view, had no place in professional sport.

Henry didn't need to be convinced that Smith was right, and a few weeks after the team returned to New Zealand, the three coaches met with the senior players and ripped up the old ways of doing things. There was going to be a new way – one where the players would be given greater responsibility to lead themselves and each other.

A nine-strong leadership group was installed, and these players would work more directly with the coaches to establish acceptable codes of conduct off the field, but they would also have input into the team's game plan and how training would look.

They were going to be more hands-on in driving the standards of the team – both on and off the field – than any All Blacks leadership group had ever been. There would be zero tolerance of court sessions or any heavy, collective drinking. Players could enjoy a few drinks, but alcohol was to be used responsibly. As adults and high-performance athletes, the players themselves would determine what responsible meant. This was going to be the new way: the players would be treated as adults, but they had to repay the trust by behaving like adults.

Henry hoped that this empowerment would lead individuals to develop wider interests that might broaden their horizons. The mantra that buzzed about the team was 'better people make better All Blacks'. While cultural change wouldn't necessarily happen overnight, and inevitably there would be a few stragglers slow to adapt to the new regime, November 2004 became a massive moment in both the commercial and high-performance history of the All Blacks.

The shift in leadership to a collaborative model where the players and coaches worked in partnership was revolutionary. The All Blacks now had the values system that Smith wanted to embed in his stint as head coach. There was strong buy-in from the players, who accepted that they had to be better people – more engaged with their fans, more amenable to their employer's needs, and more willing to conduct themselves generally to a higher standard, one that better reflected the core qualities and values of the All Blacks.

The reason this all mattered commercially was that the All Blacks not only had an even better story to tell, now that they had installed a groundbreaking leadership model, they presented a lower risk to any corporation wanting to back them. There would still be the odd indiscretion, the occasional time when a player let himself down and made headlines for the wrong reason, but by and large the All Blacks presented from 2004 as a team who tackled everything with the utmost professionalism. They were clean-cut, approachable, amenable, determined to accommodate, and humble while being successful.

They were now a team that got the big picture – the players saw, finally, the totality of what being an All Black meant. It wasn't just training, conditioning, playing and recovering. It was all those things plus promoting products, giving media interviews and signing autographs – and understanding that those things mattered too.

*

THE SHIFT TO A new leadership model inadvertently had a second major impact on the commercialisation of the sport in New Zealand. It ignited the first moves towards high-profile players becoming marketable brands in their own right.

Once the coaching trio had determined that they needed to make significant shifts in the team's culture, they concluded that they would also need to axe a few senior figures to facilitate the change. The team wasn't riddled with bad eggs, but it did have dominant personalities who were influencing, and not always in a good way, the younger players. The team needed new leaders, younger men who, although they had only known adult life as professional rugby players, had at least come through well-considered development programmes.

The real catalyst for this new era of individual commercialisation was the arrival of two special players, who were instant superstars on the field and highly marketable and presentable off it. These young men were Richie McCaw and Daniel Carter, who in time would become the two greatest All Blacks in history.

McCaw was chisel-jawed, fearless and breathtakingly good at making himself the most influential figure in every Test he played. His work ethic made him the player he was, and that grit, determination and desire to play for his teammates gave him enormous appeal. He was also academically bright, polite, clean-living and, from his early 20s, destined to become the All Blacks' captain.

Carter appealed to a slightly different demographic. He shared McCaw's work ethic, but he was more naturally talented. He'd found his rightful home in the All Blacks number 10 jersey when he was shifted there in November 2004, and became, in no time, the most exciting, dynamic and complete first five-eighth in the world. He was flamboyant but never played outside the confines of the team's game plan. He kicked goals, made tackles, could split a defence with his running game and was remarkably easy on the eye. He too was humble and, despite his success, never lost his boy-next-door appeal.

These two young players led the All Blacks' destruction of the British and Irish Lions in 2005, and in doing so endeared themselves to the New Zealand rugby public in a way no others ever had. Neither had set out to become a 'brand' player, but became so because of the way they played and how they conducted themselves.

Before them, Jonah Lomu had easily been the biggest star in the game. He had an incredible global profile, and after he came home from the 1995 World Cup, the endorsement offers flooded in. He signed deals with Reebok, McDonald's and Adidas. He was a phenomenon in France, the United Kingdom and even the United States, having been flown to San Francisco by NZR for a photo opportunity with actor Robin Williams after it learned that the Hollywood star was a massive fan.

But Lomu's brand never endured in New Zealand beyond that initial surge of mania. He was hugely well-known, but a combination of his illness, which impacted his ability to play at his best consistently, and a few dramas in his love life, dented his popularity in his home country. Consequently, he didn't have the universal appeal of McCaw and Carter.

The national body wasn't keen on the idea of individuals building their own, separate brands. The system was set up to maximise the power of the All Blacks and strike collective sponsorship deals that funnelled all the money into NZR's coffers, from where it could determine how funds were distributed. That made sense to NZR – it was cleaner, easier to control and fitted more neatly into the ruling body's view that it owned all the intellectual property connected to the All Blacks, including the players. Individual sponsorships, as far as NZR was concerned, came with two major issues: they created inequity, in that some players could exploit their status as All Blacks while others couldn't, and they risked conflicting with or negatively impacting the higher-value collective deals.

It was the second point that troubled NZR the most. In the past, individual deals – such as Nike's footwear agreements with Wilson, Kronfeld and Jones – had created tension, conflict and difficulty, and hardened an aggressive, almost belligerent mindset within the national body to protect what it saw as its property. The surging corporate interest in McCaw and Carter would have troubled NZR more but for the fact that it quickly proved to be, somewhat surprisingly, highly beneficial in fostering a culture of respecting sponsors and commercial opportunities among the wider All Blacks squad.

In what proved to be an inspired piece of thinking, Adidas was the first big mover in getting itself a slice of McCaw and Carter, by offering them both substantial individual contracts that were complementary to but separate from the collective deal with the All Blacks. The individual contracts were mostly about giving Adidas the ability to leverage the higher-profile All Blacks players offshore. The secondary benefit was that other players saw what McCaw and Carter had, and wanted it for themselves. And to get it, they realised, they not only had to throw everything into their rugby, they also had to prove they were worthy brand ambassadors. This meant being upstanding corporate citizens whenever they had to execute a collective commercial promotion for Adidas. These All Blacks, in this new era of individual opportunity, were going the extra mile when they were on commercial duty. There was no chance of Henry's

All Blacks failing to turn up in the right gear or make ill-advised comments about the quality of Adidas products.

Another additional benefit was that these individual sponsors ended up doing a bit of the heavy financial lifting by supplementing the incomes of the game's biggest stars. Carter was the sort of player for whom every major European club would have paid handsomely, and he fielded offers throughout his career. Eventually, in 2015, at the ripe old age of 34 and sure he'd given all his best years to New Zealand, Carter signed with Racing Paris for a deal that was reportedly worth close to $3 million a season. NZR was never able to offer anywhere near that sort of money, but back in 2005, when the big clubs would have been dangling about $1 million a year in front of Carter, the national body could respond with about $500,000 in wages and leave the likes of Adidas, Mastercard and Jockey to make up the difference. Individual sponsors became a vital tool in the battle to retain the best talent, and there were no two players more talented or more vital to the All Blacks cause between 2005 and 2015 than Carter and McCaw.

One of NZR's other fears about individuals becoming commercial entities was that it might erode the team ethos of the All Blacks. The brand had been built on unity and equity – no one being bigger than the team. American athletes such as Michael Jordan and Tom Brady had built individual brands, but this was never a concept that was going to sit easily with the All Blacks' ethos of humility, where self-promotion was not encouraged. But self-promotion was never an issue with either McCaw or Carter, as neither allowed their personal business activities to compromise their commitment and dedication to the team.

Conrad Smith, who won his first cap in 2004, before going on to win 93 more and become an integral part of two successful World Cup campaigns, says that both Carter and McCaw had a rare ability to keep their individual brands away from the team environment.

'In New Zealand it was limited by the fact there are only so many sponsors,' he says, 'and if they were team sponsors, you couldn't chase them individually. But Adidas offered worldwide individual contracts and those sort of things guys liked. I steered clear because I didn't like the idea of being a commercial asset. It was not something that interested me, but others would jump at it. Richie and Dan were the biggest stars, but they were the most selfless and anyone who knew them, played with them, was in an environment with them, they absolutely saw that the team came first to them. The moment the star of a team or a leader started putting themselves first and at the same time was saying "team first", the whole thing falls apart. Dan was doing his thing commercially and building his own brand and you would see him doing that, but as soon as he was in with the All Blacks, there was a clear line where you knew what he was all about.'

Ironically, for all NZR's fears about individuals trying to build sustainable and financially backable brands, it was ultimately McCaw and Carter who became victims of their own growing fame and marketability. Warren Alcock, who is agent to both men, says it became increasingly apparent that team sponsors were pushing the boundaries of the collective agreement by monopolising Carter and McCaw in their promotional work. The rules were clear that team sponsors needed to use three players equally in any promotion, but regularly that was abused by some sponsors, who seemed to think they had bought individual rights to Carter, in particular.

'When Dan and Richie first came on to the scene, we were negotiating with NZR about putting limits on use of players because sponsors kept asking for the same guys,' says Alcock. 'And in those early days, even with the collective, there might be the ability to have three players in an ad but if one player was the focus and one was way in the distance, I guess technically you might satisfy that. I do remember us putting into Dan and Richie's contracts that there had to be equitable use to stop that kind of thing. I can remember seeing an ad that Canterbury did with Anchor milk, and it was a video of Dan talking about how tall he is, and it had a picture of Dan standing there on his own. And it's going on about how Dan had got taller and taller as he grew up, and it was all about Dan Carter, and then these two other players barely featured. We said, "Hang on, there is not equitable use – it's all about using Dan Carter's profile," so we were having to negotiate these things with NZR and provinces and franchises to supplement the collective.'

Alcock would soon find that most of his time was spent battling with NZR over individual sponsorships his clients had secured. Carter and McCaw, as they so often did, had broken new ground, and while they were able to move smoothly between promoting themselves and being a member of the All Blacks, the next generation would prove not so adept at getting that balance right. The commercial landscape would become tense and fraught as the national union and the players were in an almost permanent state of conflict over the increasing number of individuals who were out to build their own brand.

But in November 2004, no one knew that trouble lay down the track. It was a good month for New Zealand rugby. A great month, indeed, as the All Blacks not only revolutionised their leadership model, but breezed through their European tour, thumping France in Paris in their final game in a coming-of-age performance. Chris Moller, not to be outdone, pulled off two of the most decisive and important acts of his tenure as CEO, both strengthening the balance sheet and restoring New Zealand rugby's global reputation.

CHAPTER TEN

A WORLD OF COMMERCIAL POSSIBILITY

THE ALL BLACKS WERE certainly in great shape by the end of 2004, but the real star that year was NZR's accounts. For the first time in history, revenue exceeded $100 million, with total income coming in at $104.9 million, $20.4 million of which was profit. The primary goal for Chris Moller in 2004 had been, however, to renegotiate a broadcast deal, as the initial ten-year contract was due to end in late 2005. The revenue numbers testified that the All Blacks were growing as a business and as a brand, but the reality from which Moller could never escape was that broadcast income accounted for around 60 per cent of the total.

Professional rugby remained wedded to a relatively simple financial model of selling sponsorships, tickets, merchandise and broadcast rights. And of those respective revenue streams, broadcast remained the single most lucrative and important contract, so it was critical that Moller at least maintain the current levels in the new deal. The business simply couldn't afford a reduction. The pressure was firmly on the chief executive and his chosen offsider, Greg Peters, who had been tasked with leading the negotiation, because compounding matters were the relative strength of the Kiwi dollar against the US dollar, and a softer market for sports broadcasting rights.

Much had changed in the wider sports broadcast rights market since that first deal had been signed. Back in 1995, the content arms race was in its infancy: pay TV operators were the new kids on the block, and there was a scramble to win the broadcast rights for the new professional competitions. In that first phase, companies were bidding mostly with borrowed money, aware they had to snare premium assets on which they could build their businesses. By the mid-2000s, even though the market for sports rights had become more competitive – which was, broadly speaking, to the advantage of the sellers – the buyers had more mature and complex balance sheets, and greater pressure to make returns for their shareholders.

The all-out bidding wars were reserved for the content that could be relied on to maintain and grow subscribers: the English Premier League, the Champions League and the four major sports leagues in the United States. There was still big money to be made in selling broadcast rights, but the major TV stations were more discerning, and more focused on extracting value for money.

The SANZAR situation was yet more complicated, as the three member nations had vastly different rugby audiences and populations and yet were selling the rights to Super Rugby and the Tri-Nations collectively to one buyer, News International, which would then look to on-sell the rights to domestic operators in each country. SANZAR would also additionally sell Super Rugby and Tri-Nations rights to international markets, and all the money collected would be split between the three nations. In that first deal, the split wasn't even. South Africa took roughly 37 per cent, New Zealand 35 per cent and Australia 28 per cent – a split that all three unions felt fairly reflected their individual Super Rugby revenue contributions and cost bases.

Separately, NZR was also able to sell the rights to inbound (Tests played in NZ) All Blacks Tests and the National Provincial Championship. This was partly why another priority for Moller in 2004 had been to conduct a review of all the various competitions, with particular focus on the NPC, which was struggling to control its costs and sustain public interest. The review was effectively about finding a new, sustainable format that capped expenditure and generated greater competition between all participants. The recommendation was to create a 12-team division – which would ultimately grow to include 14 teams – that operated with a salary cap, which it was hoped would in time lead to a greater proliferation of talent, and reverse the trend of the best players heading to the major centres of Auckland, Hamilton, Wellington, Christchurch and Dunedin. And, most importantly of all, NZR wanted a format that appealed to Sky, to the extent that it would pay more for the rights when the next broadcast deal was negotiated. The NPC allocation didn't have to be shared with the SANZAR partners.

Arguably, New Zealand's media landscape had changed more than Australia's or South Africa's since 1995. New Zealand had been a sleepy media backwater prior to the arrival of professional rugby. In the early 1990s, when New Zealand's population was 3.6 million, there were three terrestrial channels – which was likely as many as the market could support. But the market was dominated by the government-owned TVNZ, which had the funding and reputation among New Zealanders to plonk pretty much whatever it felt like on the telly, knowing there was no real competition. New Zealand's TV consumers were comparatively bereft of choice, therefore, something which both shocked and excited John Fellet, the US-born-and-bred trouble-shooter who arrived in Auckland in 1991 to help Sky find a route to profitability.

Fellet, who had picked up an accountancy degree while attempting to make the big leagues in professional baseball, had stumbled into the world of pay TV after landing a job with the Arizona-based cable-operator TCI. He became the guy who was assigned to spend 12 to 18 months at troubled companies and find ways to turn them around. Sky was one of the operators who called on his services. Set up in the late 1980s, it was losing about $1 million a week.

'I was really nervous about coming down to New Zealand,' says Fellet. 'I had a fantastic job in the States. My son had just been born and I said, "Jeez, do I want to do this to my beloved wife and yank my daughter out of school?" I turned on the TV on a Sunday night when I got to Auckland – and Sunday night is the most competitive night of TV in the States – and here, they had dog trials. Nobody loves border collies more than I do. They are insanely bright, but I am thinking, "Oh my God, this place has dog trials in the middle of Sunday nights." That was a sign from God I should stay here and build this thing up.'

TVNZ's control of the market extended to sports coverage, and until the mid-1990s it had a monopoly on broadcasting rugby. Back then, the jewel in the broadcast crown was the National Provincial Championship. The Kiwi rugby consumer felt well catered for, knowing that throughout the winter months there would be a live provincial game on the national broadcaster every Sunday afternoon.

This was at a time when international matches took place somewhat sporadically, with the schedule nowhere near as structured as it is today. Prior to the inauguration of the Tri-Nations in 1996, there was no regular competition in which the All Blacks took part. The Southern Hemisphere didn't have an equivalent of the Northern Hemisphere's Five Nations (later expanded to six), and the All Blacks' schedule was made up on the fly, with everyone seemingly grateful to get what they were given. The world champion All Blacks played just five Tests in 1988, for instance, and seven in each of 1989 and 1990, before playing just once at home in 1991. So when Sky launched in the late 1980s, the rugby it was most interested in buying was the NPC.

When Fellet arrived at Sky, the company's content offering was eclectic and confused across all genres, but particularly so when it came to sport. 'Our sports right was the ESPN channel,' he says, 'and it jumped from Ajax to a badminton tournament in Malaysia to an MBL game in the States. It was a global sports network.'

Having been around the pay TV scene for years, Fellet knew the potential impact the acquisition of valued sports rights could have on subscriber numbers. Sport, as he saw it, was a means to break inertia, and in New Zealand, the best sport to compel consumers to act – indeed, maybe the only sport that could – was rugby. A pay TV operator could advertise and promote its movies, dramas and factual content in all the right places to all the right people, but it still, more often than not, took a fear of missing out on seeing much-loved sports competitions to spark potential customers into reaching for their wallet.

'Sports got you off the couch and onto the phone,' says Fellet. 'People would say, "I need this before the World Cup starts." Or "I need this before rugby season starts." And what we really need for pay TV is sport week in and week out, [but] back then there weren't a lot of Tests being played the way they are now.'

But throughout the early 1990s, rugby was the nut Sky couldn't crack. No one within NZR saw Sky as a realistic or appropriate home for provincial rugby. The establishment was wedded to the tradition of showing just one live game every weekend on TVNZ. This was a time, of course, when there were disruptors all over the rugby landscape, and Fellet says plenty of people knocked on Sky's door looking to sell them a rebel competition to broadcast, but it was always a hard no, because he could see no value in antagonising NZR.

'All this went nowhere until someone started the World Rugby Corporation, who started signing up everybody,' says Fellet. 'They had most of the All Blacks already signed up until Jock Hobbs went up to South Africa and got them to tear up their contracts, and that was the break we needed. Because all of a sudden, they said, "Shit, how are we going to pay for all this?"

News International came to us and TVNZ, and I would imagine [the NZ radio network] MediaWorks, and said, "Anybody in?" We quickly raised our hands. I don't think TVNZ was crazy about the concept, and MediaWorks just didn't have the financial clout. We didn't have it either, but that content allowed us to go out and finance it.'

The impact of buying those rights was dramatic. Sky became the home of rugby in New Zealand: it owned all the rugby content that mattered. Having been happy to have one live game a weekend on TVNZ, New Zealanders now, for the price of a monthly subscription, could have wall-to-wall Super Rugby, with every match live, from February through to late May. Then they could have every All Blacks Test live. This was Sky's business model: it provided dedicated sports channels that were content hungry. From being a novelty, loss-making concept that no one quite understood in the early 1990s, Sky was suddenly the most profitable media company in the country by the end of the decade.

Sky had revolutionised the way Kiwis consumed rugby and had got rich doing so. Its rise and rise as the country's premier sports channel also saw TVNZ collapse as a rugby broadcaster. Rugby on free-to-air TV became anathema to Kiwis by the early 2000s, mostly because none of the terrestrial channels had anywhere near the sort of money they needed to buy, produce and deliver live rugby content.

This was why the media market was so different in 2004, when NZR began renegotiating its broadcast contract: it was no longer competitive. Both NZR and Sky knew it, yet this was not the disadvantage it appeared because both organisations were still highly dependent on one other: their respective needs were strongly aligned.

Sky had boomed on the back of rugby, and having won a huge subscription base, it needed to retain it. It had weaned almost half the country onto its satellite TV network and got them used to wall-to-wall rugby, so while it knew that neither TVNZ nor the privately owned TV3 could compete for rights – and there were no other pay TV operators in the country – it had inextricably linked the sustainability of its business to rugby. For its part, NZR had inextricably linked the sustainability of its business to the value of those broadcast rights.

The two organisations were now in a symbiotic relationship, where they were financially aligned, so the nature of the renegotiation was entirely different to the initial deal. Discussions were more collaborative, conducted in partnership, openly and robustly, with a recognition that the content and the price had to work for all parties. But the problem was that not all markets had the same needs, and NZR's aspirations didn't always naturally fit with Sky's preferences.

The Australians, who had no provincial competition, and the South Africans, who had a sociopolitical need to create a fifth team, wanted to expand Super Rugby. New Zealand, however, was lukewarm on the idea, as a longer competition would further squeeze the period in which the NPC was played. Sky, on the other hand, was relatively supportive of extending Super Rugby, as what drove and retained subscribers were season-long, compelling competitions.

NZR also wanted and needed to leverage the power of the All Blacks and maximise the number of Tests they played each year. The All Blacks were the key driver of the whole financial system, and so NZR wanted the national team to be playing a minimum of 12 Tests annually. New Zealand pushed, therefore, to expand the Tri-Nations from two rounds to three rounds. And the art of the SANZAR broadcast deal was being able to agree compromised decisions so each nation walked away with something they wanted.

But compromise also led to consequences, and an expanded Super Rugby and an expanded Tri-Nations meant the season had to extend to accommodate the extra matches. Super Rugby had to commence earlier in the year, so from 2006 the Kiwi players would be in action from mid-February until late November. Those picked by the All Blacks would no longer be able to feature in the NPC, because the Tri-Nations was going to have to overlap the domestic competition.

The extension of the Tri-Nations confirmed that international rugby had usurped the NPC as the primary rugby property in New Zealand, and that the value proposition of Southern Hemisphere rugby had changed enormously during the first decade of professional rugby. In this new era, Super Rugby and the Tri-Nations were definitively the two biggest assets.

For NZR, the challenge was finding the sweet spot of giving Sky more games to broadcast without devaluing the various properties within it. Sky wanted more content, but not so much as to turn it into wallpaper or see All Blacks Tests lose their allure. A balance had to be struck between quality and quantity, but the expansion of Super Rugby from 12 to 14 teams and the Tri-Nations from two rounds to three was pushing that to the limit. There had been high-performance give to enable commercial take – but not so much as to overly stress or hinder either. The new-look season was, just, a win for all three nations and their broadcasters.

Proof of this came when News International agreed to pay US$323 million (NZ$452 million) for a five-year rights extension. That was a 16 per cent lift on the initial deal, but the amount of cash it netted NZR came in at about the same as the first deal in real terms. Given the increased costs that South Africa and Australia would be facing, the revenue split was altered to give South Africa 38 per cent, Australia almost 30 per cent and New Zealand a slight drop to 32 per cent. Altering the revenue split was the way to get all parties over the line, and while NZR had conceded ground, it didn't suffer a drop in income.

'Because the market was softer, we ended up with more content,' says Moller. 'We increased the Tri-Nations from two games to three and added more teams in Super Rugby. That made it possible to strike a reasonable deal that protected the income. Being a negotiation between the Australians and South Africans and ourselves, we had to ask: "What was a fair split of the money?" In the end, it was pretty much line ball, adjusted for the exchange rate, in terms of income coming to NZR.'

It was a win for the fans, as Super Rugby had a freshen-up without losing its essence or becoming so bloated as to become long and boring. It's hard to say it was a win for the players, though, because it left them facing a longer season and shorter recovery times. But it was most definitely a win for Moller personally. While Peters had handled the numbers and the detail, Moller had played a critical role in rebuilding what was a badly damaged relationship with the partners, particularly Australia. The damage caused by the World Cup hosting debacle had been extensive, and it had taken a considerable and skilled diplomatic effort by Moller to restore good relations between the two nations.

The broadcast deal highlighted the skill set Moller had brought to NZR: he was supremely professional, focused, disciplined and strategic, and critically he was also likeable, relatable and ready to concede that mistakes had been made in the past. He listened to stakeholders and key partners who felt they had been wronged in the past, acknowledged their right to feel the way they did about NZR, and by doing so forged trust, goodwill and a new confidence that people could do business with him and his organisation and not regret it.

Moller was a bridge-builder – a corporate beast, yes, but a social one, with an old-school appreciation that people always preferred doing business with people they liked. In his first two years in the job, he and Jock Hobbs had made a point of rebuilding relationships, not just with their counterparts at Rugby Australia, but with the key people at all the major rugby unions. New Zealand had embarrassed itself on the global stage with the way it behaved in late 2001 and early 2002, but by December 2004 Moller and Hobbs had successfully repaired the damage. They did their bit around the board table, but they also went the extra mile after hours, wining and dining stakeholders, partners and officials from other unions, rebuilding New Zealand's reputation and winning new friends.

All this diplomacy didn't just help NZR land a broadcast deal that met its primary goal of preserving its income. It also persuaded Moller that New Zealand was ready to do what no one had imagined they ever would, and bid once again to host the World Cup.

*

GIVEN THE DAMAGE THAT losing the co-hosting rights to the 2003 World Cup had caused NZR, Moller was taking a giant risk by dipping the country's toe back into the bidding process. Why would New Zealand put itself through that again? And, more pertinently, why would the rest of the rugby world give them that chance? There were so many reasons why it felt like a bad idea when Moller, in late 2004, with no fanfare or heightened media interest, quietly announced that New Zealand had registered its interest in bidding to host the 2011 event. He noted that its interest didn't commit NZR to making a formal bid; it was more an indication that NZR was willing to consider doing so.

But even to have registered an interest was a bold move, as the wounds inflicted by the catastrophe of 2003 were still fresh. Could New Zealand really be taken seriously after all that had happened? That was a question Moller had been thinking deeply about after attending the 2003 tournament in Australia, where he saw how it had galvanised the nation, put rugby at the forefront of the sports news and invigorated the cities in which games were played. It was impossible not to see how the tournament not only fostered a sense of Australian pride in the Wallabies, but also how effectively it marketed the country to the rest of the world.

The Rugby World Cup was undeniably big business, and Australia was undeniably a big country – an economic heavyweight with the stadia, transport networks and accommodation to host such a huge event. Moller realised that hosting the 2011 tournament would stress New Zealand's smaller infrastructure – but it was the very scale of the challenge that attracted him to the idea.

It would be audacious for New Zealand to show how much it had learned in a short space of time, and how it had matured in the three years since it had disgraced itself. 'Humility is so important in the rugby world and New Zealand had lost its humility through the World Cup saga,' says Moller. 'If you slam your fist on the table and call Vernon Pugh, the chairman of the IRB, a bloody idiot, then you have done a whole lot of damage. After RWC 2003, I started talking to the board about it and we formed a RWC steering committee – all people who were not on the board, because I knew I had a challenge after the last experience of getting the board to agree to it.'

The committee included former prime minister of New Zealand Jim Bolger; chair of Air New Zealand John Palmer; businessman Paul Collins; sports administrator John Wells; and several others prominent business figures such as Brian Roche and Bruce Wattie.

Winning the NZR board over was going to prove as hard as, if not harder than, winning the actual bid. There was trepidation among the directors about New Zealand having another go, but Moller made a compelling case.

'The prime driver for me was the key thing about the All Blacks brand: winning. Having talked to a lot of rugby people and the All Blacks captains on the board, they said, "We reckon the best chance of winning the World Cup is to host it in New Zealand." So, for me, it was about winning, winning, winning. But I was also committed to winning something for the country because of the national significance. And also, equally importantly, proving that we had recovered from the depths of despair with the rugby world. Those were the three motivations.'

In early 2005, the board signed off on making a formal bid, and New Zealand found itself in a three-way contest with South Africa and Japan – the latter quicky establishing itself as the local and international media's favourite. Despite having secured its government's commitment to underwrite the tournament, the New Zealand bid was mostly written off by media analysts. The time zone was unfavourable to the key European markets, which would impact the value of the broadcast deals World Rugby would be able to sell, and the stadia were too small. Even if every ticket to every game were sold, the tournament was forecasting a $30-million loss. The New Zealand government would pick up the tab for that loss, which meant World Rugby would receive its £48 million (NZ$122 million) fee and was forecasting it would make close to £120 million in total, but that was significantly less than it would make if the tournament were played in Japan.

But the media hadn't factored in the power of New Zealand's allure as the spiritual home of rugby, and the even greater pulling power of the All Blacks. New Zealand was also enjoying something of a global awakening as a tourist destination following the hugely successful *Lord of the Rings* movie trilogy, which had wowed audiences with the natural beauty of the landscapes. People who had never heard of New Zealand were suddenly desperate to go there, and that no doubt gave World Rugby some confidence that the numbers of foreign visitors during the tournament might be higher than initially predicted.

But what gave World Rugby the greatest confidence in New Zealand was the way the country had hosted the British and Irish Lions in 2005. The tour effectively served as a trial of the nation's ability to host a big event, and NZR received a high pass mark.

'We proved we could faultlessly run a major tour and it produced a lot of the content we were able to use as part of our bid presentation,' says Moller. 'We were able to host the whole of World Rugby for a week. We helicoptered them across to the Wairarapa Coast and had a lunch where you could almost see Antarctica, and put the bid to them. We worked closely with Tourism NZ.'

In November 2005, New Zealand was voted by the World Rugby membership as the host of the 2011 World Cup. The Lions tour and the tireless work of Moller and Hobbs in selling the bid, the country and themselves to the people who would be voting proved decisive. Japan had run a global PR campaign, using prominent names – such as former England and Lions captain Martin Johnson – as ambassadors who promoted the bid and told the media it was time for World Rugby to take their showpiece to Asia. But Moller and Hobbs wanted to directly influence the executives who would be casting their country's votes. In the end, this personal, intimate approach won them the support New Zealand needed.

And so the All Blacks were going to be showcased in their own backyard, and the branding possibilities were endless. The impact of New Zealand hosting the tournament and the All Blacks winning it would no doubt be unimaginably lucrative, both in the direct financial returns and in the indirect reputational growth that would follow. But there was the 2007 Rugby World Cup to be played before then, and it was front of mind for Moller when All Blacks coach Graham Henry knocked on his door in early 2006, hoping to have a chat.

CHAPTER ELEVEN

DESPERATE TIMES REQUIRE DESPERATE MEASURES

IN EARLY 2006, AS All Blacks coach Graham Henry cast his thoughts ahead to the World Cup the following year, he saw catastrophe looming. Such a gloomy portent was hard for others to understand given the way the All Blacks had stormed their way through 2005, hammering the British and Irish Lions, then picking up the Tri-Nations title before heading to the United Kingdom, where they beat Wales, Ireland, England and Scotland to win a coveted Grand Slam. They had suffered just one loss, had played sublime rugby and seemed to have superstars in every position. The one negative was that captain Tana Umaga had retired, but in Richie McCaw, aged only 24, the All Blacks had a replacement who seemed poised to become the greatest leader the game had known. So what was troubling Graham Henry?

Henry was worried about fatigue and the impact the longer season was almost certainly going to have on his players. His

All Blacks had returned from their Grand Slam venture in early December 2005, and the opening round of the expanded Super Rugby tournament was played on 10 February – two weeks earlier than the previous year. All the best medical advice recommended that players be given a minimum of 12 weeks off between seasons – a three-month gap in which they could rest, recover from injuries and recondition themselves. A decade of professionalism had seen the athletes become bigger, stronger and more powerful, and the physical impacts more ferocious. Space on the field was becoming harder to find. Henry was conscious that there were more collisions in every game, and that they were happening in more areas of the field.

He was also conscious that his top players would be involved in two additional Super Rugby games and two additional Tri-Nations games. NZR had also agreed to play an additional third Bledisloe Cup Test that year, and to ready themselves for the World Cup, the All Blacks were going to play a second Test against France on their end-of-season tour. In total, they would be playing 14 Tests. The toll it would take on the athletes would be considerable. Cutting back the pre-season break to nine weeks and then playing more games would increase the risk of injury exponentially.

This was always the danger in changing the balance between the commercial and high-performance worlds. In the first broadcast deal in 1995, NZR had got the balance right in terms of the amount of content they sold and the price they received for it. The top players typically had 12 to 14 weeks off between seasons, and the maximum workload for any one player would be 13 Super Rugby games (if their team made the final) and ten or 11 Test matches. In 2006, the maximum workload jumped to 15 Super Rugby games and 14 Tests, on the back of a shortened pre-season. There was medical advice coming out of the UK at the time that total player workloads in a season should not exceed 30 games; New Zealand's best players would be right up against that mark. Of even greater concern was that almost half of the overall workload for some players would be made up of Test matches, which had incredible physical and mental intensity.

This was the burden the players had to carry to secure the broadcast contract and to ensure that the same volume of TV money was flowing into the game. As Henry sat in the grandstand at Eden Park on 10 February 2006 to watch the Blues play the Hurricanes in the year's opening Super Rugby match, the heat of a scorching Auckland day was still in the air. It didn't feel right to Henry that rugby, a winter code, was being played at the height of summer – and that his team would still be playing in late November.

What troubled him even more, however, was that the 2007 Super Rugby season was going to kick off even earlier. The first games were scheduled for 2 February in order to accommodate the World Cup, which would begin on 7 September. Those who would tour with the All Blacks later that year would only have a seven-week break before they were expected to be back playing Super Rugby again. The All Blacks were scheduled to play three Tests in June 2007 – against France twice and Canada – before a two-round Tri-Nations, ahead of the World Cup in France, where they would begin their campaign against Italy in Marseille on 8 September.

So there were 21 Tests to be played before the All Blacks even went to the World Cup, and some players might also be involved in 30 Super Rugby games across 2006 and 2007.

No wonder Henry had a bad feeling about what might transpire at the World Cup. He could see his best players being drained long before they got on the plane to France. He could also see many of them never making it onto that plane, because of the increased likelihood of them being injured, given the volume of games and the lack of rest periods.

The more Henry saw of the early Super Rugby rounds in 2006, the more he, along with his fellow coaches Steve Hansen and Wayne Smith, became convinced that the All Blacks would not win the 2007 World Cup if they didn't mandate a rest period for their leading players. The question was: when could this happen?

In 2002, All Blacks coach John Mitchell had left many of his first-choice players at home when the team travelled to Europe in November for Tests against England, France and Wales. Henry wasn't keen on doing the same. He wanted his best team in Europe in November 2006 so they could spend a prolonged period in France. There were also too many commercial obligations attached to the All Blacks for them to seriously consider sending a side overseas without their superstars. Sky and Adidas would have legitimate complaints if the All Blacks were at half-strength in Europe.

The only option, as Henry saw it, was for many of his leading players to make a late entry into Super Rugby in 2007.

That would have the dual benefit of affording his best players the 12 weeks they needed to rest and recondition, and cutting down the total number of games they would play before the World Cup. And so, in mid-April 2006, Henry presented his plan to Moller, which was to remove 22 players of Henry's selection from the first seven rounds of Super Rugby in 2007.

It was a huge ask, with significant commercial ramifications. Taking so many players out of Super Rugby was going to seriously dilute the quality of the competition and upset every company that had invested in it financially. It was going to create friction with the other SANZAR partners, as their respective broadcasters and various sponsors would feel equally duped that the Kiwi sides were not at full strength. Fans would feel ripped off, and would likely sense that NZR did not value Super Rugby.

As Henry made his pitch, Moller knew immediately that if he supported this high-performance plan, it would come with commercial consequences. But two factors made him willing to consider it. First, the business was in great shape. The new TV deal had preserved long-term revenue at historic levels, and the British and Irish Lions tour had provided $25 million of additional profit. Second, he rationalised that the financial benefits of winning the 2007 World Cup would far exceed, in the longer term, whatever commercial damage and costs were incurred by pulling players out of Super Rugby.

'I talked to Jock about it and the board at length,' says Moller. 'We agonised over it. But go back to the situation of having not won a World Cup since 1987, and there was this constant narrative of "20 years". The coaching staff and the people who knew rugby, as opposed to me knowing business, were adamant this was necessary. The people who requested it and were adamant about it were the All Blacks ... [T]he rhetoric was: "That this is the only way we are going to win the World Cup in the Northern Hemisphere. You either back us or we are probably not going to win." We took a risk, and it was a big risk.'

Moller took it upon himself to manage the communication strategy to key stakeholders. The two partners from whom he needed approval were Adidas and Sky, as they had the biggest financial risk.

Since taking over as chief executive, Moller had built a personal relationship with Herbert Heiner at Adidas, which had enabled a strong bond of trust to develop. On hearing the reasoning behind the move, and because he had inordinate faith that the All Blacks would only be recommending this path if they were sure it was the right one, Heiner was supportive. While Adidas was the apparel partner for all New Zealand's Super Rugby sides, it was the All Blacks that carried the value. Heiner was happy to get behind a strategy that enhanced the prospects of that elusive World Cup being delivered.

Moller had also gained the respect and trust of Sky chief executive John Fellet, but he knew this conversation was likely to be the harder one, as the pay TV operator was going to find it hard to sell subscriptions to a compromised Super Rugby competition. Sky had bought the rights to all of NZR's content, and while the All Blacks Tests were the most valuable asset in the portfolio, Super Rugby was still of considerable importance in driving a return on investment.

But Fellet, too, was ready to play the long game. In fact, he'd long anticipated that the day would come when the NZR chief executive knocked on his door with this request. Despite his lack of affinity for the code when he first arrived in the country, Fellet had recognised early that the game was making demands of its leading players that would not have been tolerated by athletes in other major codes. He'd been aware of the problem ever since bumping into a bruised, bloodied and half-broken Zinzan Brooke in the car park at Sky's headquarters one Monday morning in the early 1990s.

Sky's marketing department had persuaded Fellet that the company, although unable at that time to get its hands on any major content rights, could employ an All Black as an ambassador for the network. On hearing that such a deal would only cost $25,000 a year, Fellet signed off on hiring Brooke. It was extraordinarily good value at that price, and earned Sky huge brownie points with NZR, as that cash went a long way towards persuading Brooke to turn down offers to play professionally elsewhere.

When Fellet saw a limping Brooke, he asked what had happened. Brooke had played on the weekend, and pointed out how oppositions always targeted the high-profile All Blacks.

'But NPC isn't even on, so who were you playing for?' Fellet asked.

It turned out Brooke had been playing for his club side.

'It's like asking Michael Jordan to go back and play high school basketball with a high school team when he's not playing for the Chicago Bulls,' Fellet says. 'I couldn't believe it. Chris

Moller, when Graham Henry was the coach, was quite clear. Chris would say to me, "Look, these guys can only play X number of games, John." Now, my contract required NZR to play their best players, but I never enforced it because I recognised the dilemma. Look at the NFL guys – they play, what, 16, 17 games a year and I just did not want to become that guy, the one where everyone says we lost the World Cup because Fellet made us play. It was a big risk, but I wanted what was best for the rugby union because that would ultimately help me.'

When the All Blacks lost their play-off game for third place at the 1999 World Cup, Fellet explained, he'd been pounded by a loss of subscribers.

'The Kiwi fan gets so high by the highs and so low by the lows that I had people lined up out the door saying, "I'll never watch rugby again. That Hart!" If I could be guaranteed the All Blacks could win every World Cup or at least get to the final, that was a plus for me. The World Cup required so many games to be played on free-to-air, so I was better off, I thought, starting to sell Super Rugby packages the next year with the fact the All Blacks had won the World Cup or were the current holders of the World Cup.'

While NZR received buy-in for its high-performance plan from the two most critical commercial partners, not all stakeholders approved of the players being withdrawn. Rebel Sport, the Australasian sports retailer, had bought the naming rights to Super Rugby in New Zealand, and somehow Rod Duke, the multimillionaire owner of the business, only knew of NZR's plans when he read about them in the *New Zealand Herald*.

'I personally went to see John Fellet because I had a good and close relationship with John,' says Moller. 'Rebel Sport, I didn't have the same relationship with Rod Duke, but I think it would be nuts if someone hadn't talked to him. Now, whether they talked to the right people and whether the right people talked to Rod, I can't comment.'

The other source of heat Moller felt was from the SANZAR partners and News International. The latter's gripe was that while NZR may have built a strong and trusting relationship with Sky and sought its domestic broadcaster's approval to withdraw the players, the impact would be felt more widely than in New Zealand alone – and should the All Blacks go on to win the World Cup in 2007, the benefits would not be felt in Australia or South Africa. NZR was, according to News International, taking a commercial risk that had no upside for any stakeholder outside New Zealand.

The whole episode perhaps demonstrated to News International the risks it was taking by buying content rights from a partnership that had so many disparate needs and that had become considerably more unpredictable and volatile than it was back in 1995. The next SANZAR rights negotiation, in 2010, was conducted directly between the member unions and their respective domestic broadcasters. News International would no longer be at the negotiating table.

Justifiably, Rugby Australia and the South African Rugby Board were both irate that New Zealand had unilaterally decided to diminish the quality of its five sides. If they too had decided to risk the credibility of Super Rugby by withdrawing most of their best players for so long, the consequences for the competition would have been catastrophic. Why did New Zealand think it had the right to behave in this way when it was in a partnership? Surely the partner unions' consent was required before such actions were taken?

Having worked so hard to restore trust and confidence in the wake of the co-hosting debacle, this was a serious setback for trans-Tasman relations – as was evidenced when NZR needed a favour from their friends across the ditch. NZR wanted to play the final Bledisloe encounter of 2006 at Eden Park with a 2.30 pm kick-off. The All Blacks were due to fly to South Africa the following morning and were booked on a 6 am flight to Sydney. The early kick-off would at least give the players a chance to go to bed before the arduous trip, whereas the usual 7.35 pm kick-off would see players manage, at best, only two to three hours' sleep before they had to be at the airport.

Rugby Australia wasn't inclined to grant the request, as a 2.30 pm kick-off in New Zealand would be 12.30 pm in its key rugby territories along the eastern seaboard. The Australian broadcaster, Rugby Australia argued, shouldn't have to agree to any more Kiwi-requested changes. In the end, agreement was reached to kick off at 5.30 pm New Zealand time, and Rugby Australia was able to use this early-evening compromise as another stick with which to beat NZR in the media.

And this was the problem for NZR: Rebel Sport, News International and the SANZAR partners had all generated negative media coverage about the high-performance plan, and with it they intensified the pressure on the All Blacks to justify their decision by winning the 2007 World Cup. NZR accepted it had taken a risk by signing off on Henry's demand, but once the news became public, the narrative about this being a supremely bad idea began to build.

*

IN THEORY, THE HIGH-PERFORMANCE side of the business had been granted a massive victory when the NZR board signed off on the 22 All Blacks having what would be known as an extended rest and reconditioning window in early 2007. The logic behind the plan made sense, but ultimately it was only ever going to be judged a smart decision if it led to the All Blacks winning the World Cup. But as the athletes saw it, a decision had been made with their welfare in mind. Their performance had been prioritised over commercial obligations.

But this wasn't the biggest high-performance victory of the year. The ultimate acknowledgement of the athletes came when details of the new collective employment agreement were revealed: NZR had consented to a revenue-sharing model with the players. Under the new terms of the agreement, 33 per cent of all NZR revenue that was considered to have been player-generated would belong to the athletes. Player-generated revenue was any income that the athletes had a direct role in driving, so included broadcast, sponsorship, gate revenue and merchandise. It was, essentially, all revenue bar government and World Rugby grants, and foreign currency exchange gains. Once this new deal kicked in, 33 cents in every dollar would be assigned to what would be known as the Player Payment Pool – which was the fund from which all salaries would be drawn.

The new arrangement, while commonplace in US sports, was new to rugby. The exciting thing for the players was that it would formally align them in a partnership with their employer. And the alignment was critical as it meant that the players were incentivised to deliver for commercial partners. There was now a direct commercial link between the success they delivered on the field and the financial returns it would lead to. Again, there was a simple but irrefutable logic that sat well with the players: success attracted investment, and they would get an agreed share of any lift in NZR broadcast, sponsorship and ticket revenue. This meant the players, via the Rugby Players' Association, were contractually obliged to be consulted about any measures that might materially impact their share of the revenue.

'There were lots of examples of it around the world,' says Moller, 'and what I particularly liked about it – and this came from my business background – was it effectively created a joint venture. And for a joint venture to work, you need to have an alignment of interests, particularly financial interests. That started to help [the players] understand the importance of sponsorship, of broadcasters and to come out of the Mitchell era where the All Blacks had a culture of "We don't want these enemies near us", to this new empowered, collaborative leadership culture instilled by Graham, Steve and Smithy and then putting in a mechanism that shared the dollars. It felt like we were heading in a much better direction.'

A year out from the 2007 World Cup, the situation could hardly have been any more different to that ahead of the 2003 World Cup. In late 2002, the All Blacks were being run almost as if they were not connected at all to NZR. They were barely servicing the needs of commercial partners under the guidance of a dictatorial coaching regime. By late 2006, the All Blacks had a leadership group that was working in tandem with the coaches and management team, and which understood the players' obligations to deliver what NZR's commercial partners needed. The team was guided by Henry's mantra that 'better people make better All Blacks'.

New Zealand was miles ahead of the rest of the world, too. The All Blacks had again collected the Tri-Nations and Bledisloe cups, and then swept through Europe on a frightening rampage that saw them post a record score against France and hammer both England and Wales. What truly set New Zealand apart was the collaborative and unified relationship between the players and their employer. However much the playing demands had increased in New Zealand, they were significantly worse in France and England, where some individuals were being asked to play more than 40 games a season. The clubs had commercial obligations to meet, as did the national unions. Both tried to ram more content into the season and then fight for the services of the players, who had no protection from this madness.

Financially, too, New Zealand was the envy of the rugby world in late 2006. NZR had $50 million of cash reserves in the bank, and while it had stretched the season to ten months and pushed the players close to the 30-game season limit to win these commercial gains, it had also been willing to redress the balance by agreeing to the World Cup reconditioning window. Whether NZR was getting the balance right between high-performance needs and commercial imperatives was open to debate, but it was at least – and unlike other nations – willing and able to make compromises when it felt there was an imbalance that might upset the whole ecosystem.

When the All Blacks flew home from Europe in late 2006, they were red-hot favourites to win the World Cup. They had lost two games in two years, and with their star-studded squad back in New Zealand, 22 of them were afforded a 16-week rest and reconditioning period to ensure they were fresh for the World Cup the following September. Surely, after finding novel and unexpected ways to blow up at the 1991, 1995, 1999 and 2003 World Cups, the All Blacks would at last be crowned world champions once again, and open the door to untold commercial riches.

But the 2007 tournament turned out to be the worst campaign of all. The All Blacks were beaten in the quarter-final by France, and the media, fans and former players all turned sour on NZR's decision to sanction the rest and reconditioning window. The board had taken what it felt was a logical, well-considered and justifiable risk, but that didn't matter when the All Blacks had not even made the last four.

NZR had indulged Henry and he'd failed to repay them. That was the main media narrative in the weeks following the World Cup calamity, and equally predictably, it transformed into demands that Henry and his coaching team, who were all out of contract, not be reappointed.

Moller had signalled earlier in 2007 that he would be stepping down after the World Cup and would be replaced by his deputy, Steve Tew. And so the new chief executive and the board had an incredibly tough choice to make in December. Henry had reapplied to keep his job but was being challenged by the long-term Crusaders supremo, Robbie Deans, who had been Mitchell's All Blacks assistant.

Deans was hugely popular in Canterbury, and well respected nationwide. He didn't have the same depth of experience as Henry, but he had at least previously been involved with the All Blacks, albeit briefly. Appointing Deans would have appeased the large swathes of followers who had turned on Henry. It would also have served as an admission that NZR had been wrong to grant the reconditioning window – that it was an ill-conceived concept that had unnecessarily and unjustifiably caused commercial harm for no high-performance gain.

But Tew and the board reasoned that the reconditioning window wasn't ill-conceived, just poorly executed. The communication between the All Blacks and Super Rugby coaches about how and when players would return to action was poor, and in some cases non-existent. The programme had also been a little too long, and should have been tailored to suit individuals rather than being of uniform length for everyone. The basic principle of wanting to manage player workloads, however, was one NZR continued to want to support, and given how much progress Henry had made in transforming the wider culture of the All Blacks and growing the players into better leaders and more rounded people, there was some reluctance to bring in a new coach and risk all that being derailed. Some held the view that Henry and his coaching team needed an opportunity to learn from what had gone wrong, and to adapt their thinking around what constitutes best high-performance strategies.

'We had done things differently – rightly or wrongly – leading up to 2007,' says Tew. 'We never quite clicked at that tournament, and the things we did that were aimed at us being in good nick for that tournament, they never quite worked. I know the conditioning window was not everyone's cup of tea – but that was all about being able to play three big Tests at the end and being fresh for the last minute of the third one. But we didn't get past the first one, so you have to say it failed. The big issue when I took over was how we were going to get back up from that.

'We had to appoint coaches – I acted as the CEO during that process. The board made the decision, and while it was brave, it was also relatively straightforward. If you sat through the process, there was no comparison between the two interviews. Ted [Henry] came in and had his team organised and had banked what he thought the lessons were from the last four years. And it was a compelling team. It was the strongest coaching group in the world, and Robbie didn't front with it, and I know Robbie well and he is not a poorly prepared person. He didn't front with it. He didn't have a definitive support team with him, and if I was a conspiracy theorist, I'd say he'd already decided his future lay elsewhere.'

When everything was considered, the board felt that Henry and his coaching team were best placed to drive high-performance outcomes. If the brand was going to bounce back from the World Cup disaster of 2007, Henry needed to be reappointed, and on 17 December the board voted 7–1 to do just that, with Hobbs recusing himself as Deans was his brother-in-law.

'If I was asked whether I would do it again, I would, because of the unique circumstances we were in,' says Moller of the decision to sign off on the reconditioning window. 'This country was desperate to win a World Cup, and we had been told by the experts – the All Blacks – that this was the way to do it. Given my time over again, I would do the same thing. Had we won, no one would have thought about it again.'

CHAPTER TWELVE

THINK BIG, SPEND BIG

THE ALL BLACKS HAD an amazing story to tell. The brand was undeniably powerful and New Zealand Rugby had punched far above its weight financially on the back of the disproportionate strength of its key asset.

When the game had turned professional, there had been frequent opinion pieces from analysts warning that the All Blacks would be left behind in this brave new world. The stronger economies of the UK nations, France, Australia and even South Africa would enable them to build commercial empires, with which they would be able to better fund their high-performance programmes. The argument was always the same: money would become the greater enabler and determine results on the field. But 12 years into the professional age, the All Blacks had improved their win ratio from 71 per cent in the amateur era to 80 per cent since 1996. They were a much-loved brand and investors were attracted by the longevity of the All Blacks success.

'The deepness of the legacy, of the story, and the long-standing success ratio despite the World Cups ... that's what opened doors,' says Steve Tew. 'You put a slide up even in a cold call that says here is a national team that plays ten-plus games a year and we win 80 per cent of those games. They go, "That can't be right." But we say, "It is. Here's the record, and we are captained by a guy who has played 84 Tests and lost four." Crazy.'

But for all that the All Blacks' brand resonated with people in every corner of the globe, it was missing something. It needed the validation of a World Cup: definitive proof that the All Blacks were the best in the world. Just as importantly, the All Blacks, for all their brilliance and ability to dazzle, had to kill the rising fear that they had developed a psychological fault line preventing them from winning a World Cup. They continued to trade on the back of the tagline that they were the best team in the world, and yet every four years they couldn't prove that they were. They had won the inaugural World Cup in 1987 but then had conjured magnificently imaginative ways to blow their chances in 1991, 1995, 1999, 2003 and 2007.

There was surely a point in time when prospective commercial partners would ask why NZR continued to pitch the All Blacks as the greatest rugby brand on the planet when 20 years had passed since they had last won a World Cup.

Adidas chief executive Herbert Heiner didn't ask that question directly after the All Blacks bombed out of the 2007 tournament, but he did turn up at a lunch NZR hosted on the day of the final and reminded Tew that Kevin Roberts had promised two World Cups in the first decade of the partnership. 'It was lovely of him to come to that event in Paris, but he basically said, "You know you owe me two World Cups?"' says Tew.

The brand story needed a World Cup win.

And there was a deeper concern for NZR, which was that the next World Cup would be played in New Zealand. If they couldn't win that one, on home soil, then the brand value really would be challenged, as 24 years without a world title would discourage potential investors from supporting the All Blacks even if their win ratio was 80 per cent. Tew wasn't fearful that the commercial enterprise would collapse if the All Blacks didn't win in 2011, but he was certain it would be better if his confidence didn't have to be tested.

'While a company like Adidas gets a bit grumpy that they don't have the photographs of you picking up the cup, they are long-term serious players in the market and they get it,' says Tew. 'Two World Cups [playing badly] was not ideal but we still had this magical black jersey and this mystique that came with the All Blacks. I wasn't worried that we had a major problem ... but a home World Cup in 2011 would not have been a good time for another poor campaign.'

Winning the 2011 World Cup would be the key to the All Blacks opening the door to bigger and better commercial opportunities, and would close the gap between the brand's recognition and its financial returns. This inability to convert profile to dollars was a continual source of frustration. NZR's revenue had doubled since the game had turned professional, but the All Blacks remained a global brand with a local cashflow. The research continued to show that the All Blacks, in terms of profile and recognition, were still comparable with the likes of Manchester United, Ferrari and the Chicago Bulls.

But the economics also told the same story it had 12 years earlier: the international brands continued to drive considerably higher revenue flows. And despite NZR doubling its revenue, the financial power of the All Blacks was falling further behind that of sporting brands in major leagues that had seen an explosion in broadcast money and sponsorship deals over the same period. These leagues had also begun successful globalisation programmes, with the NFL playing exhibition games in London and the major English Premier League clubs turning up in Asia most off-seasons. The All Blacks brand was growing, NZR's revenue was growing, but there remained a sense in Wellington that neither was growing quickly enough. Perhaps a World Cup win would prove to be the required accelerant.

There was total alignment on this with the high-performance team. Henry, Hansen and Smith were the first coaching group to survive a failed World Cup campaign, and having done so, against public opinion, they were under incredible pressure to justify NZR's faith. And the only way they could do that was to win the 2011 World Cup. Their motivation to win, therefore, was equally high, so in early 2008, Tew and his management team met with Henry and built a plan to win the World Cup. The first step was to identify the players they felt they would need to be successful in 2011.

Player retention had become something of a losing battle for NZR. There was an expectation that senior players would move on after a World Cup. But 2007 saw a new and worrying trend develop, in which a handful of young players who still had much to offer chose to leave New Zealand. Carl Hayman, rated the best tighthead prop in the world and still only 27, signed with Newcastle. Aaron Mauger, who was only 26 and an integral part of the All Blacks' midfield configuration, signed with Leicester. And 24-year-old Luke McAlister, who Henry felt would be a superstar of the world game, shocked everyone when he announced he was leaving for Sale. Other World Cup squad members Chris Jack, Doug Howlett, Anton Oliver and Keith Robinson were also either leaving or retiring. In early 2008, Jerry Collins and Chris Masoe, both 28, signalled to the All Blacks' coaches that they would be leaving after Super Rugby.

The money being offered by European clubs was just too good to turn down. In the case of Hayman, it was life-changing; he was offered £350,000 a year, which at the time converted to close to $1 million and made him one of the best-paid players in the world. The big clubs of Europe not only had incredible budgets to recruit players, they also had a desire to come after younger All Blacks, who presented better long-term value than the older veterans they had previously been keen on for the profile they carried.

NZR had the budget to offer its top players – its most senior All Blacks – anything between $600,000 and $750,000 a season, but those figures dropped considerably for younger, emerging All Blacks such as McAlister. He would have been on a package worth around $300,000 a year in New Zealand, whereas Sale were believed to have offered him close to double that amount. Certainly, by early 2008 it had become clear to NZR that its labour force was vulnerable to offshore predators.

The board had two options for protecting the All Blacks' supply of labour. Option one was to amend its eligibility policy of only allowing those contracted to NZR to be selected by the All Blacks. It was a subject that had frequently come up at board meetings, and was again under serious consideration in 2008. But change was again rejected, for all the same reasons it had been in the past.

'I believe that if we had opened the door, then I think we would have destroyed the pipeline,' says Tew. 'To keep the best players eligible for the All Blacks despite them playing in Japan or the UK – if you did that, then a big group would leave, and all of a sudden, how good is Super Rugby? Dominating that competition was an important part of the All Blacks being ready to go midyear in June.'

The second and preferred option was for NZR to be more resourceful in retaining talent. What woke the union up to the danger it faced was when the All Blacks' coaches, in early 2008, conducted a series of meetings with the wider group of players they were likely to select. When they met with Daniel Carter, their star playmaker and someone absolutely fundamental to their World Cup ambitions, he told them he wanted to leave New Zealand at the end of the year and commit to a three-year contract in France. It was an enormous shock, and came the day after the All Blacks had learned that the squad's other playmaker, Nick Evans, was advanced in negotiations to join English club Harlequins.

This was a potentially catastrophic scenario for the All Blacks. To paraphrase Oscar Wilde's famous line, to lose one first five-eighth would be unfortunate, but to lose two would be careless. Carter had just turned 26, was easily the best No. 10 in the world, and destined to become one of the greatest All Blacks in history. He and Richie McCaw were the two players the coaching group had identified as the most critical in the quest to win the 2011 World Cup. Henry was clear with Tew that losing either of those two to a foreign club might be a terminal blow to the All Blacks' hopes of winning.

NZR's plan was to target McCaw and Carter first, and lock them into contracts that would keep them in the country until 2011. With those two on board, it was hoped, another identified group of players – including Mils Muliaina, Ali Williams, Rodney So'oialo and Tony Woodcock – would be encouraged to commit. This would give the All Blacks a senior, experienced core, around which they would build the rest of their team.

In February 2008, the focus became persuading Carter to change his mind, and it was perhaps fortunate that the All Blacks' coaches, having seen the changing nature of the player exodus in 2007, had already spent considerable time discussing innovative ways in which contracts could be sweetened to better compete with the higher dollar values offered by European and Japanese clubs. One idea they hit on was to emulate the setup in Ireland, where professional players could claim back the tax they paid for as long as they were contracted to an Irish club.

Says Wayne Smith: 'Steve, Graham and I approached the Labour government and put an idea to them similar to the Irish model, where if you play out your whole career in Ireland you get all your tax back. If you play a lesser amount of your career, you get less of your tax back. I liked that model in Ireland because it promotes loyalty, and it is essentially keeping your rugby icons in the country. Rugby, though, was seen to be self-sufficient, and there was no appetite for them to help us out. The following week we met with the National leaders and they had a huge appetite for it, but when they got into power it didn't happen.'

Another idea Smith came up with was to allow senior players to take a 'sabbatical' if they committed to a long-term contract with NZR. A sabbatical in a rugby sense would be a six-month period in which the individual could either play offshore or take a break from the game and still be paid. An offer was put to Carter whereby, instead of joining Perpignan for three years, he could play there for six months as part of a three-year contract to stay in New Zealand until the World Cup. In practice, that meant Carter would play the 2008 season in New Zealand, then in late November he would join Perpignan, play there until the end of the French season in May, and return to New Zealand and be immediately available for the All Blacks. The deal was painted as a win-win. Carter would earn a reported $1.4 million for his six-month contract and be afforded the European adventure he craved, while NZR would be able to keep him until 2011 without him missing any Tests.

After giving this proposal extensive thought, Carter decided to talk it over with McCaw. The All Blacks skipper had been offered a deal thought to be worth around $850,000 per season through to the World Cup, with the right to take a six-month sabbatical if he wanted one. If Carter was ready to commit, then so too was McCaw. Each man knew the All Blacks wouldn't win the World Cup without the other. They agreed to sign. With those two locked in, NZR was able to secure the other senior players the coaches had identified.

Given the buying power of foreign clubs, securing so many big-name players through to 2011 was an enormous victory for NZR, and specifically for the high-performance side. But it came at a cost. A literal one, as the new contract offers were all significantly higher than they'd previously been. Having put the wage bill under greater duress, NZR needed to find more income to pay for its largesse, but the wider economic picture was grim.

While the All Blacks had been at the World Cup, the TV news in the UK had been showing long queues of people standing outside banks trying to access their savings amid fears that some of the major financial institutions in the country were going to collapse. It was the beginning of the global financial crisis, or GFC as it would become known. By 2008, there were serious headwinds in most developed economies, as heavyweight banks, insurers and even national governments had to be bailed out by governments desperate to avoid a worldwide depression equal to the one experienced in the wake of the 1929 Wall Street crash. Economies were plunging into recession and the economic outlook was bleak, and yet here was NZR burdening itself with higher costs. It was a high-risk strategy, albeit with a potentially high reward of winning the World Cup.

Steve Tew knew he had to offset that risk by finding more money.

*

GENERATING MORE INCOME DURING a global recession was never going to be easy. Nor did NZR necessarily have a wide array of options. The broadcast contract was locked in until 2010, and the All Blacks had collected so many domestic sponsors that Tew felt the local market was saturated. Three avenues were open to NZR. First, improve the Adidas contract, which was due to expire at the end of 2011, but the Germans were open to an early renegotiation. Second, look for new international sponsors. And third, play more Tests.

Persuading Adidas to extend its association proved remarkably easy and painless. It was at the Beijing Olympics in July 2008 that the two parties brought up the idea of extending the contract early. The previous deals, particularly the initial one, had taken time to work through, but by 2008 Adidas and the All Blacks had been together for almost ten years, and the parties had built trust, understanding and respect for one another. And while the broader economic climate was not necessarily the right one for NZR to be trying to lengthen and improve a critical contract with a global behemoth, Tew had reason to be confident that the All Blacks remained a strong asset for Adidas.

When Heiner met Tew in China, he revealed that All Blacks replica jersey sales had climbed to record levels in the lead-up to the 2007 World Cup – to numbers that were in line with those achieved by European football giants AC Milan and Bayern Munich. Just as significantly, however, the Germans had fallen for the whole humility and respect theme of the All Blacks. Adidas had come to value and embrace, as best they could understand, the quintessential Kiwiness of the athletes and the brand.

It had become a legendary tale among Adidas staff that in 2002, after the All Blacks had played England at Twickenham, NZR chair Jock Hobbs, with a few drinks on board, had taken to explaining the finer points of attack play to Heiner and his executive team in the lobby of a five-star hotel in London. There they were, in suits and ties, faces beaming with the red wine and exertion of playing what may have become full-contact rugby with a cushion serving as the ball. And each time All Blacks players had visited Herzogenaurach, the staff were blown away by the easygoing nature of the superstars of the global game. Staff in Germany were used to dealing with world-famous footballers, who could be surly and difficult and particular about what they would and wouldn't do. The All Blacks became renowned and revered for their politeness and professionalism.

'That was one of the things I often heard, particularly from companies that deal with other big sports ... there is no comparison dealing with our athletes,' says Tew. 'We have the odd ratbag who doesn't do what they are supposed to do, but largely our guys, and increasingly our women, are just great ambassadors. Genuine, real people who make an effort and do the mahi when they have to do it but have fun and enjoy themselves.'

The combination of the players' relatability, the team's continued on-field success and the growing commercial returns from replica sales meant Adidas was eager to extend its commitment to the All Blacks. Once the parties began talking after the Olympics, it became clear that the only real points that needed to be figured out were the length of the deal and the price. In

November 2008, it was revealed that the term would be 11 years, and while Tew wouldn't reveal the value of the extension, he did confirm that it was an uplift on the existing deal.

Other than Adidas, NZR hadn't previously devoted many resources to securing international sponsors. The focus had been on domestic partnerships. But when Tew took over, he could see that would have to change. 'We knew we would need to have more international sponsors as we were outgrowing the NZ market really quickly,' he says. And, in an almost freakish coincidence, one came knocking on their door. It was Iveco, the Italian-based heavy vehicle manufacturer. The Italian theme continued when, shortly after Iveco came on board, luxury brand Louis Vuitton signed up too. These deals didn't have enormous monetary value, but they exposed the All Blacks to an international audience – many of whom likely had little knowledge of rugby. It was also felt that having prestigious, well-known brands in the sponsorship portfolio made the team more attractive to other prestigious brands.

But two problems emerged as the All Blacks added to their portfolio of domestic and international sponsors. Firstly, the number of hours some players were having to spend promoting these deals was rising. Sponsors typically negotiated a specific number of hours that All Blacks would be available to directly promote their association. As more sponsors were added, more promotional hours had to be fulfilled.

The second issue, as Tew would discover when he went to Turin to sign off on the Iveco deal, was that international companies were often attracted to New Zealand's cultural heritage, and wanted to create advertising collateral using protected iconography, motifs and other sensitive intellectual property.

'Iveco's guy had had a bit of exposure to the All Blacks,' says Tew. 'He loved the story, the imagery and he pretty much knocked on our door. I went to their headquarters just outside of Milan. It was a truck factory and it wasn't small, acres of stuff, and he said he had something to show me. So we go out to this internal roadway thing and he's got three trucks all painted up with Māori motifs and whatnot. It looks like we are going to do a deal, but we can't have that ... a bit of a cultural issue here. That is one of the things that is most difficult commercially: part of the attraction offshore is our Māori culture and heritage, [but] people are truly connected to that; [companies] want to be able to use it, but it is a fine line between being part of it and exploiting it.'

So these international deals gave NZR more money and more exposure, but also more headaches. It wasn't just that the players had to spend more time on promotional work, but more NZR staff had to spend more time managing these relationships and ensuring that IP was not used inappropriately. Playing more Test matches in some ways added to that problem, as it burdened the players with more activity, but it was at least the right sort of activity, and it was lucrative. A Test match, played under the right commercial agreements, could net NZR anything between $2 million and $4 million.

International rugby was still operating on the amateur financial model of centralised control and reciprocation.

World Rugby designated three weeks in June and three weeks in November to what it called the 'international window'. It would then randomly schedule, often ten years in advance, Tests between Northern Hemisphere and Southern Hemisphere countries, where the home side kept all the gate money but also met all the associated costs. It was a slightly archaic setup, but it mostly worked. Where the opportunity to make additional money existed was to play additional Tests outside of that official window. These could be played under any commercial terms that were agreed, and the All Blacks, with their brand power and ability to fill a stadium, had plenty of leverage to negotiate additional Tests on advantageous financial arrangements.

In 2005, the side had played Wales in Cardiff under agreed terms where the All Blacks took a share of the gate, which was the case again in London the following year, when they played England. But in 2008, NZR ramped up the additional content: the All Blacks would not only play an additional commercial Test on their end-of-year tour to create a Grand Slam itinerary, they would also play a fourth Bledisloe Cup game against the Wallabies. This would be played at a neutral venue – in this case, Hong Kong – and it would be part of a three-year agreement between NZR and Rugby Australia to play an offshore Test.

This new agreement meant the All Blacks would play the Wallabies four times in each of 2008, 2009 and 2010, with the final Test of each series to be played in a neutral venue, to expose a new audience to the rivalry. Asia and the United States were the territories both nations agreed they were most interested in exploring. The strategy of building the brand overseas by playing

Test matches made sense, at least in theory. This was showcasing the actual product, literally putting boots on the ground so interested locals in Hong Kong could meet the athletes, see the size of them and watch them play.

But even if the theory was right, the All Blacks were being locked into playing 14 Test matches a year. In the late amateur years, the All Blacks were sometimes only playing five Tests a year. Even in the early professional years they mostly played a maximum of ten. And now, in 2008, there was a 50 per cent increase in Test commitments. That all-important balance between commercial and high-performance needs was being challenged.

'We agreed to the four-Test Bledisloe Cup cycle because the Australians needed it,' says Tew. 'It was another of those moments where Australia asked for help and we said yes. We started to talk about a strategy ... if we are going to be any more relevant globally as a brand, and then financially/commercially, we needed to have more presence offshore. The problem with the rugby market is – when you are the All Blacks – you play in a narrow corridor. It is very select: you play in Europe – UK, France and Italy – South Africa, Australia and sometimes Argentina. You can't grow the market. Japan is a big rugby market, huge economic market and is time-zone-friendly. USA is more complicated, but it is the Holy Grail of sports markets.

'Australia was keen, and John O'Neill [then CEO of Rugby Australia] was ambitious and entrepreneurial, and so from that point of view those discussions were easy. That's where the understanding of the bigger picture from the coaches and athletes became important. They needed to understand where it all sat, because there is no doubt it put more pressure on performances – more travel, more time away from home, different environments and unknown grounds, and all that kind of stuff. Did we go close to overcooking the golden goose? Too many games? We were pushing it. No doubt about that.'

*

PERHAPS IT WAS THE strength of the headwinds being generated by the GFC, but for all the extra running NZR was doing to increase revenue, it didn't appear to be making any progress. In 2008, despite playing a record 15 Test matches and an additional game against Munster in Limerick, NZR posted a tiny profit of $300,000 off turnover of $102 million. In 2004, when the union had, for the first time, generated more than $100 million of revenue in a financial year, the profit was $20.4 million. Four years on and there were more sponsors, more Tests and more playing and commercial obligation thrust upon the players, and yet revenue was down by $2 million and profit virtually wiped out. In 2009 the figures were decidedly more worrying as revenue was down to $97.1 million – the All Blacks played 14 Tests – and there was a $9.5-million loss posted. The underlying picture was starting to emerge that the business had operational costs that exceeded its income, and that it was hard to grow revenue without an exponential rise in costs.

An additional Bledisloe Test in Hong Kong could generate $2 million to $3 million of income, but the players had to get to Asia in business-class seats, they had to be accommodated, fed, watered, massaged and medically looked after, and they had to be paid. Under the terms of the collective agreement, each All Black received $7500 for every week they were assembled with the team. The All Blacks' coaches also argued they needed larger squads to deal with the extra matches and promotional work, so instead of touring with the typical 30 players, by 2008 there were 35 on the plane to Hong Kong, with 12 coaching and management staff. That extra Test cost NZR $262,500 in player payments alone.

High performance wasn't cheap, and the profit margins on those additional games the All Blacks were playing were not as great as the headline figures suggested. By late 2009, Tew realised, just as his predecessors in the role had, that the single most effective way to change the P&L favourably was by striking an improved broadcast deal.

Broadcast was still where the real money lay in professional rugby. TV had the power to make or break the game, and while NZR had lured new and exotic sponsors and was playing Tests in far-flung lands and talking about international brand exposure, the health of its business was determined by the strength of its broadcast deal.

By early 2010, when SANZAR was in full swing with its negotiations, the global economic outlook had brightened. Mostly the world was in recovery mode, and consumer confidence and spending power were returning to pre-GFC levels. That buoyant mood was felt around the negotiating table in April 2010, when it was announced that the partners had extracted an improved deal from their broadcast partners. They had agreed to a US$437 million (NZ$620 million), five-year deal, which represented a 35 per cent increase on the existing contract.

But – and it was a big but – both the Super Rugby and the Tri-Nations competitions were expanding. The former was going to become a 15-team competition, as the Melbourne Rebels would be joining. This meant the three partners would run five teams each, hence the revenue would be split evenly: 33.3 per cent each. Perhaps more significantly, Argentina would be joining the Tri-Nations, which would be renamed the Rugby Championship.

That wouldn't add to the overall content burden, as the new format would see each team play each other at home and away, for six Tests in total. It would, however, add a significant travel burden, and initially at least, while rugby tried to grow its profile, the Argentinian union would need some help meeting its share of the costs. Once again, there would be more money coming in but also more money going out.

Rugby in the Southern Hemisphere was starting to feel like it was dangerously close to breaking point, where the weight of its commercial enterprise threatened to crush its high-performance aspirations.

CHAPTER THIRTEEN

AIG CALL THE SHOTS

OF ALL THE DECISIONS NZR had made since that fateful day in 1995 when World Rugby declared the game 'open', none proved more astute than the reappointment of Graham Henry, Steve Hansen and Wayne Smith after the All Blacks had failed at the 2007 World Cup. Equally astute was the decision to throw money at Richie McCaw, Dan Carter and a handful of their senior peers, to keep them in New Zealand until 2011.

Retaining Henry and his coaching team had not endeared NZR to its public. It was a decision that also had a direct financial impact, as the mood was so febrile and the fans' faith in the All Blacks so shaken that there were thousands of empty seats when they played Italy in Christchurch in 2009. The balance sheet had been stressed by the improved payments made to keep the talent, but when McCaw – after a clumsy three-way handshake with New Zealand prime minister John Key and World Rugby chair Bernard Lapasset – hoisted the Webb Ellis Cup on 23 October 2011 at Eden Park, there was massive relief alongside widespread joy.

The reward of winning the World Cup justified the risks that had been taken to do so. Chris Moller had been brave enough to persuade his board to consider a bid to host the 2011 tournament, and Steve Tew had followed up with a determined player and coach retention strategy in 2008. But the real vindication for NZR chasing that World Cup title as hard as it did came in April 2012, when Tew, while he was in the United Kingdom attending World Rugby meetings, fielded a call from a number he didn't recognise. The caller, an American, said he worked for a company called AIG, and that his boss was interested in discussing a sponsorship deal.

Tew drew a blank at the name. He was aware of IAG Insurance in New Zealand, but was not familiar with AIG. And with plenty on his plate, he wasn't sure this was going to go anywhere. But the caller was insistent that his boss was eager to talk, so Tew relented. He would be flying home via the United States, and could perhaps divert to somewhere convenient for both parties. But the caller said no: if Tew could get to Stanstead Airport in London, a private jet would be waiting to take him to Dubrovnik, Croatia.

The boss to whom the caller referred was Bob Benmosche, the chief executive of American International Group. Benmosche had been appointed to take over the insurer – one of the largest in the world – in 2009, after it had received a US$182-billion (NZ$248-billion) bailout from the US government. AIG had been pilloried in the States and in other major financial markets for taking high-risk bets on poorly secured mortgage debt, which had forced the US Federal Reserve to intervene in 2008. It was an ugly scenario, one that former Federal Reserve chairman Ben Bernanke said in his memoir made him angrier than anything else in the recession.

Benmosche was the safe pair of untainted hands appointed to rebuild AIG's reputation. Having managed to clean things up financially in his first three years in charge and repay the government its US$182 billion, the CEO was looking for a way to rebuild staff morale, which had understandably plunged in the wake of the bailout and the company being branded a corporate pariah. Prior to the GFC, AIG had its name on the front of Manchester United's jersey. That deal was all about exposure: a huge price paid to have those three letters displayed on the apparel of one of football's most revered clubs. A deal with the All Blacks would be driven by different imperatives.

Benmosche, after being made aware of the All Blacks through research conducted by his marketing team, had familiarised himself with the culture and success of the brand. He loved the way the team had thrived on cohesion, unity and pride, and he felt that an association with the All Blacks would foster a sense of pride within AIG. He wanted to put the company's name on the All Blacks jersey not for the traditional exposure such a sponsorship would bring, but for the access it would provide to the players and the 'feelgood' it would deliver to his almost 40,000 staff.

A few days after the mystery call, Tew found himself at Villa Splendid, the former discotheque that Benmosche had converted following his decision to retire from corporate life in 2006, before he was persuaded to take the AIG job. 'I spent a day there with him and we talked it all through,' says Tew. 'I met him for lunch and he thought it was a great story – the winning legacy, the cultural stuff, the diversity and the men and women. It was almost perfect for what they were looking for.'

Tew returned to New Zealand confident that AIG was likely to commit. But there were several barriers for NZR to clear before any deal could be done. The first was to meet with Adidas to gain its approval, as the Germans had effectively bought the naming rights to the All Blacks jersey. NZR would be asking Adidas to share space on the jersey, which wouldn't require a reconfiguration of assets as such, but would mean the AIG logo occupied the centre of the jersey, the most prominent real estate. Certainly, if AIG came on board, it would materially alter the terms that Adidas had agreed to. Even asking the Germans to consider the proposal would be a genuine test of the relationship.

Tew flew to London in late July to meet with Herbert Heiner. 'We had to negotiate with Adidas because it had already bought the jersey,' he recalls. 'So, it was another trip to see Herbert. We were in London at the Olympics, and I was in their hospitality tent at the top of some building not far from the stadium. I sat down with Herbert and explained what we were doing, and that AIG were kind of a possibility. He said, "I am not too concerned about who it is because you will get that right. But it has got to be a win-win-win."' Ultimately, Adidas gave its approval for NZR to negotiate with AIG, in return for a five-year extension with the All Blacks through to the end of 2024.

One of the other significant barriers to a deal had been cleared in late May 2012, after Tew had returned from Dubrovnik. That was the issue of inventory – and the issue was that NZR did not have enough of it to offer AIG.

While it was the story of the All Blacks that had attracted AIG, the Americans liked the idea of having a relationship with the Black Ferns too, and with New Zealand's national male and female rugby sevens teams. The rationale for sponsoring the All Blacks was to drive staff morale, so there was a strong desire to include female athletes in the package. There were also geographical imperatives, as both sevens teams played regularly in Asia and the United States – the two key markets for AIG's business, but also, importantly, where most of its staff were located. AIG was interested in sponsoring the whole national team family, as it were, and so in May 2012 Tew announced that the two sevens teams, the Black Ferns and the New Zealand Māori team would all carry the name All Blacks.

It was a move that had fierce critics, with strong arguments made by media commentators and former players that this was cheapening the brand. Many felt it wasn't appropriate to bestow the name on other national teams who hadn't delivered the same volume of success over the same period. It risked tarnishing the All Blacks' legacy, some argued, and NZR was accused of diluting its most lucrative and important asset.

Tew disagreed. 'You can't expand your commercial programme unless you have something to sell,' he says. 'You can't go past 14 or 15 Test matches – that was already pushing the boundaries in terms of exposure and who you could legitimately play, and also what you could expect our guys to do in a year and still play Super Rugby. We had to have more inventory, and the reality for me was that the men's sevens was already known as the All Blacks. If you travelled with them and you went to their table at their hotel at lunch, they had All Blacks on it. The growth of the Black Ferns and the establishment of the women's sevens and the great job our girls did there gave us a lot more breadth of exposure, because they played in Asia and America and Canada. That gave us more inventory.'

NZR didn't have the green light for the deal to progress, however. Arguably, the most important factor was gaining the approval of the players. The All Blacks jersey was a precious icon, and – as had been apparent throughout the initial negotiations with Adidas back in 1997 – preserving its classic black simplicity was hugely important. The jersey was almost sacred, and the few times it had been altered – most notably with the addition of the Steinlager and then Adidas logos – there had been uproar among sections of the public and the media. Any changes had to be carefully considered, particularly when they involved the addition of a corporate logo.

In late July 2012, when a deal with AIG was becoming a distinct possibility, Tew sought the opinions of former All Blacks, men who had become what he called 'touchstones'. He talked the matter through with, among others, former captains Sir Brian Lochore and Sir Colin Meads, as well as Sir John Graham, who had played for and captained the All Blacks before becoming headmaster at Auckland Grammar School and serving on the NZR board. The old guard were fine with the idea, so the day after the All Blacks had beaten the Wallabies 22–0 at Eden Park in August, the current generation of players were brought into the fold and told a deal was in the offing. What did they think about it?

Whether or not the players had any real power to stop a deal going ahead if they objected was unclear. Under the terms of the collective agreement and the revenue-sharing clause, they had to be consulted. But this deal was going to improve their position significantly, not damage it, so if they did have any objection, it would be on the grounds that they considered AIG an inappropriate partner, given its recent need to have been bailed out by the US taxpayer.

Tew and the board had grappled with that very issue themselves. 'It was a fair question,' he says. 'Was it appropriate to put an American insurance and finance company on the All Blacks' shirt who had to be bailed out during the GFC? Given that AIG had paid the money back, and they weren't the only company impacted, and they didn't create the crisis, we felt we made a balanced decision.'

As it turned out, the players did have an objection – but it concerned the size and style of the logo. AIG had just finished a corporate rebranding when Tew first met Benmosche, and the jersey the players were shown had AIG in pale blue inside a pale blue box. Kieran Read, a senior player at the time and a future All Blacks captain, remembers being slightly aghast when he first clapped eyes on the jersey.

'Initially, when they had the big old slogan on it and it was massive, there was a bit of a pushback from us,' he says. 'It was AIG but it was big and boxed, covering most of the front of the jersey.'

Tew took the feedback to AIG, and it was agreed that the logo would shrink and lose the box, and that the three letters would be in white.

'Once they got that sorted out and it turned to be what it was, that alleviated a few fears,' says Read. 'I would rather have not been playing with a corporate sponsor on the jersey, but I was comfortable with it. I think it was a natural progression of where the game was heading, and you looked around at that time, and every team in the world had one. I had the old '90s jersey with Steinlager across the front. As a player all you wanted was the chance to have your say. Decisions that are made without that chance, that is when there is pushback. The players are the ones wearing the All Blacks jersey, so having a say and hearing us out was important. And we had to consider the whole corporate thing. These guys were a company that had just come out of a massive thing in America around the GFC and it impacted a lot of people.'

By the end of the Rugby Championship, which the All Blacks won with a Grand Slam, NZR had all the approvals it needed to sign off on the new deal with AIG, which was worth US$70 million (NZ$105 million) over five years.

This was the first significant deal struck in the wake of the All Blacks becoming world champions. Perhaps AIG would have been drawn to the All Blacks had the national team not won the 2011 World Cup, but the pictures of McCaw with the Webb Ellis Cup had gone around the world, exposing the All Blacks to new audiences. The brand benefitted further when stories about what had happened during the campaign filtered into global circulation. Stories such as McCaw playing the entire tournament with a broken foot. Maybe best of all was the Stephen Donald story: once pilloried by an angry public, he was recalled to the team while he was on a fishing trip in the middle of nowhere. Having not played for five weeks – and, judging by the muffin top hanging over his shorts, having not trained much either – he'd played the last 50 minutes of the final and kicked the winning penalty goal. So it's fair to say winning the World Cup brought AIG to the All Blacks, and delivered a pile of cash to NZR that was desperately needed. As Tew says: 'The numbers were trending in the wrong direction as we were running deficits. We needed this.'

*

AS THE TALKS WITH AIG neared their conclusion in August 2012, NZR received a letter from the Fiji Rugby Union. It would be celebrating its centenary in 2013, and was writing to see whether a Test match in Suva between Fiji and the All Blacks could be arranged to mark the occasion.

NZR's relationship with and treatment of Fiji and the other Pacific Islands nations of Samoa and Tonga was a fraught topic. All three were geographically and culturally close to New Zealand, and Auckland was the world's largest Polynesian city, yet all three had been snubbed by SANZAR when the game had turned professional. Most rugby fans had assumed that a team, whether a composite from the three islands or a national team from one of them, would one day be invited into Super

Rugby. But although room had been found to accommodate two new Australian sides, one more from South Africa and a place for Argentina in the Rugby Championship, the Pacific Islands nations were still out in the cold. They had seen money flow into New Zealand and Australia since 1996, but none of it had made its way to them.

In fact, the only thing that flowed in the Islands was human traffic and it was all going one way – out of Fiji, Samoa and Tonga and into the All Blacks and Wallabies. Neither NZR nor Rugby Australia directly recruited talent from the wider Pacific region, but they were the beneficiaries of wider socioeconomic imbalances that drove immigration and saw hundreds, if not thousands, of people leave the Islands each year in search of better education and higher-paying employment.

Among those leaving were droves of school-aged boys who took up scholarships at renowned institutions in New Zealand. While the intent of these ventures was to provide the recipients with a holistic education, it was surprising how often the boys who came over were oversized, athletic and fantastic at rugby. And while NZR wasn't involved in this, it had no qualms about helping itself to Island talent once it was in the country. Fijian-born players such as Joe Rokocoko and Sitiveni Sivivatu had made rich contributions to the All Blacks, as had Samoan-born players Mils Muliaina, Jerry Collins and Jerome Kaino.

The accusation flung at NZR was that it exploited the Islands by giving the three national sides of Fiji, Samoa and Tonga no access to regular competitions in the region – a scenario that drove promising players to New Zealand in search of professional contracts, where they would then be captured by the All Blacks. To compound matters, NZR had never thrown any of the Island nations even the smallest bone by taking the All Blacks to Fiji, Samoa or Tonga to play a Test match. So when the Fiji Rugby Union's invitation to play in Suva arrived, it seemed like a golden opportunity to redress one of many historical injustices.

But the invitation was rebuffed by NZR. Fiji were offered the 'Classic All Blacks' – an ageing and mostly retired group of New Zealanders well past their best. In writing back, NZR's general manager of strategic relationships and partnerships, Nigel Cass, regretfully informed the Fijians that the All Blacks already had a full Test schedule for 2013. The All Blacks did indeed have a full card, with a three-Test series planned against France in June, the Rugby Championship followed by a third Bledisloe Cup Test, and then matches against France, England and Ireland in November. There were 13 Tests planned and so no room for Fiji.

Yet in April 2013 NZR announced that the All Blacks would be playing Japan in Tokyo on their way to Europe at the end of the year. It turned out that the All Blacks' calendar was not actually full at 13 Tests – they just hadn't been made an attractive enough offer to convince them to expand their commitments. It was a bad look for NZR to say no to Fiji but yes to Japan, as it highlighted how commercialised and corporatised the organisation's decision-making about high-performance commitments had become.

A Test in Suva would have netted the All Blacks zero dollars, but it would have generated untold goodwill by finally respecting and valuing a Pacific partner in the way most rugby followers wanted to see. Rugby had long been built on the values of fraternity and unity, and these qualities absolutely defined the All Blacks. Seeing them play a Test in Fiji would have been an acknowledgement of the strong links between the two countries, but also a recognition that New Zealand needed to give something back.

But a Test in Tokyo, on the other hand, came with a $1-million payday, and it aligned with NZR's longer-term aim of growing the All Blacks' brand in Asia – and specifically in Japan, which was going to host the 2019 World Cup. Japan was seen as a potential goldmine for the All Blacks. It had the third-largest economy in the world, already had a professional rugby framework funded by heavyweight corporations such as Toyota, Panasonic and Mitsubishi, and a fan base that was increasingly interested in the sport. And, most importantly, Japan was AIG's second-most important market, and a country in which it had a significant and growing number of staff. AIG didn't do any business in Fiji, or have any staff there. Clearly, the All Blacks venues and opponents would be determined by the specific returns they could provide, and the value they could deliver to commercial partners.

The All Blacks players, many of whom had strong familial and cultural ties to the Islands, would have chosen to play in Fiji rather than Japan. The coaching staff would have chosen to play Fiji too, as they would have presented a genuine challenge that would have tested the character of a few young players. But NZR's commercial team, with its ambition to conquer Japan, and AIG's desire to be visible in one of its key markets, meant the All Blacks were off to Tokyo.

AIG had signed up as a jersey sponsor, but it was clear by April 2013 that it was much more than that. It had a veritable seat at the board table: a hand on the tiller of the Good Ship All Blacks, and a licence to steer the team in the directions it wanted. NZR would carefully remind sceptical opinion writers that it was the dog, AIG was the tail, and the decision to play in Japan was a win-win, but where the balance of power between the two lay was impossible to know.

By the time the All Blacks were in Japan in early November 2013, plans were already in motion to play a Test in the United States in November 2014. Again, NZR could justifiably say that breaking into America had been a long-held ambition. If the All Blacks could establish a brand presence there, the rewards would be enormous. But however great NZR's desire was to establish a presence in the USA, AIG's desire was obviously greater as its initials had barely been on the jersey for a year, and an All Blacks match there was about to become a reality.

NZR wanted the All Blacks to play a composite or invitational XV, but that idea was kiboshed by Kevin Roberts, who, having shifted to the United States to take up his role as global chief executive of Saatchi & Saatchi, had also become the chair of USA Rugby. He argued that if the All Blacks were going to play in the States, it should be against the national side, the US Eagles. Showing that he'd lost none of his flair for the dramatic, he said it had to be at an iconic stadium. AIG agreed, and so the search began for a high-profile venue that would be available to host the All Blacks and Eagles on 1 November 2014.

As fate would have it, what was formerly known as Giants Stadium, on the outskirts of New York, would be free that weekend. But the reason it was formerly known as Giants Stadium was because it had been renamed MetLife Stadium – MetLife being AIG's largest insurance rival in the United States. The All Blacks didn't play in New York in 2014. Instead they played in Chicago, at Soldier Field, and while the Test match sold out and rugby had its day in the Windy City, the influence of AIG in determining the high-performance fate of the All Blacks was undeniable.

This was the new world in which NZR was living. It had taken US$70 million (NZ$105 million) of investment from a global insurance firm to plug a gap in its accounts, but had perhaps underestimated the demands that would come with the money. NZR was doing its level best, in those first years with AIG, to convince itself that it was determining and executing a well-considered strategy to grow the brand in the key offshore markets of Japan and the United States. AIG just happened to be aligned in its strategic objectives.

But as hard as NZR wanted to believe it was in control, AIG tested the boundaries of the relationship on multiple fronts. In November 2013, the week after the All Blacks had been in Tokyo, AIG took staff and clients to watch the team's final training session before a Test against France. This was already a major source of concern for Steve Hansen, who had been promoted to the head coaching role at the end of 2011. And like all international coaches, he was wary of his team's preparations being observed by outsiders. He knew it might seem paranoid to think that what an uninitiated AIG staffer saw at a training session might become useful intelligence for the French, but his point was: why take the risk? He wanted the All Blacks' training to be entirely off-limits, or at his discretion as to who could observe it and under what conditions.

Whatever discomfort he and the players were feeling when they began that final training session in Paris multiplied when the AIG contingent began popping champagne bottles and gorging on a lavish picnic, becoming a little raucous in the process. This was not the high-performance environment the All Blacks needed or wanted. It was as if they were the conscientious kids going to study in the quiet of the library, only to find that the cool kids had decided to throw a party there. But the deeper concern was that the All Blacks were being associated with behaviour that ran contrary to their ethos and culture.

The world was rebuilding after the GFC, but even in 2013 there were remnants of its impact. In Paris, the Metro system had become an underground home for thousands who had lost everything – their jobs, their homes and their dignity. These people had been reduced to riding trains all day, every day, begging for money. In Ireland, where the All Blacks would play their final game of 2013, the team saw homes either boarded up and abandoned or falling into a state of disrepair as the owners could no longer pay their mortgages. Those suffering financially still blamed the mess on the greed and recklessness of companies such as AIG. To embitter an already nasty broth, it transpired that many of the executives responsible for plunging the global economy into freefall were being paid enormous bonuses. AIG was one of the worst in this regard, using US$218 million (NZ$300 million) of its government bailout to reward staff in its financial services division. The All Blacks finished their training that day angry about being made to feel complicit in something they wanted no part of.

This was the risk NZR had taken in partnering with a massive international firm. The two organisations may have been aligned strategically, in that they both wanted to do business in the United States and Japan, but culturally they weren't always on the same page.

That became apparent again in October 2014, when the All Blacks were training in Johannesburg ahead of their final Rugby Championship Test. Hansen could hardly believe what he saw when he arrived at the training ground. AIG had erected a marquee at one end of the field – this much he had been made aware of. But what he hadn't known was that former All Blacks coach John Mitchell would be regaling AIG's staff and guests with a running commentary of what the team were doing.

This was totally unacceptable. Mitchell was a highly skilled rugby analyst, having spent the past three years coaching the Lions in Super Rugby. He now lived in South Africa and was plugged into their professional network, with contacts and friends within the Springboks. The All Blacks kimono hadn't been opened so much as totally discarded.

Hansen was furious, and so too was Tew, who had not been informed about Mitchell's presence. Even in his fury, the irony wasn't lost on the chief executive that this former All Black coach who had never been keen on doing any commercial activity was now being well paid by an All Blacks sponsor to potentially spy on the team.

'We had no idea that was happening until after it happened and we weren't happy,' says Hansen. 'But that was the sort of stuff we had to put up with, and that is when you are told you are just paranoid. I'm not. Games are won and lost on little margins. That was unacceptable.'

Unwanted spectators at training wasn't a problem specific to the AIG sponsorship. NZR had taken a majority stake in a company called All Blacks Tours – a tourism operator that organised holiday packages around All Blacks Tests. These packages came with match tickets, and to sweeten the pot they also included exclusive access to watch the team train. One such tour was to Edinburgh in November 2014. A Test against Scotland wouldn't usually have the All Blacks on edge, but for this encounter at Murrayfield, Hansen was giving a handful of fringe players their last chance to persuade him that they should be included in his 2015 World Cup planning.

Hansen was taking something of a selection risk by picking a weakened team in the hope it would lead to World Cup reward, and as the early evening winter gloom descended across the University of Edinburgh ground at Peffermill, the head coach was in his element. His language was direct and colourful. He wanted his young players to feel his presence, and while those who knew Hansen and rugby would understand that this was his style – and how effective it had been, as the All Blacks had only lost two games in the three years he'd been head coach – if any video of this session had been put on social media without context, it would have been hugely damaging to his reputation.

And the danger of that happening was high, as there was no one supervising the 100 or so All Blacks Tours guests as they watched training unfold. Although they were mostly quite old and so probably somewhat technically challenged, there was nothing stopping any of them from taking images or video and sending them into cyberspace.

No footage of Hansen barking his orders and commanding the training ground appeared on the internet from that day, and the All Blacks managed, after a nervy start, to squeeze past Scotland. So while there was general unhappiness among the coaching and management staff at this open-door policy, which afforded paying stakeholders behind-the-scenes access, and a growing unease at the ability of commercial partners to dictate terms and flout established protocols, it had no impact on the team's performance.

In 2012, when Hansen took over as head coach, the All Blacks lost just one of 14 Tests and drew another. In 2013, they became the first team to go through a calendar year without a defeat, winning all their 14 Tests. In 2014, they reproduced the same overall results they had in 2012, and by the time they headed to London for the 2015 World Cup, their win ratio since the last tournament had jumped to 91 per cent.

NZR's finances had enjoyed an equally strong revival, with a profit of $3.2 million in 2012, $2.8 million in 2013 and $300,000 in 2014. These figures were all produced off higher revenue, as income had grown from $103 million in 2012, to $117 million in 2013 and to $120 million in 2014. The commercial strategy was delivering financial rewards, and while it had provoked unprecedented friction with the team, the All Blacks were winning at a rate they previously never had.

The results on and off the field said NZR was getting the balance right between its commercial and high-performance objectives. The two, despite some tense moments, remained in equilibrium. But Hansen knew that this balance was only being maintained by the fact he had in his midst a once-in-a-generation group of senior players, and a captain who was already destined to leave the game as the best leader the All Blacks had ever known.

CHAPTER FOURTEEN

AROUND THE
WORLD IN 80 DAYS

ON 31 OCTOBER 2015, Adidas got what it had been promised when Richie McCaw became the first captain in history to lift the Webb Ellis Cup at successive tournaments. Back in 1997, Kevin Roberts had promised the All Blacks would deliver Adidas two World Cups, and while it had taken longer than either party would have liked, the Germans were, strangely, delighted to be paying out the estimated $5 million win bonus offered as an incentive.

The 34–17 defeat of the Wallabies at Twickenham had brought the most amazing World Cup cycle to a close. The All Blacks had played 56 Tests, won 51, lost three and drawn two for a win ratio of 91 per cent. Financially, across the same cycle, NZR had grown its revenue from $103 million in 2012 to $133 million in 2015 – a 23 per cent rise – and had accumulated profit of $6 million. This compared with the last World Cup cycle, in which the All Blacks had played 55 Tests, winning 46 and losing nine for a success ratio of 84 per cent. Revenue had effectively flatlined at around $100 million. NZR had lost $15 million in total across the four years from 2008 to 2011. The last eight years, but especially the last four, had been a golden age for the All Blacks.

The days following the World Cup victory were devoted to long and deserved celebrations. But as much as the mood was triumphant, there was also a sense of something having come to an end. McCaw, the greatest captain in history, confirmed he was retiring. His long-serving teammates Dan Carter, Keven Mealamu, Ma'a Nonu, Conrad Smith and Tony Woodcock were either retiring or moving overseas to play, so the All Blacks would be losing six players who between them had almost 700 Test caps. It was going to be a battle to replace that volume of experience and leadership.

But the bigger worry for Hansen, who was contracted through to 2017, was what his players would be facing when they returned to action in 2016. The stress points in the last World Cup cycle had come from the incursion of new sponsors and stakeholders into the team's inner sanctum. A much bigger threat, however, awaited the high-performance world in 2016, which was a wildly and almost madly expanded Super Rugby, the scale and ambition of which was vast.

A competition that began life with 12 teams spread across three countries would now have 18 spread across five, as teams from Japan and Argentina joined. With so many teams, separated by enormous physical distances, a new format was conceived with four conferences. While the SANZAAR – the organisation added an additional A into its name to reflect the presence of Argentina – bosses who came up with it felt they had created something compelling, everyone else was baffled. It was convoluted and riddled with inequities, epitomised by the crazy decision to guarantee individual conference winners the right to host a play-off. This agreement had been reached to satisfy broadcasters, but it would lead to teams with more competition points having to play quarter-finals at the home grounds of teams that had finished beneath them. This was the most egregious example of commercial imperatives impacting high performance.

SANZAAR thought the new Super 18 stood as a monument to its strategic vision to grow the game across the Southern Hemisphere and plant a flag in Asia, but it really was a symbol of compromised decision-making among increasingly ill-suited partners, greed, hubris and an expansion plan that had no other purpose but to try to grab yet more yen from the corporate heavyweights of Japan. The justification for the expansion was that it had enabled NZR to double its broadcast revenue to about $70 million a year from 2016. On the face of it, NZR had struck a stunning deal. But it had perhaps misunderstood two key elements, each of which promised trouble down the track.

The first mistake NZR made was to interpret Sky's willingness to double the value of its contract as an endorsement of Super Rugby's expansion strategy. The SANZAAR partners had convinced themselves that their respective domestic broadcasters would all see incredible value in having the rights to broadcast matches with new teams from exotic lands. Bringing in the

Sunwolves from Japan and Jaguares from Argentina was giving Super Rugby exposure in countries with a combined population of 170 million, almost double the combined total populations of South Africa, Australia and New Zealand. But Sky saw precisely zero value in bringing in these new teams, and if anything was puzzled as to why NZR and its partners thought it was a good idea. Sky upped the value of the contract not because of the increased exposure Super Rugby would enjoy in new markets – that was effectively worthless – but simply because there was more content.

'In my mind, your decision to keep Sky or not would be based around how many hours you watched,' says John Fellet, former chief executive of Sky. 'It wasn't a movie contract or a rugby contract, it was hours, and I had the best detailed records because I had more homes hooked up. I knew a lot more than my competitors, and for that matter the suppliers. I wasn't buying the Cartoon Network or rugby – I was buying viewer hours ...

'I had a *Money Ball* approach to it about the price we could afford to pay. I was happy to tell [SANZAAR] when they came and said, "We have a team in Japan now – how much extra is that going to be worth?" And I would say, "Guys, that's not going to be worth anything extra to me. It is out of our time zone, people are not going to stay up to watch them at 1 am in the morning." I would rather have them play prime time. We didn't get much viewership for the Crusaders, one of the strongest [teams], when they played in Cape Town at 1 am. If it was up to me, we would have had all games in Australia and New Zealand.

'The rugby union viewed that as a huge breakthrough, having a team that played in Japan, but I thought, economically, you can't have games spread through that many time zones. The EPL is good not because it runs from China to London. Everybody sees every team.'

The second thing NZR misunderstood, or perhaps was just happy to live with, is that the increased fee came with significant additional costs, both financial and human. NZR's annual accounts show that expenditure on competitions in 2016 was $82 million, compared with $62 million in 2015. Most of that increase related to Super Rugby, which had become easily the most expensive competition in world rugby.

Back in 1996, a total of 69 games were played. The Blues, who won the competition, played 13, beginning in mid-March and finishing in late May. In 2016, the new format would see a total of 134 games played. The Hurricanes, the eventual winners, played the first of their 18 games in mid-February and the last in early August. They ended up with a relatively kind schedule, in comparison with that of the defending champion, the Highlanders, who travelled to South Africa in early July for two games, then on to Argentina, before returning for one last round-robin game in New Zealand, before having to play a quarter-final in Australia and then a semi-final in Johannesburg. The constant long-haul travel was horrendous for the environment, for the bank balance and for the welfare of the players.

It was the last part that troubled Steve Hansen the most. In his first year with the All Blacks, players were nowhere near the 30-game season limit, and the travel was manageable. Now, Super Rugby winners played 18 games and there were 14 Tests a season. But worse was the air miles that had to be endured: some teams would make at least two trips to South Africa during Super Rugby, plus one to Argentina or Japan. The inclusion of the Pumas in the Rugby Championship meant some players would have to go to Argentina twice in a season. As the All Blacks had discovered, getting from South America to South Africa, as they had to do every year to play Argentina and the Springboks in successive weekends, was a brutal and disorientating journey, given the time differences.

It seemed that every additional dollar that had been gained in the new broadcast contract came with increased costs, making it questionable as to whether the deal was actually worthwhile. The headline figure was impressive, but for those having to manage the players and deliver All Blacks Test wins, it was a false economy of ever-diminishing returns. More was being sold, but the exponential costs that came with it swallowed the gains. Crucially, it was the All Blacks players and coaching staff who had to endure the increased game time, travel and commercial activity.

The looming player welfare catastrophe in 2016 was headed off by the long pre-season the All Blacks players were afforded following the World Cup. That was the beauty of World Cup years: the players were granted the 16 weeks they needed to rest and recondition before playing Super Rugby again. It was only at the end of the year that fatigue hit – and it hit hard.

As usual, the All Blacks had to play their last two Rugby Championship games in Argentina and South Africa in successive weekends in late September, early October. For some in the team, it was their third trip to South Africa in as many months, and their second to Argentina. After a week off, they had to play Australia in Auckland, before flying to Chicago to play Ireland in early November; then they faced Italy, Ireland again and France in Europe. That last run of games was particularly gruelling, and the All Blacks lost to Ireland for the first time in history when the teams met at Soldier Field.

Almost unbelievably, the defeat in Chicago was just the fourth in Hansen's five-year tenure, and ended the All Blacks world-record run of 18 consecutive victories. And it most certainly had not escaped Hansen's attention that two of the four losses the All Blacks had suffered on his watch had been in Tests that were arranged with the sole purpose of making money. The first defeat had come at Twickenham in 2012, when NZR had negotiated a fee of $4 million to play in London. The Soldier Field game against Ireland had netted about $3 million, but the money was in danger of becoming a mere sugar hit. There were longer-term implications for the value of the brand if the All Blacks' winning record declined as a direct consequence of the team being stretched too far physically and mentally by these additional matches.

The All Blacks were starting to feel like a dancing bear, being dragged around the world to perform for money. 'We noticed it,' says Kieran Read, who captained the All Blacks in 2016. 'I think guys noticed we were playing these extra Tests and it made it quite a massive year, especially with the nature of the Super Rugby landscape that year and with the Rugby Championship. Suddenly we are flying around the world three times a year, or four with Super Rugby, and it just turned it into a massive thing, and you can't help but notice and think, "I hope they are making some money from this because we are doing a tonne of work for them."'

That the All Blacks finished 2016 with 13 wins from 14 Tests was a minor miracle. South Africa and Australia had both underestimated them because the All Blacks had lost so much experience and leadership after the World Cup. And the All Blacks had doubly benefitted from the detailed planning and preparation Hansen and his coaching team had done in late 2015 and early 2016 to ready the team to play without McCaw and co. The All Blacks had at times played breathtakingly good rugby, scoring an average of 5.7 tries a game. But as well as they had played, Hansen could see that his team had begun to decline in the last five or six Tests of the year, as all the travel and all the rugby caught up with the players. In the final Test of 2016, in Paris, it was obvious to anyone who had followed the All Blacks that they lacked energy. The All Blacks scraped home against an ordinary French team.

When Hansen presented his review of the 2016 season to the NZR board, he detailed changes he wanted to make in 2017 – which loomed as a huge year, given the British and Irish Lions were coming to New Zealand for a three-Test series. Hansen, in conjunction with NZR's high-performance director, Don Tricker, felt there had to be agreed protocols with the Super Rugby clubs to limit the game time of Test players. Some players would start the season a few weeks late, and for every All Black there would be a graduated formula in the first three weeks whereby they could play no more than 180 minutes in total.

No All Black would be allowed to play more than four weeks consecutively, and it would be mandatory for them to sit out two games entirely.

Hansen also wanted to try something different in the Rugby Championship – which was to not take all his best players to Argentina. The All Blacks typically ran a weakened side against the Pumas, so there was no point dragging superstars such as Beauden Barrett, Brodie Retallick, Sam Cane and Rieko Ioane there if they were unlikely to play. Those players could instead fly from New Zealand to South Africa and meet the rest of the squad there.

These were all common-sense measures to protect the players from burnout and give the All Blacks the high-performance agreements they needed to perform at their best. The system was asking too much of the players, so the system had to be manipulated to give the All Blacks what they needed. Hansen does not dispute that his plans prioritised the All Blacks ahead of Super Rugby, and that resting players was a big sacrifice for the clubs to make. But he knew the pressure he was under to deliver results, and, more importantly, he knew the importance of a successful All Blacks side to the overall health of New Zealand's rugby economy.

'You are making decisions about how you get these guys to survive,' he says. 'With the massive travel miles and massive playing time, it is accumulative. It builds up. It doesn't affect you today, but eventually it will rear its head and bite you in the bum because the guys were physically and mentally fatigued. Then, on top of that, you have to say, "These guys can't start the Super Rugby competition, they need a break." Then you have got everyone moaning, "Why aren't they playing for their franchises?" You have got to understand that commercialism has created this, and the by-product of that is, "Do we cook the golden goose that lays the egg, or do we look after it?" I chose to look after it and stand up for it.

'We managed to get through that period because we were smart, and we prepared for it. We put things in place that not everybody liked, but it gave us the ability to get through the year and survive and perform. And while the All Blacks are performing, they are a commercial commodity.'

*

FOR THE THREE ORIGINAL SANZAR nations, hosting a British and Irish Lions tour was the golden ticket. The Lions had an enormous following of loyal and passionate fans, who loved the sense that this composite side was the strongest and maybe the only living reminder of the amateur days that many longed to see return. The Lions were the rugby equivalent of vinyl, and nostalgia was big business. NZR had made a record profit of $23.6 million when the Lions had toured in 2005, off a record turnover of $147 million. The 2017 tour was forecast to make NZR a new record turnover of $257 million and a record profit of almost $34 million. This additional money was the result of a $31-million increase in broadcast revenue and a $7-million increase in sponsorship and licensed sales, but the real kicker was the extra $47 million that came from ticket sales.

Given the enormous fan interest in a rare Lions tour, the All Blacks players and management viewed the Test series almost on a par with a World Cup. Hansen had made clear in his presentation to the NZR board at the end of 2016 that a series victory was the highest priority of the year for the All Blacks. The team were enormously motivated to test themselves against the best of Britain and Ireland, who, Hansen suspected, were going to be the best Lions side ever assembled. This was a series the All Blacks were desperate to win: they wanted to throw the kitchen sink at the visitors and unleash rugby hell.

In 2016, the All Blacks had swept through their Tests, losing just once – in defiance of those who said they would struggle without McCaw, Carter and the rest of the golden generation. It had given the team enormous satisfaction to prove their doubters wrong; defeating the Lions would be the perfect way for this young All Blacks side to stick their flag at the summit of the rugby world and make a statement: anything their predecessors could do, they could do better.

Having made his pitch that preparation was the key to winning the series, Hansen was partly bemused but also partly angry that he, his management team and the players were being asked in early 2017 to give their thoughts about a proposal NZR had received from the corporate giant Amazon, which wanted to make a behind-the-scenes documentary about the All Blacks during the Lions tour and the Rugby Championship. Amazon had made similar programmes with other major sporting clubs such as Manchester City and the Los Angeles Rams, with cameras poking into areas they were not normally allowed, to give global audiences an insight into the inner workings of these iconic teams. The docuseries would be called *All or Nothing*.

While NZR's commercial team were presenting the idea as a proposal on which everyone was being consulted, the All Blacks coaches, management and players knew that the deal with Amazon was all but done. This wasn't a consultative process in the true sense – more a communications exercise where everyone was being told what was happening.

This was indicative of where the balance of power now lay between the commercial and high-performance teams. The All Blacks knew they had consultative rights over most commercial initiatives that impacted the team, but they suspected they were only told about things to create the right optics – to demonstrate that they had been involved in the decision-making process. No one on the high-performance side knew what would happen if they strenuously objected to a commercial proposal. They suspected, however, that they were powerless to stop anything they didn't like. When NZR put a proposal to play an additional Test match in front of the coaching team, it was presented in such a way as to make them think they had no choice but to agree.

It was the same with the AIG deal: the players had been asked to give their feedback, but would NZR really have walked away from US$70 million (NZ$105 million) because the players objected to the association? Negotiations for the Amazon proposal were at an advanced stage, and NZR laid out in clear terms why it wanted to do the deal.

'Amazon was important for two reasons,' says Tew. 'It was a significant injection of cash. It paid well. They were also going to make the All Blacks visible in markets we previously never had been. It then became: how do we do justice to it, and how much of the inner sanctum were we prepared to share? How intrusive would that be? We made significant concessions to make sure that worked. We had significant people hired to manage the process, and [ensure] that the guys doing the work had a clear understanding what was on the table and what was off it. We had quite strong editing rights, a whole lot of protections put in place. But it was another set of obligations, more intrusion, and it was a potential seepage of intellectual property, but again the guys were careful about that too.'

The consensus among the senior players and coaches was that they didn't want to do it, but they were, however, acutely aware that they weren't really being asked but told, and therefore the smarter political play was to show willingness and then control things as best they could.

'Initially I was sceptical,' says Kieran Read. 'We were asked our opinion. They kept coming back saying they wanted more, and I guess we decided that if we were going to do it, then we had to be able to do it our way. Potentially it was a distraction, when you look back, but we were professionals, and when you were in there, I don't think it was. They would come into a meeting for two minutes, Steve would crack a joke and then they would be sent out. When the coaches were miked up, they might say "fuck" at training a few times but that was about it, but you didn't notice them much.

'My wife watched it and thought it was interesting. I watched it and I don't think it revealed much. We gave nothing away because we could dictate how it worked. Do it again in another ten years, and I don't think you would be able to do it that way. I don't think you want to be selling your IP. The IP of who we are – it is shown in the way teams play against us ... [I]f you don't quite have that fear factor, then it is an advantage you have lost.'

The series with the Lions was drawn, but for the All Blacks it felt like it had been lost. After a solid start, where they won the first Test with relative ease, they never again played at their full potential. Mostly, Hansen blames himself for that. He admits that his desire to win got the better of him and that 2017 was the worst year in his coaching tenure. The players, too, felt responsible for the series not going the way they wanted, as they didn't play with discipline and tactical awareness. The resilience of the Lions must also be acknowledged, as they defended brilliantly and offered more attacking spark than most had predicted.

But two other factors undoubtedly played a role in the series playing out the way it did. The first was a genuinely inexplicable refereeing decision in the last play of the third Test that denied the All Blacks a penalty they had fairly won. The second was the volume of distractions inside the All Blacks camp caused by Amazon and other commercial pressures.

Wayne Smith, who had rejoined the All Blacks in 2015 as defence coach, was stunned by NZR's decision to sanction the Amazon documentary. Selling IP and All Blacks secrets would, he felt, only lead to trouble for NZR. He had experienced the dangers that could arise from efforts to commercialise the culture and dynamic of the team.

He'd been assistant coach in 2010, when NZR commissioned photographer Nick Danziger and author James Kerr to produce a coffee table book called *Mana*, a pictorial essay of life with the All Blacks. Both men spent a few weeks with the team, and when Kerr began interviewing Smith later that year, he assumed it was for the text that would be published alongside the photographs in *Mana*. Unbeknown to Smith or NZR, it turned out that Kerr was in fact writing a different book, called *Legacy*, which was a deep dive into the culture and mechanics of the All Blacks, and what the business world could learn from them. It would go on to become a global bestseller, but the circumstances in which the intelligence was gathered and the means by which the author gained access never sat well with the All Blacks – and with Smith in particular.

'There is a lot of stuff in *Legacy*, for example, that was the start of this – of taking the blackness out of the All Blacks,' he says. 'It became a bible for some people around the world in terms of how to get your team to perform. It put a lot of pressure on us, I felt, to innovate, to try different things and to add to the legacy in different ways. Which was probably a good thing, but there was a lot of information that has gone out and *Legacy* is a difficult one. I was rung up quite a bit when we were out of camp, thinking I was doing interviews for *Mana*, and then a year later *Legacy* comes out and NZR starts asking us questions about who did this – "Why did you guys give interviews for this book?" We were really caught off-guard because it was the same bloke who was writing *Mana*. It was a warning shot for me that there was a real change going on in this area, and that more of it was going to be intrusive. It was going to be difficult to retain the inner sanctum of the All Blacks and keep it away from the public eye.'

Smith's concerns were not confined to the documentary. He was ideally placed, having been head coach of the team as far back as 2000, to see how the commercial landscape had changed so dramatically in the past 17 years. Read may not have found the Amazon crew being inside the camp that much of a distraction, but Smith did, and he felt it was illustrative of a wider incursion of commercial interests impacting negatively on the high-performance ability of the All Blacks.

'There was no comparison at all,' Smith says of what he encountered in 2000 and what he experienced in 2017. 'The obligations on us were few and far between, as I remember it. If you compare that with 2017, where we had something that I was against, but it got voted on, which was being followed around by Amazon to do that documentary – having been an All Black and then a coach for so long, I found that intrusive and it was difficult. It changed behaviours to the extent that guys that you would joke with on the field previously wouldn't come over because it would come over on my mic what they were saying. It changed everything.

'It was a microcosm, I think, of where the pressures have ramped up. As the money has got bigger, the obligations have got bigger, and that is just the nature of it. If you put $15 million into a team, you are going to expect a fair bit back from them. It is the evolution of sponsorship. Sponsors of my time were buying the mystique in many ways, and they didn't want everything exposed. They liked the black shroud, that whole persona of the All Blacks. I think it should be maintained.'

Amazon had paid $3 million to make *All or Nothing*, but by the time unforeseen costs had arisen, the profit NZR made was only around $1 million. No one had publicly said that if NZR was going to sell its soul to the devil, it should at least get a good price – but by the end of 2017, there were plenty of people close to the All Blacks thinking exactly that.

CHAPTER FIFTEEN

BUDGET ALL BLACKS

WHEN NZR CHIEF EXECUTIVE Steve Tew announced in March 2018 that the previous financial year had produced a record profit of $33.2 million from a record turnover of $257 million, the mood should have been celebratory. But in making these figures public, Tew carried a somewhat sombre air, as he had a sense of foreboding about the dangers ahead. He stressed that the numbers weren't illusionary as such, but they reflected the fact that NZR had hosted a lucrative British and Irish Lions tour, and this was a one-off. There thus was a bit of smoke and mirrors about the balance sheet, and anyone who dug into the accounts would easily discover that more money was going out than was coming in.

The evidence was there, in black and white, that NZR was operating a business model that had become overly reliant on the Lions cash dump every 12 years. In 2005, the Lions had delivered NZR a profit of $23.6 million, and the national body had lost $22.8 million over the next 11 years. NZR had picked carefully at the carcass to make it last until the next kill. But this wasn't a sustainable strategy, as even though the Lions tour of 2017 brought in $33.2 million of profit, the surplus was never going to last another 11 years. NZR was forecasting it would lose $1.8 million in 2018 and $7.3 million in 2019, so a third of the carcass would be eaten after just two years.

It was hard to fathom how the cash was being burned up so voraciously, as NZR had doubled its broadcast contract in 2016. It had renegotiated a five-year extension with AIG in the same year, which was believed to have come with a slight uplift from US$14 million (NZ$22.5 million) a year to US$16 million (NZ$25.7 million) a year, and the Adidas agreement was still understood to be easily the most lucrative in world rugby. There were more domestic and international sponsors than there ever had been, and the average revenue between 2012 and 2017 had climbed to $149 million, up 51 per cent in the five years between 2006 and 2011. The problem was that while income was growing, outgoings were rising faster: a business that had cost $134 million to run in 2015 had total expenses of $169 million in 2016, and NZR was forecasting those would rise to $194 million by 2019. 'Post-2020 we've got a deficit projected which we can't live with,' Tew stressed. 'That means we either change the expenditure model or find ways to generate more money.'

Finding more money had been a perennial objective for NZR from the first days of professionalism, so Tew's lament didn't resonate with the media. It was seen as a standard play from a sports body's chief executive – a warning that tough times were ahead, in order to temper his players' salary expectations and build a platform from which he could underpromise and overdeliver. But Tew wasn't bluffing. NZR was running out of levers to pull to magic more cash. It had exhausted almost every conceivable means to make more money, and in early 2018 there was no quick fix to boost revenue.

To put it in household terms, NZR was mortgaged to the hilt and had maxed out every credit card. Its most valuable contracts were all locked in, with both Sky and AIG fixed until the end of 2021 and Adidas until the end of 2024. The All Blacks were due to play two Tests for cash in 2018, both in Japan. The commercial team would be out knocking on doors, hustling as usual, but Tew couldn't see that a landscape-changing sponsorship or opportunity would be coming in the next 12 to 18 months.

NZR had more ability to take immediate action with its expenditure. Cutting costs would be the short-term focus in the quest to balance the books, and the high-performance budget had been put under intense scrutiny by chief financial officer Nicki Nicol after she arrived in the role in late 2016. Player payments were fixed and effectively outside her control, but operational budgets – the money spent on travel, training equipment, nutrition, analysis, technology and the like – was an area where cuts could be made. Or at least a halt could be put on the increased budget the All Blacks seemingly asked for every year. There had been exponential creep in expenditure without it being clear what the extra money was being spent on.

The desire to get a handle on operational costs led to a proposal being tabled by the NZR executive that the All Blacks give up flying business class and get themselves around the world in the economy cabin. Shifting the athletes into economy would deliver significant cost savings. A squad of 33 players plus 15 management dropping from business to economy would have saved $1 million to $1.5 million a year. But it wasn't going to happen on Hansen's watch. That was a concession he was never going to agree to, as he was sure it would immediately and catastrophically impact the ability of the All Blacks to perform in offshore venues.

The All Blacks management fought the idea aggressively and relentlessly, as it was their view that high-performance athletes most definitely should not be flying economy. Many of the All Blacks' long-haul flights came the day after a Test match – a day when the players' bodies were recovering from the intense battering they had taken. Given the weight, power and speed of the athletes, the force of the collisions was incredible: the impact of a Test match, according to the medics, left some players with the same sort of physical trauma as burns victims. It was tough enough trying to travel directly after a Test in business class – so how athletes the size of Brodie Retallick and Sam Whitelock would cope in economy was unimaginable. It was a health and safety issue, as far as the All Blacks were concerned, and a sacrifice that simply couldn't be made if NZR was serious about high performance.

The ferocity of the All Blacks' resistance led to the proposal being amended: the athletes could stay in business, but some coaching and management personnel would be relegated to economy. Again, knowing the volume of work required by every member of the team, this was another concession the All Blacks weren't willing to make.

But justifying why all staff had to fly business class was a tougher battle to win simply by the power of argument, so Nicol was invited to spend a week with the squad in South Africa. There, she experienced the nonstop, frantic, exhausting pace of life with the team, and came to appreciate that no one had an easy ride. Business class wasn't a perk, it was a necessity. The proposal to shift people to the back of the plane was dropped, but NZR still requested that the All Blacks cut $800,000 out of their operations budget.

This was a significant amount of money for the All Blacks to lose. Although they were the number one team in the world, they operated on a relatively lean model in comparison with some of the Six Nations sides. It seemed dangerous for NZR to hack away at the money available to the All Blacks given how reliant the organisation's financial model was on them being successful.

But while the All Blacks were the financial linchpin of the New Zealand rugby economy, new cultural pressures were weighing upon NZR that demanded a reallocation of high-performance resources.

*

THERE WAS, AMONG THE anger and disappointment, utter astonishment that the Chiefs Super Rugby team had thought it acceptable to pay a stripper to perform at their end-of-season function in 2016. The story became one of the biggest scandals of the year after the performer they had hired laid a complaint against the team for lewd and offensive behaviour that sparked a police inquiry. The whole business demanded questions be asked about attitudes within professional rugby teams.

When, a few weeks later, it came to light that All Blacks halfback Aaron Smith had been involved in an unsavoury tryst in a disabled toilet at Christchurch airport the day after a Test match, professional rugby had an undeniable cultural problem. Specifically, there was an undertone of misogyny, apparent not just in the behaviours of the players, but in the way administrators and executives responded to the public outcry with disdain when these incidents became public.

In November 2016, Tew announced that NZR had commissioned an independent panel to conduct a 'Respect and Responsibility' review. This was to be a drill-deep investigation into the core of professional rugby to see what could be done to make it more inclusive, and to rid it of the toxic masculinity that was clearly in the system. This work was ongoing when the Black Ferns won the 2017 World Cup in Northern Ireland, beating England in an epic final that produced record viewing numbers.

It was an achievement that highlighted the inequity between the Black Ferns and the All Blacks, and the extraordinary difference in how they were respectively funded by their employer. When the All Blacks won the 2015 World Cup in England, each player was paid $7500 per week for the time they were there, on top of their retainer contracts, which ranged in value from about $200,000 to $800,000. They also each received a bonus of $100,000. The Black Ferns, on the other hand, received $2000 per week and had no retainer contracts. There was no bonus payment when they won, and they flew home in economy class. Unlike for their male counterparts, there was no civic parade in New Zealand. To put it into perspective, All Blacks captain Richie McCaw would likely have earned about $1.1 million in 2015 from playing rugby, while Black Ferns captain Fiao'o Fa'amausili, a full-time police officer, earned about $12,000 from rugby in 2017.

NZR was desperately trying to present itself as an equal-opportunity employer and a champion of diversity, but there was plenty of hard evidence to suggest its efforts were cosmetic only. The impression that NZR was an organisation failing to break free from its male-dominated past was enhanced by the composition of its board of directors. It took until late 2016 for NZR to appoint its first female director, and this despite gender diversification of the board having been stated as a priority aim of chairman Brent Impey when he took the hot seat in 2013. Having just one female director – the legendary former Black Fern Farah Palmer – on a nine-person board left NZR nowhere near the 40 per cent female representation that most major corporates were aiming for.

The bigger picture was yet more revealing, as across the whole professional rugby landscape female representation in governance positions was just 6 per cent. Women were the ghost in boardrooms but not on the playing field, as by the end of 2016 there were 21,000 registered female players. The projections suggested that by 2025 there would be almost as many girls playing as boys.

Rugby, as everyone could see, was a game administered by men, coached by men, managed by men and governed by men.

Its culture was characterised by men looking after men, and this jarred with a country that had, in September 2017, elected its third female prime minister – one who was young, charismatic and a champion of inclusivity and diversity. NZR needed to change, and not just to say it was changing. The public needed tangible evidence that money was being invested, opportunities provided and female faces welcomed in the decision-making chamber.

This was largely why Nicki Nicol was trying to put the brakes on All Blacks expenditure – it would enable NZR to divert money to the Black Ferns' operational budget. It was untenable for NZR to throw so much cash at the All Blacks when the Black Ferns were battling for basic provisions and living off so little. This wasn't just about conforming to societal pressure, however. Overall participation numbers were stagnating, and the only growth area was women. If rugby wanted to remain relevant as a community and participation sport, it needed to invest in growing female participation. The Black Ferns, as the most visible element of the women's game, had to be better looked after.

The All Blacks were going to feel this cultural shift because the Black Ferns, still in the infancy of their professional development, didn't have the brand profile to generate much, if any, of their own revenue. There was little doubt that the Black Ferns had the potential to become an income driver, a standalone entity independently attractive to broadcasters and sponsors. In time, the Black Ferns were expected to become self-sustaining, but the money to build the brand initially was going to have to come out of the existing pot.

*

BACK IN 2012, NZR had slapped the All Blacks name on all of its national teams to give AIG the inventory it needed to invest US$70 million (NZ$105 million). But that didn't create a universal All Blacks family in the way NZR had hoped. The market still knew that there were the All Blacks and a host of other national teams that carried the name but weren't the All Blacks.

In the 22 years since the game had turned professional, the All Blacks had become almost Herculean in their ability to put their shoulder into the money wheel. NZR generated almost $190 million of revenue in 2018 and (excluding the $18 million that came from interest, foreign exchange gains and government grants) about 80 per cent was directly attributable to the All Blacks – as in the All Blacks side that Steve Hansen was coaching.

The All Blacks were the ATM for the whole New Zealand rugby family, and also bore the burden of servicing the increasing number of sponsorship contracts. The All Blacks' players were doing more than their fair share of the heavy lifting when it came to commercial work – and by 2018 there was more commercial work than ever before.

The balance of NZR's income had changed significantly in the 11 years since Chris Moller had stood down as chief executive. In his day, broadcast income had accounted for more than 60 per cent of all income. But in 2018, NZR took $73 million in broadcast revenue and $68 million in sponsorship and licensing. The portfolio of sponsors was enormous, and included Air New

Zealand, Steinlager, Tudor, Ford, Gatorade, Vodafone, Iveco, Barkers, ASB, Rexona, Sanitarium, Apple, Jockey, Nissui and Nouriz. And, of course, there were also the main players, AIG and Adidas.

Some of the contracts were relatively small in monetary terms, but every company with an investment had a right to utilise the players in some way. Unlike in the early days of professionalism, the players' collective agreement had ensured there was a heavily regulated and detailed framework around the fulfilment of commercial duties. There was a maximum number of 'commercial hours' individuals were required to fulfil in a year. This was critical in restricting the commercial team from selling to sponsors and other stakeholders more time than the All Blacks could collectively service.

Other compromise agreements had been reached between the All Blacks and NZR's commercial team to try to keep interference in high-performance needs to a minimum. A two-week period in the off-season in January was devoted to executing what the marketers called 'above-the-line activity'. The second key agreement was that sponsors would have access to players for a maximum of two hours on the day before a Test match, where they could use them in 'below-the-line activity', which might be going to an Adidas store to meet fans, attending an ASB branch to engage with staff, or spending time with prize winners. These activities were contractually required to take no longer than the two hours allocated.

'We were trying to build a win-win scenario, so that for the partners having an activity close to match day is really important to them because there is the atmosphere and the build-up and they get to utilise the players at that time,' says All Blacks manager Darren Shand. 'The benefit of that for us was that window then allowed us to say, "If we give you Friday, then we would prefer not to have to do things during the week, particularly at night. Sometimes that meant me and the coaches talking to partners about performance and what does that mean and what does a week look like, to build an understanding for them about the pressures we face and the time constraints we have and what does building up to a Test look like for a player. The idea is that they get the players at their best and we get the players at their best.'

The impact of having more sponsors was unquestionably being felt within the All Blacks squad in 2018. 'As the amount of money has grown, the volume of activity has increased,' says Shand. 'A player that would do 75 per cent of the activity has seen that incrementally grow. If we have a three-Test series, a player a while ago would have been doing one Friday; now it is more likely they will be doing two, if not three.'

Other issues were cropping up regularly too. The planning for all commercial activity was typically done months in advance and signed off by Shand. And mostly things ran to plan once the season began. But with more sponsors, there were more relationships to manage, and it became more likely a stakeholder would look to push the boundaries of the agreement or change arrangements late in the piece. While there were strict rules around how long players should be on their feet at an activity, and an obligation to keep them out of the sun, to hydrate them and not ask them to travel overly far, it was increasingly hard to police all of this and make sure sponsors adhered to the rules.

Hansen, bullish and fiercely protective, had enough confidence in his position and a strong enough relationship with Tew to push back against what he says were increasingly ill-considered commercial requests. By early 2018 he felt he was under siege – that the need to make money and balance the books was starting to cloud NZR's judgement. He felt like the Jack Nicholson character in *A Few Good Men*, standing alone on the wall protecting high performance from the commercial enemy. It seemed to him that NZR's commercial team had all the power within the organisation, but little idea about what it took to prepare a team to play a Test match. That was a dangerous combination. More of Hansen's time was spent fighting commercial requests that he felt pushed the boundaries of the collective agreement and would negatively impact the performance of the team.

'The one thing that changed the most was the commercial side of the game because of the need for money,' he said in a 2021 interview for *Steve Hansen: The Legacy*. 'You have high-performance on one side and commercialism on the other. Whether people like it or not, the only real commercial commodity that the NZR has is the All Blacks, and personally I think that is where most of the pressure came from, because it became a real battle to get the balance right. And once the balance goes in favour of commercialism over high performance, then it is interfering with how you can play. And I believe my job was to make sure that never happened. But I think at times that got very close. People didn't understand that what they were doing was demanding more and more of the players, that they were looking to sell more and more of our IP to make a dollar, and the risk of that is that the brand would be damaged if we got beaten. It was about making sure that doesn't happen.'

Hansen was shielding his players best he could, but it was impossible to hide the tension that was building. The players, and in particular the senior leaders, were aware that their coach was scrapping to protect the sanctity of the high-performance environment.

'We knew it was going on, but he kept it away from the team,' says Kieran Read. 'In the environment we wouldn't speak ill of the commercial stuff because it was the reality of what we had to do. And because we had to do it, if you were pissed off about doing it, then it was going to affect your next training or your next game, because that whole mindset thing carries on. We never spoke about it in the team, but I think we could feel it and there was a sense of it, and it was turning a little bit.

'You were aware of the extra expectations on you. How you spun that was crucial as All Blacks. You can look at promotional work in two ways. It is a distraction that shouldn't be happening, or you embrace it. We weren't going to be able to change them because of what they had sold to these guys, so we had to just roll with it.

'In the perfect world you wouldn't have them, would you? If your one goal is to play well, then you would do everything in your week to get to that point. So there is that side of it, and then there is the commercial reality side of it. Because we always had these things, and I had always understood the value, it was more a case of flipping the narrative in your head to try to get something out of it and try to embrace it. That's why we had a yes attitude within the All Blacks towards them.'

*

BY THE END OF 2018, the All Blacks were starting to feel each of the multiple pressure points that were squeezing them. The players were physically and mentally exhausted by the volume of rugby they'd had to play and the amount of travel that had come with it. They had finished the 2018 season with a five-week road trip that saw them spend two weeks in Japan, before playing England, Ireland and Italy. They'd lost in Dublin – for the first time in history – and while the Irish deserved their win, there was no question the All Blacks were low on energy. Just four days before the game, All Blacks flanker Liam Squire was seen literally hauling himself up the stairs of the team hotel one at a time. He looked broken – and yet he ran out at Aviva Stadium.

This was the reality for the All Blacks now: managing players through long seasons where the physical and mental toll was colossal. Two of those five games had been arranged purely to make money – and while the All Blacks won the two Tests, the impact of additional gametime was felt when the team played in Dublin. More games also meant more training hours, and while the early generation of professional All Blacks had plenty of time for golf, PlayStation and even a few nights out, that was not the case for the team by 2018. They earned considerably more than their forebearers, but they had to do considerably more to earn it. Between the training, the recovery, the commercial work and the travel – not to mention the heightened exposure that came with social media – life for the modern All Black was mentally and physically exhausting. And it could have been more draining still had the All Blacks not had a coach with the desire and ability to prevent yet more commercial intrusion into the high-performance side.

But Hansen also knew that he had his finger in the dyke. The battery life of his players was shorter than that of their predecessors – the game was grinding them down quickly and, in one case, totally. Squire, after making his debut in 2016, wouldn't play another Test after that 2018 game in Dublin. He wasn't quite 30, but the injuries, the battering, the stress, the time on planes and the endless commitments were too much for him.

The days of the best players giving their best years to New Zealand were over. The intensity of being an All Black was so great that players who entered the Test arena in their early 20s were unlikely to still be there in their mid-30s. A decade was about the maximum players could feasibly manage before they needed a break. Hansen could see trouble ahead.

By late 2018, almost half the All Blacks squad were considering playing in Japan after the 2019 World Cup. The Japanese clubs had enormous budgets and an insatiable desire for world-class talent. They were offering anything from $1.5 million to $2 million a season, and the rugby was less physical and the season just four months long. Beauden Barrett, Sam Whitelock and Brodie Retallick were looking to sign contracts that would allow them to play one or even two seasons in Japan as part of a four-year extension to stay in New Zealand through to the 2023 World Cup.

This, Hansen feared, was likely to be the future: NZR paying its best talent more than it ever had, but still having to make compromise deals to allow players to spend one or more seasons in Japan as part of any longer-term contract. NZR argued that these compromise deals were helping it win the battle to retain talent, but Hansen and others weren't so sure. Was NZR kidding itself that it was a good idea to let Whitelock stay in Japan after the 2019 World Cup, go straight into a club season there and then be immediately available for the All Blacks when he returned to New Zealand in May 2020? He would have no off-season – no break at all, really – and come July 2020 he'd have been playing for 18 months straight. How was this good for the All Blacks? And how was it a victory to offer Retallick a four-year deal, but one which would see him spend almost 40 per cent of the contract period in Japan?

When Hansen surveyed the likely lie of the land in late 2018, he knew that while his heart told him he wanted to negotiate a contract extension, his head told him it was time to move on. He saw a team that appeared destined to be crushed under the weight of the commercial demands being placed upon it, and he felt NZR was chasing dollars in a self-destructive manner. Hansen therefore announced on 13 December 2018 that he would be stepping down after the World Cup.

*

A WEEK LATER, ARGUABLY the biggest rugby story of the year broke in the *New Zealand Herald*. The paper revealed that St Kentigern College, a fee-paying school in South Auckland, was effectively being kicked out of the prestigious 1A First XV competition because of gratuitous recruitment of pupils.

The issue of private schools bolstering their First XV by offering scholarships had long been an issue, but in this case St Kent's, after losing in the final earlier in the year, had headhunted six players from around the country. They targeted boys who were either in their last or penultimate year at school and had already played First XV rugby. It was deliberate, aggressive, egregious recruitment that was designed specifically to pick up the best players in New Zealand in positions in which the school felt it was weak. The other schools in the competition decided they couldn't condone that policy in what was a school competition, so they all agreed to boycott their fixtures against St Kent's.

The story was significant because it illustrated that both sides of the game – professional and community – were broken. At the community level, participation rates among boys were plummeting. On the surface, the numbers appeared concerning rather than catastrophic. The number of registered male school-age players had dropped 8 per cent over a decade from 25,836 in 2009 to 23,813 in 2018. But what the numbers didn't show was the incredible drop-off rate: more than 50 per cent of the 13-year-olds playing in 2018 wouldn't be five years later. Rugby was doing well at finding new recruits, but it just couldn't keep them: teenagers were leaving the sport at an unprecedented rate.

They were quitting mostly because rugby at the school level had professionalised itself. Schools had become obsessed with winning and producing players good enough to play professionally, and their programmes were set up for the elite only. Most schools only cared about and catered for the top team in each year group; those deemed not good enough were handed over to the bemused geography teacher who had little interest in coaching. The kids who did make the cut were asked to specialise in rugby and train excessively; many revealed in an NZR-commissioned report in 2020 that they hated the pressure and expectation placed upon them.

What happened at St Kentigern illustrated the scale of the problem facing NZR. They had a game that was dying as a participation sport among males, as schools were madly investing everything in elite players only. The community game was breaking itself to provide a tiny number of players who would graduate into a broken professional model. Something had to change, and in a transformative way.

Rugby was trapped in a broken financial merry-go-round, where its traditional income sources of broadcast, sponsorship and licensing, merchandise and ticket sales weren't bringing enough in to cover its costs. And NZR had realised that supersizing everything didn't work, as the more Tests the All Blacks played, the more sponsors they took on, the more their costs went up, and the more demands were placed on them, endangering their high-performance ability.

More worrying still was that the community game was dying and needed investment – but from where would that money come? Without a healthy community game, how long before the All Blacks' famed production line of talent failed? Or before the nation simply stopped caring about the All Blacks because rugby was no longer a national obsession?

All these questions were mounting at the end of 2018, and so in early 2019 the NZR began seriously considering engaging a private-equity partner to buy a stake in the commercial assets of the national body. Things had reached the point where the board felt there was no other option.

CHAPTER SIXTEEN

WE HAVE A DEAL

ONE OF THE MOST overt syndromes spawned by the arrival of social media is the fear of missing out – or FOMO, as it's known in digital abbreviation. It's a syndrome that typically affects teenagers, who sit angst-ridden on couches in suburban households wondering how and when they should seek parental permission to attend what their phones are telling them is likely to be the greatest event in human history. Strangely, though, by early 2019, NZR was suffering from FOMO, as it saw how private-equity investment was revolutionising Northern Hemisphere rugby.

The English Premiership had signed a £225-million (NZ$450-million) deal with the private-equity firm CVC Capital Partners in December 2018. The France/Luxembourg-based investment group had taken a stake in Formula 1 in 2006 and made US$8.2 billion when it exited the sport, which equated to a 750 per cent return on its initial investment. But city analysts and Formula 1 enthusiasts were divided as to whether CVC's investment had been good for the sport or just for the investor.

Clearly, though, the Premiership felt that both the competition and the investor had benefitted, and sold 27 per cent of itself to CVC. The premise of the investment was that the clubs would take an immediate cash injection and that CVC would become a major influence in driving future revenue. Its expertise was in negotiating broadcast deals, building audience and monetising the greater profile of the sport. The concept appealed to the Premiership because, just like rugby in New Zealand, the professional game in the Northern Hemisphere had also realised its financial model was failing, with costs exceeding income.

The ink on the EPL deal was barely dry when the UK media began reporting that CVC was lining up more rugby investment, with the ProD12 – a league featuring the best teams from Scotland, Ireland, Wales and Italy – and also that it was eyeing a deal with the Six Nations.

Steve Tew and the NZR board were watching this play out, and given the financial stress gripping the professional game in New Zealand, the national body developed a serious case of FOMO. 'You can't have a major initiative change the shape of the game in Europe and ignore it down here,' says Tew. 'It was so hard to retain talent, and while we enjoyed some success, we couldn't afford to go backwards any further. South Africa and England and all the Six Nations had cashed up. We had to explore it.'

That exploration began with Tew travelling to Los Angeles in February 2019 to attend a private-equity conference. It was an informal meet and greet, a chance to see which investment firms had an interest in pumping cash into sport, and to let it be known that NZR – or, more accurately, the All Blacks – might come onto the market. He returned home encouraged by the initial interest, which was hardly a surprise, given how private-equity firms were crawling all over professional sport.

The All Blacks had the global profile to excite those in the investment world who were looking for the next big opportunity to make some serious cash. The brand was huge and the growth potentially significant, because rugby didn't have the capital base to invest in all the potential business initiatives it could. This was a combination investment firms liked – and it helped, of course, that rugby had already established a global presence, but its administration was still, to some extent, stuck in the amateur era.

Private equity wasn't in the market for top performers with world-class management. Those sorts of companies were for listed stock markets. The money swirling around in private funds was attracted to underperformance: to businesses that were battling, and which could obviously benefit from leadership and expertise. This is how private equity rolled – it didn't just dump cash in and sit back; it threw people into the mix, typically putting a few of its own trusted people to sit on the board in order to do something about the balance sheet.

Collectively, global rugby didn't have its administrative act together. There were three major showpiece tournaments – the World Cup, the Six Nations and the Rugby Championship – but the July and November windows for Test matches remained ad hoc, and so were hit and miss as to whether they engaged people.

There had been attempts over the years to agree what everyone called a 'global season' – a unification of the Northern and Southern Hemisphere playing calendars, to provide a definitive off-season for everyone – but every attempt had failed. And as a result, the same nations that dominated the sport at the beginning of professionalism continued to dominate in 2019.

More than 20 years had passed since Kevin Roberts had pitched to Nike in 1997, but by 2019 his words were just as relevant: rugby was still, potentially, the next big sport behind football. And the All Blacks were still the jewel in rugby's crown.

An investment partnership of some kind was gaining traction. Board director Mark Robinson and chair Brent Impey were despatched to the United Kingdom a few months after Tew returned from the United States. They were tasked with meeting investors who had been identified as the most likely partners, should NZR elect to proceed with a capital raise.

'Brent and I accompanied [US private-equity investor] Silver Lake to dinner and had an initial chat about what a partnership might look like,' says Robinson. 'We shared some things about NZR and they shared some insights about what they were seeing in the sporting world, and that was part of a conversation with different parties who were potential partners. At that stage, private equity was not seen as the absolute final solution in all this, but it was clear that sport as an industry was changing rapidly, and we were beginning to form a view that the principle of partnership was going to be critical.'

What also became clear about the same time was that Tew would not be part of NZR's future. Tew had been at the helm since late 2007, and his tenure had overseen many landmark successes. New Zealand had hosted a successful World Cup in 2011 and the All Blacks had won consecutive tournaments, holding their number one ranking for ten years. Rarely had the country lost a key player in his prime, and NZR had more than $100 million in cash reserves in early 2019. Key sponsors such as AIG and Tudor had been engaged, and the relationship with Adidas had been maintained. He'd steered the organisation through the global financial crisis, commissioned the 'Respect and Responsibility' review and maintained strong and productive relationships with other national unions.

But for all that he had achieved, and as well as he had managed the business, the feeling had grown around the board table that he was no longer the right man to steer NZR through what was shaping as a period of transformation.

Tew certainly fitted the euphemistic definition of being 'old school'. He had been a player himself, making a few appearances for Wellington's B team, and he brought the work hard, play hard mindsight of his amateur rugby days to his role as chief executive. Those who sat across from Tew in negotiations say he was tough – sometimes to the point that he came across as aggressive – and unflinching, operating mostly on the force of his personality and desire to get things done. Yet however tense and fraught a day at the office may have been, Tew would always drop his weaponry and hold court in the bar with his fellow protagonists, with no hard feelings lingering. He was good company, engaging, funny and usually the last one to go to bed. This was precisely the ethos on which rugby had been built: two teams smashing each other black and blue for 80 minutes, before retreating to the bar to build lifelong friendships.

Tew was all about relationships. He believed wholeheartedly in their power and importance, and he was a handshake guy, doing deals mostly on the strength of his conviction that if anything went wrong, he would have a direct line to his CEO counterpart, whom he could look in the eye and ask what was going on.

There was growing concern among the board members that this method of operating wouldn't be right in the coming years. Frustration had built that Tew might have left money on the table. In 2016, when NZR had been negotiating with AIG about extending the sponsorship for another five years, some board members had wanted independent research to determine what the naming rights for the All Blacks jersey were worth. AIG had been paying US$14 million a year since 2012, which seemed a lot of money – but was it actually good value? No one really knew, because the market hadn't been tested. Yet when AIG offered a slight uplift in 2016, Tew was happy to take it.

The extended deal was announced when the All Blacks were in Chicago to play Ireland in a Test that was going to net NZR $3 million, so it felt like it was raining cash. But again, while $3 million seemed like a lot of money, it could have been more, as NZR had outsourced the management of the Test to a third party, with Tew arguing that the national body didn't have the expertise to organise big games in foreign markets. NZR was happy to take a smaller, guaranteed fee rather than incur the risk of having to promote ticket sales, find sponsors and a broadcast partner, and manage hospitality packages. Being risk-averse meant the promoter probably made at least double, if not three times the cash out of the Test than NZR had.

It also transpired that Amazon had offered Manchester City closer to $10 million to produce an *All or Nothing* documentary, with NZR taking just $3 million because that was what it was offered.

And so in March 2019 Impey sat down with Tew at the Koru Lounge at Auckland Airport to discuss the chief executive's future. The chair felt the organisation needed strong succession planning and long lead times to make changes in key roles. Hansen had given more than a year's notice that he would be stepping down, and Impey felt Tew needed to do the same. The chief executive wasn't being pushed out; it was more that he was being encouraged to accept the need for the organisation to make a change after the World Cup, and for that to be communicated with as much notice as possible.

In early June, Tew announced he would step down after the World Cup. This opened the way for the board to take control of the upcoming broadcast negotiation. Given the importance of getting maximum value, this was not a deal that could be struck on the strength of light research, gut feel and a firm handshake.

*

THE FINANCIAL HISTORY OF NZR wasn't such a hard study. Since the earliest professional days, when News International tipped in US$555 million to get the SANZAR ball rolling back in 1995, income from broadcast rights had been critical to the financial wellbeing of the entire Southern Hemisphere rugby ecosystem. That was as true in New Zealand as anywhere else, and Sky had ploughed more cash into professional rugby than Adidas and AIG combined. The total value of NZR's sponsorship contracts had risen exponentially in the seven years since 2012, and in 2018 it accounted for 36 per cent of total revenue. But broadcast rights, which sat at $73 million a year, were still the most valuable revenue-generating asset NZR had, comprising 39 per cent of its annual income.

NZR's fundamental problem was that it was spending more than it earned, and that problem could be fixed almost instantaneously if the next broadcast deal came with even a moderate lift in value. And while there may have been some frustration with Tew's preference to rely on the power of relationships, his approach seemed to work when it came to selling TV rights: NZR's broadcast income had jumped every five years when the contract was renewed.

The process of agreeing terms was more straightforward than it appeared. The SANZAAR partners had to agree a Super Rugby and Rugby Championship format for the duration of the contract, and then work out on what terms they would split the accumulated revenue. Each domestic partner would then sell their individual rights. In NZR's case, there was a contractual requirement to give the existing rights holder – which had always been Sky – an exclusive window in which it could negotiate an extension. If NZR didn't like Sky's offer, it was able to go to the open market after Sky's exclusive period ended.

The process always culminated in a Hollywood-style showdown between the respective chief executives. NZR would dedicate a team of people, and might even engage an external consultant to work through the probable value of the five-year rights, and would then come up with a ballpark figure. Sky would do the same. The two teams would meet during the exclusive window and discuss big-picture stuff, before Tew and Sky chief executive John Fellet would take themselves off to a separate room. At this point, Fellet would state what Sky was willing to pay, and in both 2010 and 2014 Tew had been happy to reach across the table and shake Fellet's hand, saying, 'We have a deal.'

By mid-2019, much of the hard work had already been done. The last broadcast deal had brought in more money, but of course it had also come with a significant lift in costs, as Super Rugby had expanded from a 15-team competition played in three countries to an 18-team competition played in five. Unsurprisingly, Super Rugby collapsed under its own weight long before the end of the contract: in late 2017, Rugby Australia agreed to axe the Western Force, while South Africa withdrew the Cheetahs and the Southern Kings, and the competition reverted to the 15-team, three-conference format it had used between 2011 and 2015. From 2021, when the new deal kicked in, it was agreed to keep Super Rugby at 15 teams, but to operate the competition as a straight round-robin.

But two far more significant changes had occurred since the last deal, and they were going to require NZR to play a smart strategic hand. Fellet had stood down as chief executive of Sky in mid-2018 and had been replaced by Martin Stewart, an Englishman who had held roles with BSkyB in the United Kingdom and with TV operators in the Middle East. Even more significantly, for the first time in the history of professionalism there was a genuine rival to Sky. Spark New Zealand, the former national telecom operator, had announced in late 2017 that it was going to launch a streaming service and so was in the market to acquire content rights, with a heavy focus on live sport. It was a natural progression: not only was the company cash-rich with deep reserves, but because of its history as the national landline telephone operator, most Kiwis had Spark packages in their homes.

How serious Spark was about challenging Sky's market position became clear in April 2018, when it announced that it had won the rights to broadcast the 2019 World Cup. Spark Sport, offering $12 million, had outbid Sky for the rights. While it had been World Rugby's decision, NZR had, informally through some personal relationships, encouraged Spark's chief executive, Simon Moutter, to build the service, and Impey had briefed key media about the new entrant's potential. NZR wanted competition in the market and was happy to give Spark Sport a helping hand to get it up and running. This was hardly corporate altruism, but a calculated strategy to increase the pressure on Sky and give NZR leverage in future broadcast negotiations.

After Spark had won the World Cup rights, and because Amazon had made its *All or Nothing* documentary and was buying live sport rights in the United Kingdom, the New Zealand media speculated that NZR would, for the first time, go to the open market and not accept whatever it was offered by Sky during its exclusive negotiation window. But internal discussions were not following the media narrative: unlike what the press was suggesting, there was no split between 'hawks' and 'doves' on the NZR board, with one faction pushing to embrace new technology and arguing to carve out all sorts of digital rights, and another championing the security and certainty of sticking with Sky.

The board had discussed all the options, including NZR building and owning its own platform, but Tew had been convinced by Fellet that the cost was prohibitive and the risks too high. Competitions such as the EPL, which ran its own platform, had massive budgets and enormous capability.

'This was happening in other countries,' says Fellet. 'They would have someone on their board who was a real high-tech guy saying, "We don't need anybody, let's just stream this baby on our own." Then they realised that while the EPL may have streaming rights, they have local people to produce the game and do all the heavy lifting. Steve would not only have to start a sales team, and NZR weren't real good at that, they would have to get into the production side of the business and that would be $50 million in vans. It was getting cheaper, but it was still not cheap, whereas I get to use the vans year-round four nights a week covering other sports, but his would be sitting around in a parking lot half the year, so I had lots of advantages. Steve understood that.'

The board was confident that a deal with Sky remained the right option, but nevertheless they wanted Sky to feel under threat during the closed period of negotiation. And because the preference was to stick with Sky but also to push for the upper limit of what the rights were worth, NZR's board commissioned detailed research that effectively stress-tested what the TV operator would likely be able to afford. Leading investment minds forensically analysed Sky's cashflow, operating assets and business model to ascertain what the company could sustainably afford. This analysis led NZR to believe that $120 million a year was Sky's limit.

When Sky put an offer of $80 million a year on the table in early October 2019, Tew and other directors were of the view that this was as far as Sky could be pushed. But as it was being debated, Spark Sport made the bombshell announcement on 10 October that it had outbid Sky for the rights to New Zealand's domestic cricket programme. This was a massive loss for Sky – one that would see it lose subscribers. It also showed how deep Spark Sport's pockets were.

The timing of the cricket rights announcement was perfect for NZR. Sky was suddenly in panic mode, because if it also lost the rugby rights, its business might no longer be viable. Its share price was already under duress, trading at just 91 cents, and NZR knew that chief executive Stewart would be feeling desperate, especially as the exclusive window would close on 11 October, the very next day.

'The pivotal moment in that decision-making process was Spark picking up cricket,' says Tew. 'That was announced at a really important time in our discussion, and I am sure Martin got surprised by that announcement and that just made it more important for him.'

Sensing the opportunity it had, NZR's negotiating team told Sky if it could up the offer to $100 million a year ($500 million in total over five years), they would have a deal. Sky had to seek approval for a sum of that magnitude but came back to NZR later the same day agreeing to the price. That wasn't the end of it, though, as the following day NZR said it also wanted a 5 per cent shareholding in the company – which was valued at $23 million. Again, desperate to get the contract signed and delivered, Sky sought approval to agree the request. On 14 October the deal was announced to the stock exchange. NZR had secured a $27-million annual uplift and an equity stake in Sky.

If there had been an increasing number of negative interactions between the commercial and high-performance teams, this one was a huge positive. Having almost $30 million more in annual income would pave the way to fund retainer contracts for the Black Ferns and would keep many players out of the clutches of Japanese predators. Money like this would reverse the equation of NZR spending more than it was earning. While there was widespread disappointment a couple of weeks later when the All Blacks failed to secure a third consecutive World Cup title, beaten in the semi-final by England, there was growing confidence that NZR was finally on a sustainable financial footing.

In December 2019, NZR took another major step towards improving its financial position by commissioning management consultant McKinsey to run a deep review of the entire rugby landscape to see where savings could be made and whether there were any revenue-generating opportunities not being explored. The world-renowned firm produced an impressively detailed report that worked out how much money was being spent on player development, talent identification, marketing and administration across the entire professional network, and identified how NZR, through a combination of cutting operational costs and some simple revenue initiatives, could be better off by anything between $31 million and $46 million per annum. McKinsey found that there was duplication of provincial back-office functions, a confused and needlessly costly player development system, and a bloated head office, where the headcount of staff and contractors had climbed to 160 from 32 in 1996. It estimated that between $11 million to $14 million could be saved in what it called 'non-player labour costs'.

The only problem with the McKinsey report was its timing, as it was presented to NZR on 25 February 2020 – just four weeks before New Zealand's government shut the border and locked the country down as protection against the Covid-19 pandemic. And, of course, the outbreak of Covid changed everything. Sport couldn't be played, and the border would likely be shut for at least a year, if not longer. This threw NZR into full crisis mode. What was going to happen to Super Rugby? And who (and where) on Earth were the All Blacks going to play – if indeed they were going to be allowed to play at all?

*

IN SEPTEMBER 2019, NZR announced that Mark Robinson would be taking over as chief executive. Robinson, a former All Black who played nine Tests between 2000 and 2002, had been on the NZR board since 2013 and a World Rugby delegate since 2014. He had degrees from Victoria University and Cambridge, and there had long been whispers in rugby circles that he was being groomed to take over from Tew.

If there was a concern about his readiness, it lay in his lack of heavyweight corporate experience. He had served as chief executive of the Taranaki Rugby Union between 2007 and 2012 before taking on various consultancy roles, so it would be a huge step up to take charge of an organisation that turned over more than $200 million annually, had a relatively complex contractual arrangement with its elite playing base, had close to 30 major commercial partners and was under intense and relentless media scrutiny. That lack of experience was thought to be the reason Robinson scored slightly lower than the other shortlisted candidate for the role, Scott Pickering, who, at the time, was chief executive of the Accident Compensation Commission (ACC) – the country's insurance scheme, which covers citizens and visitors in the event of accidental injury. NZR had been working off a skills matrix, and the two candidates are thought to have scored the same, but for one category. Robinson, however, was offered the job because it was deemed that his institutional knowledge, the depth and breadth of his relationships with existing and potential stakeholders, and his longevity in the game in various roles outweighed the findings of the skills matrix.

Having been in the job for barely a month when Covid hit, Robinson was in an impossibly difficult position. It simply wasn't feasible to have any strategic goal other than to survive.

The business was going to haemorrhage cash while no rugby was played, and so the period between March and June was focused entirely on cutting costs by shedding jobs and negotiating pay cuts. It wasn't until June 2020, when New Zealand lifted the last of its internal restrictions, which allowed the country to function as normal, albeit with a closed border, that Robinson and NZR could start to think about longer-term initiatives.

Given that NZR had publicly stated in April 2020 that revenue might decline by as much as 70 per cent, and some predictions suggested losses could push as high as $50 million, the issue of a capital raise was firmly back on the agenda. The argument had shifted: this was no longer just something to consider, it was a virtual necessity, and a tender process concluded in June with the appointment of investment bank Jefferies as NZR's adviser in the search for an investment partner.

'We were of the view that something around partnership had to be considered,' says Robinson. 'We crystalised in our own mind what a model could look like. That was to take on a partner to look to do a couple of key things: one was to provide capital to invest to stabilise the financial position; two, to make an initial investment in the game in the short term; and three, most critically, to invest in revenue-generating capability. To get hold of the skills and competencies that we thought were necessary to aggressively grow revenues.'

The process was called Project Future, and while NZR says it was open to exploring other ways to raise capital, such as taking on bank debt or floating on the stock market, its preference was always to find a private-equity partner. By the end of 2020,

Jefferies had procured three private-equity offers, the best of which had come from US firm Silver Lake Partners, which specialised in technology investments. Silver Lake had also been a key investor in the UFC and had a stake in Manchester City, and promoted the idea that sport's best financial opportunities sat with digital assets and the ability to harness new technology to drive audience growth and engagement. NZR certainly liked the pitch, and indeed the offer.

When Tew had returned from the United States in early 2019, NZR had various fundamental questions that it needed answered before it could progress any further with a private-equity sale. Most notably, how precisely would a deal be structured? What level of equity would be appropriate to sell? And what would the business be valued at? The question of structure – that is, what precisely would NZR be selling to a third party? – was the most pressing, and Silver Lake had provided an answer the board liked. Under the terms of the deal, a new entity called Commercial Company (CommCo) would be created, containing all NZR's revenue-generating assets, from broadcasting, sponsorship, ticket sales, merchandise, licensing and digital properties. CommCo would have its own chief executive and staff, its own board of directors reporting to NZR, and would be valued at $3.1 billion. Silver Lake would buy a 15 per cent stake in CommCo for $465 million.

NZR was going to be flooded with cash, and the capital would be available to patch up the holes left by Covid and then create new revenue-generating initiatives. This, on the face of it, seemed to be the win-win NZR said it was: the ultimate sweet spot where commercial intersected with high performance in a frictionless manner. If money, as Moller had said, was the great enabler of high performance, then a partnership with Silver Lake would be hugely beneficial for the All Blacks and their aspirations to bounce back to the summit of world rugby.

In January 2021, details of the deal were leaked to the *New Zealand Herald* as part of a deliberate PR strategy to sell the deal with Silver Lake as a permanent fix to the game's financial problems – a once-in-a-lifetime opportunity to keep the community game alive and well for decades. NZR wanted the public to believe that Silver Lake's money would be used to buy balls and bibs for rugby clubs around the country; that the smartest investment brains of Wall Street were going to harness the brand profile of the All Blacks and drive so much new revenue as to make rugby the lifeblood of every community again.

The implication was that the rising tension between the commercial and high-performance sides of professional rugby in New Zealand would be a thing of the past. But that wasn't going to be the case at all, because what NZR hadn't made public was that it was preparing to go to war with its players. Under the proposed terms of the Silver Lake deal, commercial ambition was going to wreak unknown havoc on high performance. The two worlds were on track for the most cataclysmic clash.

CHAPTER SEVENTEEN

SELLING THE FAMILY SILVER

IN MARK ROBINSON'S EARLIEST days as chief executive, he seemingly carried an envelope, knowing that almost everywhere he went, he'd end up giving an impromptu seminar on the back of it detailing the state of NZR's finances. What he liked to show was that the union had two distinct problems: one, it didn't have enough money coming in to sustainably fund the community game; and two, it had a distribution problem because it had too many direct costs. Robinson liked to demonstrate the latter by drawing a pie chart that showed 36.5 per cent of NZR's revenue had to be paid to the professional players under the terms of the collective employment agreement, and another 16 per cent had to be paid to the provincial unions. He would explain that this was something NZR was no longer willing to tolerate.

NZR's partnership with the professional players had long been the envy of the world. For all that there had been some angst and heat between the two sides over the years, they were bound by a mutual respect and shared a vision that managed and funded professional environments, which helped New Zealand succeed on the world stage and generate income that could sustain a vibrant community game.

Somehow, though, by early 2020 the mood around the NZR board table had changed. The back-of-the-envelope pie chart came to be seen by the executive and board as a monument to player power: a symbol of the control the New Zealand Rugby Players Association (NZRPA) had come to exert in all aspects of professional life. How could the players be commanding $1-million salaries and the right to take a sabbatical season in Japan? The narrative built that the revenue-sharing agreement between NZR and the cohort of about 300 professional players was holding the game hostage. If Silver Lake did indeed invest $465 million, then $170 million of that would go to the elite playing fraternity – and, yes, the money was being earned on the power of the brand and the reputation of the All Blacks, but in theory the workload of the players wouldn't increase once the money was banked. NZRPA chief executive Rob Nichol came to be seen not as a trusted ally helping build a vibrant game for everyone, but as an enemy, working to make 0.2 per cent of the playing base rich beyond their wildest dreams.

NZR had entered into the Silver Lake negotiations with two clear objectives. The first was to achieve the goals set out by Robinson: to stabilise the business and then to use the capital and capability of Silver Lake to identify and establish new revenue sources. Second, the deal was seen by Robinson and his board as an opportunity to rebalance the existing revenue-sharing agreement. The sales pitch would be that the players should take a smaller cut of a bigger pie.

Silver Lake was projecting that if it was brought in as a partner, revenue would grow to $270 million in 2022, then up to $305 million in 2025, and so NZR struck the deal on the basis that the players would agree to a revenue model of tiered, descending royalties, where they took 36.5 per cent of the first $200 million earned, 18.3 per cent of the next $50 million of NZR income and 9.1 per cent thereafter. This roughly equated to about 31 per cent of the total revenue NZR was forecasting it would earn over the next three years.

The problem with this, however, was that NZR didn't have a mandate to unilaterally lower the percentage paid to players. The terms were enshrined in law through the collective employment agreement and couldn't just be altered because NZR wanted them to be. Additionally, one of the reasons NZR felt the players had become too powerful was that the NZRPA had negotiated the right to be consulted about and agree with any initiative that would have a material impact on the terms of the collective agreement.

The only way the numbers stacked up on the Silver Lake deal was if the players agreed to the new payment structure, but NZR seemed determined not to negotiate or even communicate with the NZRPA about its capital-raising plans. The NZRPA accidentally became aware something was going on in June 2020, when chair David Kirk, in his capacity as the co-founder and managing partner of Sydney-based private-equity firm Bailador, was notified of a term sheet being circulated by New

Zealand–based adviser Jarden, in which NZR was touting an investment opportunity. It wasn't clear from the intel Kirk had gathered what NZR was offering, but it seemed it was looking for $200 million of investment in a range of new business initiatives.

There was limited market appetite for the opportunity, but by late September the NZRPA had learned that Jefferies was leading either a revamped or new capital raise, and that international interest was high, with bidders scheduled to pitch. It was only at this point, with the proposal well advanced and potential investors already identified, that NZR communicated directly with the NZRPA about its intentions.

After being briefed, the NZRPA wrote to NZR with a list of questions about the deal – questions which it felt NZR had not answered satisfactorily. Having not received the answers it needed, and harbouring concerns about the way NZR was handling the process with an air of secrecy and a lack of consultation, the NZRPA followed up with a second letter, in which it asked the national body to clarify the terms around which future discussion between the two entities should continue. Essentially, the NZRPA asked NZR to confirm, which the national body did in a letter dated 17 December, that it needed player approval to bring in an equity partner.

When the NZRPA's board met in 2021, it decided to inform NZR that it would not support the deal, and this was communicated in a letter dated 29 January: 'We have concluded that we will not grant approval for the restructure and sale proposed by NZR and believe we should communicate that conclusion to you now.' The letter was signed by Nichol, Kirk and the organisation's board members, who included current All Blacks Sam Cane, Sam Whitelock, Aaron Smith and Dane Coles, as well as Black Ferns Sarah Hirini and Selica Winiata.

Three days later, specific details about the Silver Lake deal – minus the player payments element – were made public in the *New Zealand Herald*. NZR was also selling the merits of the deal to the provincial unions, who between them were going to share an immediate $39-million windfall if the agreement was sanctioned. For the deal to be approved, NZR needed a 75 per cent majority of the provincial unions to vote in favour of it at the NZR annual general meeting scheduled for 29 April, and for the players to give their approval. The fact that NZR was only actively wooing one of its key stakeholders, as well as trying to win the hearts and minds of the public through certain media operators, suggested that its strategy was to win so much support for the transaction as to make the NZRPA conclude that its objection was not tenable.

But this was a gross miscalculation by NZR. Far from breaking the NZRPA, the process around the Silver Lake deal galvanised the players, past and present, who were willing to make this the hill on which they would die. At the AGM, the provinces voted unanimously to accept the deal – which had been slightly revised, with Silver Lake's stake reduced to 12.5 per cent at a price of $388 million. But the players held firm, refusing to give their blessing.

Their own remuneration was not what drove the players to war. Their concerns about NZR doing a deal with Silver Lake were broader and more significant; as Nichol would say many times, the players were destined to be well remunerated in almost any scenario. The NZRPA had questions about control of the game. How, it wanted to know, would NZR be able to manage an external investor that would have the sole goal of making money from the All Blacks brand?

Silver Lake was a genuine heavyweight in the investment world, with more than US$90 billion (NZ$131 billion) of assets under management, and while NZ$388 million did not constitute a significant amount of money, given the size of the US firm's portfolio, it would still be looking for returns of about 25 per cent per annum. For the last decade, NZR's revenue growth had averaged 8 per cent per annum, so questions about how this growth would be delivered were entirely legitimate, especially as the All Blacks were already feeling the weight of increased commercial expectations.

NZR, however, offered no hard detail on how this growth would happen. Robinson and Impey talked about Silver Lake's ability to help monetise digital assets and use its links to the technology world to enhance the audience experience, but no one was sure what that might mean in practice. There was a vague thesis that Silver Lake believed there were anything from 10 million to 60 million All Blacks fans overseas, people who were waiting to be activated and turned into paying supporters of the team.

This combination of hugely ambitious growth projections and limited detail on how it would happen alarmed the players, who felt that the risk of commercial interests overwhelming the All Blacks' high-performance needs would become dangerously high if they accepted private-equity investment.

There were other legitimate concerns, too, such as whether NZR's current board even had the legal right to sell a stake in the organisation's commercial assets. The contract may have talked about NZR, but everyone knew that Silver Lake was buying a stake in the All Blacks. The national side was NZR's only commercial asset, and the players who had worn the jersey and who had bled for the cause wondered whether the board were custodians of the brand, rather than its owners.

Then there was the question of Silver Lake's exit strategy, as private-equity investors typically looked to get their money out four to seven years after putting it in. How was NZR going to ensure that Silver Lake's stake didn't end up in the hands of a Russian oligarch or a sovereign wealth fund owned by a nation with political, social or cultural views at odds with the values and beliefs of the All Blacks?

A deal with Silver Lake would make the All Blacks the most commercialised property in global rugby, and there would no longer be any debate about whether they were a sports team or a business. If they took the money, the All Blacks would exist purely to make more money, and it wouldn't be for just a few years. There was no feasible scenario in which NZR might raise the necessary capital to buy back the equity stake. Given the magnitude and irreversible nature of the deal, the players wanted NZR to slow down. The NZRPA wasn't against Silver Lake specifically, or even dead-set against a private-equity raise, but it demanded to be treated as a valued partner. The process, it said, had to be more transparent and collaborative.

Former captain Richie McCaw, recognised as the greatest All Black and best leader in the history of the game, felt compelled to speak on the issue. McCaw was publicity-shy and naturally conservative, but having worn the All Blacks jersey 148 times, and having led the team to back-to-back World Cup triumphs, he didn't like the way NZR was trying to frog-march the players into a deal.

'The whole ethos behind the All Blacks is that you do your time, and leave it in a better place, so that the future generations can keep adding to it,' he told the *New Zealand Herald*. 'Sure, there was money that needed to go around to make it all work, but the last thing any of us ever wanted was to think that New Zealand rugby wasn't put first. We wanted it to survive not just on the field, but also financially long after we're gone. There's also the feeling of, "What happens down the track? Is it the right thing? What are the risks?" You'd like to stack it up against the other options. Being told [by NZR] that's the only option and we take it or leave it does make you wonder. I can see how a whole lot of money coming in would make people feel pretty excited. But when you talk with people about private equity, the feedback I get is to be very careful, that you have to understand the motivation, which is to make money off it. Straight away that scares me.'

But NZR appeared to have no interest in bringing the NZRPA into the fold. The executive had no empathy for the players' stance; indeed, the NZRPA's refusal to approve the deal triggered Impey and Robinson into an aggressive and almost hostile PR campaign in which they painted the players as greedy and misguided. At the AGM, Impey said the players would be 'scoring the greatest own goal in the history of sport' if they didn't give their approval. 'It would be a terrible mistake if the players don't eventually support this deal; a really bad mistake,' he said. And when he was asked whether the players were being greedy, he replied: 'I'm not going to use those words. It comes down to how the money is spent. In my view the need in the game is for clubs and teenagers.'

A week later, Robinson issued an astonishingly personal and emotive attack on Nichol after the NZRPA had sent the media details of an alternative capital-raising venture he believed NZR should consider: a stock-market flotation that would value the business at between $3.4 billion and $3.8 billion.

'We are shocked and disappointed that Rob Nichol has shared another counter proposal with media before sharing it with New Zealand Rugby,' the statement read. 'This is a fundamental breach of trust and the partnership which up until now we valued highly. Through doing this, the NZRPA leadership has unilaterally taken a decision to attempt to destroy the Silver Lake deal – and the incredible financial and capability outcomes it would provide for all of rugby. We are sorry, that for the players, their own union has put them in this position where the greatest opportunity for the future of all of rugby in New Zealand could be lost.'

When Impey followed that up by calling Kirk – a deeply intelligent and hugely revered figure in New Zealand, having been a Rhodes Scholar who led the All Blacks to World Cup glory in 1987 – 'disingenuous' on a national radio show, it was clear the sport had embarked on a toxic and bitter civil war. The partnership that had served the professional game so well was shattered, and the current players were in the unenviable position of having been publicly shamed by their employer in a way that they felt grossly misrepresented their stance and values. NZR was publicly suggesting that the revenue-sharing agreement was killing the community game, but the players believed it was protecting it, by capping expenditure on their salaries. There was a finite pot of money allocated to fund the processional game, which created certainty and security about what was left to fund the community side of the sport. And the amount of revenue the players were allocated – 36.5 per cent – was in line with the arrangements in other major sports.

Impey and Robinson's strategy of pursuing a belligerent PR campaign that belittled and berated the very people on whom the success of the Silver Lake proposal depended seemed utterly mad. NZR didn't just need the players to approve the deal, it also needed them to deliver the Test victories that Silver Lake's investment would require. No matter how clever or innovative Silver Lake was with money, its investment would flourish only if the All Blacks continued to dominate the world game.

High-performance environments need stability, and that was something the All Blacks most definitely didn't have when they assembled to play Fiji and Tonga in July 2021. Senior All Blacks Cane, Whitelock, Smith and Coles were heavily involved in the process of trying to find a way forward with NZR, and had been hurt by the comments Impey and Robinson had made. Manager Darren Shand was on the NZR executive, and therefore had to look after a disaffected playing group while also supporting his employer's position. While everyone did their best to retain their professionalism, tension within the All Blacks camp was inevitable. The players simply didn't trust their employer.

What they were about to discover, however, was that Silver Lake was effectively just the tip of the commercial iceberg that was heading inexorably towards the All Blacks, poised to rip the sort of hole in their high-performance hull from which they might not recover.

*

AS WELL AS HIRING Jefferies to begin a tender for an investment partner in June 2020, NZR had also engaged London-based consultancy TRN to find a new front-of-jersey sponsor for the All Blacks. AIG had signalled that it would not renew its contract when it expired in December 2021, and NZR decided it needed external help to ensure that it achieved full value for its next deal. And TRN wouldn't just be looking for a name for the front of the jersey: NZR would be selling a suite of assets, which included the back of the All Blacks' shorts and their training kit.

By July 2021, the UK-based petrochemical company Ineos was closing in on a $10-million-a-year deal to sponsor the back of the shorts and the training kit, and Altrad, a French-based building services company, was ready to pay $30 million annually for the front-of-jersey naming rights. With Adidas's contribution, the All Blacks kit would have close to $60 million of sponsorship splashed all over it, and between these new sponsorship deals and the improved broadcast contract, NZR's revenue was on track to jump to about $270 million in 2022. NZR's accounts looked considerably healthier than they did in early 2018, and the larger pot of money would have a direct impact on high-performance programmes.

But what had NZR sold to Ineos and Altrad to persuade them to sponsor the All Blacks for such vast sums? The players had already seen their commercial workloads pushed close to the limit of their contracts, and they were wary about the expectations two major international companies – owned by billionaires Sir Jim Ratcliffe and Mohed Altrad, respectively – would have when these sponsorships went live in 2022. It turned out, however, that the snag to these deals was not the time demands they would make of the players, but the damage the association might cause to the All Blacks brand.

Ineos was knee-deep in fossil fuels at a time when the world's collective attitude towards companies drilling, mining and processing finite and highly pollutive resources was turning. Ineos was officially the largest source of climate pollution in Scotland. Environmental organisation Greenpeace was so outraged when the *New Zealand Herald* broke the news that a deal between the world's most iconic rugby team and one of the worst polluters of the world's oceans was close to fruition that it began a petition to stop the agreement being signed. NZR, it appeared, was facilitating Ineos in a 'greenwashing' programme: the company was trying to improve its reputation through association with an iconic and trusted brand. NZR denied this, saying that it had been drawn to Ineos's quest to rebuild itself as a champion of sustainability, citing the company's ambition to shift into hydrogen and other renewable energies.

It hadn't gone unnoticed by the players, either, that on the day the Ineos deal was officially announced, Adidas was holding its annual Run for the Oceans event in Auckland. The German-based group, whose logo had sat in the middle of the jersey since 1999, was trying to raise money and awareness to clean up the world's oceans, and now it appeared that the back of the All Blacks' shorts would be advertising the company responsible for dumping the waste in there in the first place.

Altrad, however, potentially carried an even higher risk to embarrass the All Blacks, as the eponymous owner had been arrested in 2020. Investigators took Mo Altrad and Bernard Laporte, the former France coach and at the time the head of the French Rugby Federation, into custody over the nature of an agreement they struck around the front-of-jersey naming rights for the French national team. According to the prosecution, a deal under which Laporte agreed to appear in Altrad group conferences and sold his image reproduction rights in return for €180,000 (NZ$298,000) was signed in February 2017. But while that sum was paid to Laporte, prosecutors claimed that he had never provided the services, and later that year Altrad had won the sponsorship rights for the French national jersey with a $60-million offer.

The optics weren't great for NZR when the All Blacks were in Europe in November 2022, with the name Altrad prominent on their jersey and the man himself facing jail time should he be found guilty of the bribery and corruption charges he was to be tried for the following month. The optics became terrible on 15 December, when Altrad was found guilty and handed an 18-month suspended sentence and fined €50,000 (NZ$82,000).

Altrad's arrest had been front-page news around the world in 2020, and NZR knew precisely what was alleged to have happened. Robinson justified the board's decision to push ahead with the deal regardless, saying in November 2022:

> We were made aware of the allegations in our discussions with Altrad prior to them becoming the front-of-jersey sponsor, although at that time we understood no charges had been laid. Altrad's founding principles we recognised as relevant to our game and with the support of their international footprint, we will continue to build our global legacy in rugby.[1]

NZR's belligerent Silver Lake campaign, the active attacks on the players and the high-risk decision to jump into a partnership with Altrad came across as almost reckless: as if the organisation had abandoned and revolted against the steady, relationships-based tenure of Tew. As had become evident, the former CEO had been wildly underappreciated for running the business with a firm but fair hand that had won him universal respect among players, stakeholders and international partners.

Perhaps it was the impact of Covid and the additional financial pressure the lockdowns exerted, but the period from June 2020 to November 2022 was among the most turbulent and disruptive in New Zealand rugby history, and the All

Blacks' commercial and high-performance interests no longer intersected. The commercial tail was wagging the high-performance dog.

*

AS MUCH AS THE Covid-19 pandemic was an existential threat to the financial viability of professional rugby in New Zealand, it simultaneously created the sort of volatile and uncertain environment in which opportunism could thrive. New Zealand was hit by a perfect storm as Covid arrived and shut the international borders at a time when the national body was readying itself to make a transitional change to its revenue profile, reposition the players' revenue share at a lower rate and maximise its traditional income streams. And there was a new chief executive, one with no experience managing an organisation the size of NZR, being guided by a long-serving chairman who was battling, at the time, serious health issues.

It wouldn't be fair to say that this perfect storm led to a reign of chaos, but the combination of ambition, uncertainty and crisis – effectively, means, motive and opportunity – led to a period of haphazard strategic thinking in which high-performance considerations were sidelined. Super Rugby was the first point of attack in the early pandemic months: as a cross-border competition, it was no longer tenable, in the short term at least. The New Zealand government had signalled that quarantine requirements and restricted travel were likely to persist for up to two years. This provided, therefore, a golden opportunity to radically restructure a competition that had lost its way both commercially and as a high-performance entity.

Three ideas held sway inside NZR midway through 2020. The first was that South Africa was no longer a viable Super Rugby partner, due to its time zone and the low audience numbers the games there produced for Sky. Second, Australia had become a financial liability as it didn't have the money to run all the teams it wanted in the competition. The third idea was that if NZR could establish itself as the sole owner of Super Rugby, it would be significantly more attractive to the private-equity investors it was courting.

The upshot of this thinking was that in July 2020 NZR announced that it was looking to build a new Super Rugby competition with eight to ten teams. It would feature five clubs from New Zealand and one Pasifika team, and the door was open to Australian franchises to bid. This announcement doubled as notification that NZR was unilaterally breaking free from its SANZAAR obligations, and effectively kicking South Africa out of Super Rugby.

The South Africans, having already placed two provinces in European competition before Covid-19 struck, might have been planning to depart from Super Rugby anyway. However, the cold and abrupt way in which NZR announced its plans removed any prospect of a reconciliation when the international borders did eventually reopen.

The absence of South African teams from Super Rugby might have lowered the cost base of the tournament and made it more TV-friendly, but it severely damaged the All Blacks' high-performance ambitions. Throughout 2021 and the first three Tests of 2022, the All Blacks' biggest issue on the field was their lack of physical presence and their inability to compete in the set piece. They simply weren't equipped to play collision-based rugby.

This became undeniable when, after winning their first eight Tests of 2021, the All Blacks lost to South Africa, before finishing the season with back-to-back defeats to Ireland and France. In 2022, they lost the July series 2–1 to Ireland, before the Springboks beat them in Mbombela. This run of defeats – one of the worst in the side's professional history – could trace its origins back to that Super Rugby decision in July 2020. Without exposure to the bigger athletes of South Africa and their powerful and grinding approach, New Zealand's best players were no longer coming out of Super Rugby ready to compete with the best international teams. What's more, Test rugby had become somewhat obsessed with size and epic brutality. Several senior All Blacks said quite directly that they hadn't supported the move to kick the South African sides out of Super Rugby.

Yet the All Blacks' slump couldn't be blamed entirely on the revamped Super Rugby competition, as there were clearly issues with the coaching staff. But some of those issues could be traced back to NZR decisions that made little sense.

At the end of 2020 and 2021, All Blacks assistant coaches John Plumtree and Brad Mooar received poor reviews from the players about their ability and competency. This wasn't necessarily surprising, as neither man had been a first-choice pick for head coach Ian Foster when he'd won the job in 2019. Foster had initially planned to work with Jamie Joseph and Tony

Brown, but both became unavailable when they were offered increased contracts to stay with the Japanese national team. And the main reason Japan was able to recontract them was that NZR had opted to delay its process to replace Steve Hansen until after the 2019 World Cup, even though the coach had given almost 12 months' notice that he would not be seeking reappointment. A poor process had led to a poor outcome, and the All Blacks didn't get the coaches they had identified as being the best fit.

It's also questionable whether the newly installed All Blacks coaching group got the support they needed when Covid hit and NZR shifted into crisis mode. In June 2020, when New Zealand came out of lockdown, the All Blacks were looking at playing six Tests, but there was little certainty that would happen. The question was put to Foster by his employer: given the reduced Test programme, did he still need a full coaching team? Everyone was doing it tough – there had been widescale redundancies at NZR, the players had agreed pay reductions, so could the All Blacks coaching team be cut down to save some cash?

Whether it was a question or a request was never made clear, but given that Mooar had given up a three-year, well-paid head coaching contract in Wales just six months earlier to join the All Blacks, and that Plumtree had sacrificed his head coaching role at the Hurricanes at late notice, it would have been callous to axe their jobs before they'd even coached one Test together. No one, in the end, was forced out of the coaching group, because all were willing to take significant pay cuts to deliver the sort of cost-savings NZR was after. But the message from NZR's halls of power was loud and clear: high performance would be sacrificed as readily as any other part of the business.

These were unprecedented times, and the financial duress was extreme, so NZR had a real and pressing need to strip costs out of the business quickly and clinically. There were healthy cash reserves set aside for this sort of rainy day, but still there was no desire to burn through $50 million or more in one year just to avoid making unpopular decisions. NZR's loss in 2020 ended up being $34 million – a figure much lower than anticipated, and one that could be taken as a validation of the hard decision-making.

But seen through the lens of high performance, there was a pronounced sense that the All Blacks were under attack. The combination of the uncertainties produced by the pandemic and the civil war over the Silver Lake proposal was impossibly hard. And even when a truce was reached in August 2021 and the players and NZR agreed a new deal by February 2022, the tensions never fully eased. The scars were deep, and trust between NZR and the NZRPA remained at an all-time low.

The new agreement valued the business at $3.5 billion, was offering Silver Lake only a 5.7 per cent initial stake for $200 million, and included provision for local institutional investors to invest up to $100 million in a separate capital raise. The players' share of the revenue remained at the existing 36.5 per cent. Having set out to reduce its direct costs, NZR ended up growing them, as the arrival of Silver Lake meant there was one more dividend payment to be met each year.

The deal was signed off in June 2022, and the first $100 million was paid into NZR's account, but the unease about what lay ahead for the All Blacks only grew, as it still wasn't clear what Silver Lake's investment thesis would entail and how it would impact the team. NZR had completed some preliminary work in which it had identified seven new potential income streams to explore with Silver Lake. This research forecast that the national body could make $115 million of revenue over the next five years by selling executive coaching ($33.5 million), All Blacks clinics ($14.1 million), e-sports ($6.3 million), virtual signage ($10.8 million), merchandise ($3.4 million), e-commerce/ social selling ($26.9 million) and an NZR-owned and operated broadcast streaming platform ($20.4 million).

While the intent of these initiatives was to find ways to make more money without putting yet greater burden on the players, the high-performance side remained wary about what intellectual property might be given away. This concern was not without foundation, as NZR's first foray into the executive coaching market had been at the 2019 World Cup, when a leadership programme was sold to the top executives of Mitsubishi. The promotional brochure had suggested that much of what was being offered had been lifted straight from the All Blacks' inner sanctum.

Another rising concern was over what sort of demands would ultimately end up being made of the players to facilitate the creation of content for the OTT platform. There were hints about where things were heading when NZR created a new position called 'head of brand and communications' and hired two full-time content creators who travelled everywhere with the All Blacks. These moves were designed to ensure the team presented itself in line with the brand values that Silver Lake and NZR wanted to promote and to project, and to begin gathering imagery and key moments that could be used to build a standalone content platform to better engage and potentially monetise fans.

Rumours circulated that Silver Lake also wanted to encourage individuals within the All Blacks to build and promote their personal brands. This was something that had already begun to happen organically, and older, wiser heads who believed in the longstanding team-first ethos of the All Blacks were wary of encouraging it.

Kieran Read had noted a shift during his last years as All Blacks skipper, and felt that it was a high-performance risk. 'I understand the commercial strategy of the NZR and where they can utilise the All Blacks and that doesn't worry me too much,' he says. 'The thing that probably worries me is if individuals seek their own initiatives or brand, or seek their own stuff ahead of what they are doing with the All Blacks and it becomes quite a big thing. To create a brand, to keep a brand, you have got to do a lot of posting, and it becomes a question of: are you a brand ambassador or are you a rugby player?'

There was no room left in the calendar for Silver Lake to demand the All Blacks play yet more Tests, but Robinson had mentioned many times that the new investor wanted to build stronger narratives around match content, and the players and coaching staff were uncertain what their roles in this might be. Their concerns had been piqued in August 2021, when NZR, due to Covid restrictions, decided to play both its home Bledisloe Cup

Tests at Eden Park over successive weekends. After selling out the first Test, sales the following week were battling to fill even half of the stadium, and staff from the commercial side put direct pressure on coach Ian Foster to do more to promote the game.

In the face of such poor ticket sales, a serious discussion began that week as to whether the All Blacks coach should have a Twitter and/or Instagram account to communicate directly and regularly with fans. Commercial tentacles were spreading into every area of high-performance life. How long would it be before the head coach's job was rebranded as 'Chief Influencer of High Performance', their Twitter account full of sponsored, behind-the-scenes videos thought up by a marketing department eager to make them more relatable to millennials?

But the pressure of commercial imperative was most keenly felt when the All Blacks endured a prolonged form slump between November 2021 and July 2022. After the series loss to Ireland, Robinson and his second-in-charge in professional rugby matters, Chris Lendrum, had no choice but to meet Foster at his house a few days later and tell him that Plumtree and Mooar had to go. That was a valid decision, and indeed one purely based on the team's performance, but it was made seven months too late. Plumtree and Mooar should have been let go at the end of 2021, but Foster had assured the NZR board that he would mentor and upskill his two assistants. To everyone else, this had seemed like a doomed promise, but the board had signed it off – which only highlighted that, between the nine directors, not one had any experience, knowledge, history or direct involvement in the high-performance side of international rugby.

When the All Blacks then lost their next Test – against the Springboks in South Africa – NZR quietly sounded out Crusaders coach Scott Robertson. He was not being offered the job, or even interviewed for it, but he was asked to detail who he would want on his coaching team, should the role become available. With the All Blacks having lost five of their last six Tests, the decision to look at an alternative head coach was justified – but how much pressure was being exerted by investors to see a change at the helm? Or, at least, how much pressure was NZR feeling to appease Silver Lake, and indeed Ineos and Altrad, by giving them Foster's head?

This was the reality of having a heavyweight private-equity group invested in the team, along with two billionaire sponsors. They had been sold a legacy as much as anything else, a promise almost that the All Blacks didn't do prolonged defeats and wallow at number four or five in the world rankings. Big business had paid big money, and it expected big victories. When they didn't come, they needed to see big changes, or at least to know that NZR was actively managing the underperformance. Foster only survived because his recently appointed assistant, former Ireland coach Joe Schmidt, who brought inside knowledge of the Six Nations – which the board saw as invaluable, given it was France and Ireland that kept beating the All Blacks – wasn't willing to work with Robertson.

All this made it clear that a war was raging inside NZR to control the brand narrative of the All Blacks and shape the public's perception of the organisation. And it was a war the commercial team won with little resistance. Ahead of the All

Blacks' third Test against Ireland, in Wellington on 16 July 2022, NZR attempted to micromanage Foster's media performances. He should display more vulnerability, he was told, because the brand story needed a more human element of angst and despair.

A week later, having survived in the role amid heavy speculation that he wouldn't, Foster fronted a media conference at Auckland Airport before travelling to South Africa, where it appeared that he had bowed to the pressure. 'I am Ian Foster, and I am the All Blacks head coach,' he began, visibly emotional. 'Let me tell you who I am, I'm strong, I'm resilient, I think I've proven that.'

It was a clear departure from the Foster everyone knew. The tone and style he was being pressured to adopt were not naturally his, but they suited his employer's vision and served the brand strategy of engaging fans and growing the All Blacks' audience. High performance was now at the total mercy of commercial interests.

CHAPTER EIGHTEEN

DANCING WITH THE DEVIL

FROM COMING INTO THE professional age with $10 million in the bank, broadcast arrangements that were worth a few hundred thousand dollars, and an apparel deal worth $3 million a year with local company Canterbury, NZR was barely recognisable by late 2022. It had $100 million in the bank, and millions more coming via Silver Lake, a broadcast deal worth half a billion dollars, and almost 30 significant sponsors paying collectively more than $100 million a year. The organisation's commercial assets had been valued by one of the world's premium investment houses at $3.5 billion. Long before they sold an equity stake to Silver Lake, the All Blacks had become the most commercialised rugby team in the world.

The results the team has achieved in the professional age would suggest that money has indeed been the great enabler. The All Blacks have won the Rugby Championship (or the Tri-Nations, as it once was) 19 times. They have held the Bledisloe

Cup since 2003, picked up three Grand Slams, set a world record of 18 consecutive victories, and won back-to-back World Cups in 2011 and 2015. They have an 85 per cent win ratio since the game turned professional. All this stands as strong evidence that commercialisation has not killed high performance.

But there are cracks in this amazing record, little signs that hint at the impact of commercialisation and the dangers it presents. Since the All Blacks took back the Bledisloe Cup in 2003, they have beaten Australia 44 times, lost nine and drawn three. The Wallabies are the All Blacks' nearest and most treasured rugby neighbour, so it's not surprising that they've played a significant number of Tests in the professional age. But the players, and many fans, believe they have played too often against Australia.

Between 2008 and 2010, the series was extended to four matches, not at the request of the respective high-performance teams, but because both unions felt they could make money by playing additional games. Removing any doubt that these additional Tests were commercial and not high-performance ventures was the fact they were played in Hong Kong in 2008 and 2010, and in Tokyo in 2009. One of the nine losses the All Blacks suffered against the Wallabies came in Hong Kong in 2010 – a game that was played at a half-empty stadium, producing an occasion and a result that did nothing to enhance the brand.

After it had become clear that Asia didn't have much of an appetite for the Bledisloe Cup, the series reverted to three games a year between 2012 and 2018. The high-performance preference was for two, but the commercial teams on both sides of the Tasman got their way, shoehorning in a third Test without considering the consequences of that decision. The third Bledisloe Test in that six-year period served neither the All Blacks' playing ambitions nor NZR's commercial aspirations.

The coaching staff felt that so much exposure to Australia, a declining force in the global game, didn't push the All Blacks to innovate and refine their own high-performance offering. If anything, playing against a weaker team, as often as they did, forged bad habits within the All Blacks, or at least stalled their growth in developing the attributes that were needed to beat the likes of England, France, Ireland and South Africa.

They perhaps could have accepted that if the commercial returns had been astronomical, but these additional games rarely got anywhere near selling out in Australia, while in New Zealand the interest in the Bledisloe as a contest declined due to overexposure. In 2021, for instance, only 22,000 fans turned up at Eden Park. Everyone was striving for scenarios that were a win for both the commercial and high-performance teams, but the excessive Bledisloe fixtures produced something much closer to a lose-lose.

Maybe those additional Bledisloe games would have been more attractive to the high-performance team if Argentina hadn't been introduced to the Rugby Championship in 2012. The Pumas had embarrassed World Rugby in 2007 when they made the semi-finals of the World Cup at a time when neither the Six Nations nor the Tri-Nations had shown any interest in inviting them to join their respective competitions. They became the bastard child of the world game, unwanted by either hemisphere, until World Rugby stepped in, gave them some cash and promised they would continue to help them meet their ongoing high-performance costs. That was enough for SANZAR to extend the Pumas an invitation to join the Rugby Championship, and while the move was sold as the alliance doing its bit to grow the global game, and welcome an emerging nation on the basis that it was a genuine and credible high-performance force, in reality it was a commercial play to see if there was money to be made by better establishing the game in South America.

Argentina is a country beset by inequity, and while many of its 44 million people live at or below the poverty line, the rugby set are mostly obscenely wealthy corporate types. Argentina also borders Brazil, the 11th-largest economy in the world, and with the game also well established in Uruguay and Chile – both nations have qualified for the 2023 World Cup – the decision to let the Pumas join the Rugby Championship suggests NZR saw South America rather than North America as the more profitable prospect.

Whatever the motivation, bringing the Pumas into the Rugby Championship added a travel component that profoundly altered the elite players' season. And while the six titles the All Blacks won between 2012 and 2018 says they coped admirably with the arrival of Argentina, arguably the impact was felt in the last few weeks of each season, when they travelled to Asia and Europe. Except for their 2007 World Cup quarter-final, the All Blacks didn't lose a Test match in Europe between 2004 and 2010. They played 23 November Tests against Six Nations opponents and won them all. And they typically won emphatically, posting record victories against France in 2004 and then again in 2006, while also posting 25-plus-point margins of victory against England, Wales, Ireland and Scotland at various times.

The picture between 2012 and 2018 was greatly different. The All Blacks were supremely good in the Rugby Championship in those years, losing only two and drawing one of the 36 Tests played, but they lost three times in Europe in the same period, and lost and drew one of the additional Bledisloe Cup Tests they played after they had returned from Argentina.

And rarely did the All Blacks travel to Europe throughout that period and look imperious. In 2013 it took a miracle try after the final whistle to salvage a win in Dublin. In 2016 they scraped home in their final Test in Paris, thanks to a Beauden Barrett intercept on his own tryline. And in 2018 England had a late try disallowed, which enabled New Zealand to hold on for a 16–15 win.

The Northern Hemisphere sides improved greatly after the 2015 World Cup, and that partly explains why the All Blacks didn't enjoy the same success in that part of the world. But between the expansion of Super Rugby, the arrival of Argentina in the Rugby Championship and NZR's desire to play additional Tests in Asia and the United States, there is no doubt New Zealand's best players have found it hard to cope with the increased physical and mental demands of a typical season. NZR's commercial ambitions have made the season just that bit too long and demanding, stretching the players to the point that, in the final few weeks of each year, they are not as sharp or explosive as they need to be.

This was never better illustrated than the contrasting performances the All Blacks produced against Ireland in November 2018 and October 2019. In 2018 the All Blacks were beaten in Dublin. They looked physically tired and mentally flat – perhaps because they were. When the sides met 11 months later at the World Cup – with the All Blacks, free of any commercial imperatives to make money, tailoring their season to ensure they were at their high-performance peak at the tournament – Ireland were obliterated 46–14 in the quarter-final. What would the All Blacks' win–loss record look like if each season were set up exclusively for high performance?

The most damning evidence that commercialisation is hurting performance can be seen in the All Blacks' results post-2019. In the most successful commercial period of NZR's history, between early 2021 and mid-2022 – a period in which it secured a $200-million private-equity investment and six-year sponsorship deals with Ineos and Altrad worth a combined $240 million, and in which its $500-million broadcast deal kicked in – the All Blacks endured their worst run of results in the professional era. At one stage the team lost five of six Tests, as well as suffering the indignity of a first ever home defeat to Argentina. For the first time the All Blacks were beaten in three successive Tests in New Zealand. To those who say commercialisation hasn't impacted the All Blacks: these results beg to differ.

The statistic that should most alarm NZR is that the All Blacks won 90 per cent of their Tests between 2011 and 2016, but only 75 per cent between 2017 and 2022. That means their losing rate increased by 250 per cent between 2017 and 2022, compared with the six seasons from 2011 to 2016.

To some extent, this performance decline reflects the loss of key playing personnel: the retirement of McCaw, Carter and the rest of the golden generation after the 2015 World Cup. But the All Blacks went from losing four Tests in total between 2012 and 2016 to losing four from their first six matches of 2022. For all the brilliance and resilience McCaw and his peers brought to Test rugby, their absence alone doesn't explain the severe deterioration of the All Blacks' results.

The more impactful change within the All Blacks since 2016 has been the increased focus on driving revenue and keeping NZR's accounts out of the red. It was in 2017, conscious that it was forecasting big losses in the years to come, that NZR shifted its commercial programmes into top gear, ramping up the pressure on players and management to service more sponsors, to work with a greater number of stakeholders and to squeeze down high-performance costs wherever possible. Commercialism hasn't just burdened the players with too much content, it has been a major distraction. It has taken too much time and focus away from the intricate and supremely detailed high-performance routines that are all-important in preparing athletes and teams to perform at their best.

The numbers posted in the past six years allude to the new reality that the game in New Zealand is facing: that the biggest threat to the All Blacks' legacy is not the rise of the Six Nations as cohesive, destructive rugby forces, but the ambition of NZR to monetise the brand in partnership with an investor whose primary goal is to leverage the reputation of the brand to make returns of 25 per cent.

NZR, fearful it was being left behind by debt-laden Six Nations unions, which turned to private equity out of desperation, has convinced itself that Silver Lake is the panacea to all its commercial, financial and high-performance ills. Money has always been seen in New Zealand as the great enabler in professional rugby, but those who have prolonged experience of life inside the All Blacks during the past decade fear there is a time it will become the great disabler. And that time may have arrived.

This is a premise NZR has refused to consider, sticking rigidly to its conviction that a direct and correlating relationship exists between commercialisation and high-performance success – that the more money the All Blacks make, the more Test matches they will win. The alternative view is that NZR has taken a colossal risk by partnering with Silver Lake, which will intensify a commercialisation programme that was already beginning to erode the high-performance ability of the All Blacks.

The evidence to support this began to surface almost immediately after Silver Lake paid their first $100 million in mid-2022. The first change was structural, as NZR formed a new company in which it placed all its commercial assets, and then began recruiting an executive and governance team to manage it. As an organisation, NZR today is almost unrecognisable from what it was in 1996. It has a nine-person board overseeing its commercial interests, reporting to a nine-person board that manages high performance and community rugby, but the reporting lines are so confused that few are confident this new system will be well managed, able to make strong and timely decisions and operate without conflict.

Much about NZR is confusing or conflicts with its stated objectives. There's a degree of difficulty, for instance, in understanding what role chief executive Mark Robinson will now play, as the creation of a separate commercial arm means he has lost control of his revenue-generating staff and any direct ability to influence the P&L. He's also a board director of CommCo, and so is fiducially and legally bound to act in its best interests, even if those conflict with the best interests of NZR. In its quest to persuade the players and provinces to approve a deal with Silver Lake, the national body argued that it didn't have the in-house commercial personnel or acumen to drive the sort of revenues it needed, and yet Richard Thomas was promoted from his role as chief commercial officer at NZR to chief executive at CommCo. Finally, NZR's board has no one with any high-performance background, yet sitting on the board of CommCo is Richie McCaw, the greatest rugby player in history, but someone who has no corporate or big business experience.

The players, too, immediately felt the arrival of Silver Lake in 2022. A few weeks before the All Blacks set off on their end-of-season tour to Japan, Wales, Scotland and England, NZR was scrambling to find a production company to make a behind-the-scenes documentary about the team. It wasn't clear exactly what the proposal was, or where the film would be shown, but it spoke to NZR's and Silver Lake's desire to create, own, distribute and monetise All Blacks content.

The professional sports world has been alerted in recent years to the value of unique-access storytelling by the success of the *Drive to Survive* series, which has seen the popularity of Formula 1 explode. Tennis has dipped its toes into the same water with its *Break Point* documentaries, and the Six Nations struck a deal with Netflix in late 2022 to produce a series that would go behind the scenes of the 2023 competition. This sort of content has proven almost as valuable as live broadcast rights, and is exceptionally good at engaging audiences who are attracted more by human stories than by sport itself. Robinson has revealed that NZR is looking to produce 100 hours of long-form television for its own broadcast channel, which will become a key part of its revenue-generating strategy.

This means that, despite the clear warnings that were sounded by coaches and players following Amazon's *All or Nothing* series, cameras will become an almost permanent part of All Blacks life. Having Amazon around in 2017 clearly impacted the team's preparation for the British and Irish Lions series, and created tension between the All Blacks and their employer.

If the coaching staff and players were able to give an honest answer without fear of the consequences, they would say they don't want production houses behind the scenes, now or ever. As several senior members of the management group and players revealed in November 2022, their concerns are not only over the intellectual property being given away, but about the mental exhaustion that comes with the constant demands on their time and the need for them to conform to a brand narrative. But no genuine consultative process exists in a world where commercial imperatives almost always take precedence. The players and coaches will be told that the onus is on them to facilitate the making of content and still win Tests.

Another looming problem is that NZR is driving so much team-related content behind paywalls that it is distancing the All Blacks from the very audience they are trying to engage. The All Blacks are supposedly the New Zealand people's team, but for 27 years they have had no free-to-air television exposure in their home country. The national team are virtual ghosts in hundreds of thousands of lower-income living rooms. This is a frightening prospect for those who believe that young people can't be what they don't see. But NZR has forecast that it will make $20.4 million through its own broadcast platform in the next five years, so the need for paywalled content will likely grow, even if it means fewer people are paying a greater price to view it.

Built into this content plan is a need to change the lifelong key dynamic of the All Blacks' culture. For more than a century, the ethos has been team-first. But now, in a desire to sell the All Blacks to the United States and other offshore markets, the commercial team want individual players to have greater profiles and to feel empowered to build their own brands. Given how aggressively NZR has policed its own backyard in the last decade to deter players from pursuing individual commercial contracts and endorsements, the fact it is now actively encouraging players to showcase themselves represents a stunning reversal. Organisations are of course entitled to change their strategy and adapt their thinking, but some who are close to NZR believe this can only create chaos and conflict, as the biggest stars will inevitably win such profile and financial opportunity that the national body will fear money is being drawn away from the All Blacks.

But perhaps the biggest problem with commercialism is that it is an insidious force, rather than an overtly destructive one, and the damage it causes is hard to detect and easy to deny. It took a decade for the impact of Super Rugby's expansion and the All Blacks' additional Tests to manifest. NZR was slow, too, to detect that there was a cultural shift in its playing base after the 2015 World Cup. McCaw's team will be the last to define the success of a career by the number of All Blacks caps won. He and his peers saw money and commercial opportunity as the by-product of high-performance success; what they chased was rugby excellence. But the players who followed have been more willing to see their career through a broader lens, and to measure their success in money, endorsements and social media followers. They still care about results, but many would prioritise retiring from the game with enough money to know they will never have to work again ahead of winning a World Cup, something that has become apparent by the career choices young players such as Charles Piutau, Steven Luatua and Lima Sopoaga made when they headed offshore for the greater financial benefits despite being key members of the All Blacks at the time. All three were clear about why they were leaving and other players, too, now speak to the media about their desire to set themselves up for life rather than collect Test caps.

Perhaps this is simply generational – a new breed of athletes who are better tapped into the ethos of professional sport. But modern All Blacks might be a product of their environment: that is, their desire to monetise their rugby abilities might be reflective of their experience of a highly commercialised setup. That's not to say they don't treasure playing for the All Blacks, but high-performance swings on tiny margins, and the micro commitments made in training and during games can make all the difference. Sport at the highest level is determined, essentially, by the strength of the commitment of the athletes, and what they have been willing to sacrifice.

It's a big thing to lay at NZR's door, but it is impossible not to wonder whether its incessant desire to make money and drive ever greater commercial activity through the All Blacks has somehow softened the desire within the players to make the sacrifices previous generations did.

The All Blacks of even ten years ago turned up with one thing in mind: to find a way to win. Their singular and obsessive focus was epitomised by Meads playing with a broken arm, Shelford with a ripped testicle and McCaw with a broken foot. There was a mental hardness about those men and their respective teams that suggested they were willing to sacrifice everything to deliver the win. Maybe, in contrast, the current players have come to feel that making money for their employer is just as important as winning Tests – or maybe it is simply that the modern player has had to contend with having to do significantly more commercial activity, and hasn't been able to devote the same time to their high-performance preparation as the early generations of professional players did.

What we can be sure of is that keeping the two worlds of commercialisation and high performance in an amicable and sustainable equilibrium is the single greatest challenge facing NZR, and most likely will remain so. Steve Tew, whose relationships-based management style was ideally suited to finding ways to balance the two worlds through negotiated compromise, puts it best: 'As soon as you start commercialising the game and paying people to be part of it, including the coaches – and they are not the cheapest part of the investment in the game – you put pressure on yourselves. We would have those conversations all the time. "Can we fit another Test match in on the way to Europe?" You start making trade-offs. There was always a tension in delivering properly on our commercial obligations ... We pushed hard but I think we found the balance most of the time. Both sides had to give.

'All the coaches I have dealt with have been frustrated from time to time; equally, all of the really good commercial guys have been frustrated as well, because they think we could do more or could do better. Someone in the organisation has to have a role where they can see both sides of the argument ... [W]hether it is the CEO or general manager of high performance, someone has to be able to see it through both lenses.'

ENDNOTES

CHAPTER THREE – BLACK OUT
1. Vincent Hogan, 'Pressure of Kiwi perfection gives Ireland fighting chance' Irish Independent, 1991. Mentioned in https://www.independent.ie/sport/rugby/vincent-hogan-pressure-of-kiwi-perfection-gives-ireland-fighting-chance-29777777.html

CHAPTER SIX – CRY FOR HELP
1. NZPA, 'Former manager blasts Mitchell', *New Zealand Herald*, 10 December 2003.
2. Gerry Thornley, 'Mehrtens criticises yellow ball', *The Irish Times*, 18 June 2002.

CHAPTER SEVEN – AMATEUR HOUR
1. Wynne Gray, 'Cup report slams two rugby chiefs', *New Zealand Herald*, 24 July 2002.
2. Sir Thomas Eichelbaum's report on the 2003 Rugby World Cup.
3. Sir Thomas Eichelbaum's report on the 2003 Rugby World Cup.

CHAPTER SEVENTEEN – SELLING THE FAMILY SILVER
1. Gregor Paul, '$60 million burden: The greatest threat to All Blacks' performance', *New Zealand Herald*, 11 November 2022.

ACKNOWLEDGEMENTS

A significant number of people were more than generous with their time and agreed to be interviewed specifically for this book. A huge thank you to David Moffett, John Hart, Kevin Roberts, Rob Fisher, John Foley, Richard Reid, Martyn Brewer, David Jones, Andrew Gaze, Chris Moller, David Howman, Simon Johnston, Rob Nichol, Wayne Smith, Steve Tew, Kieran Read, John Fellet, Conrad Smith, Steve Hansen, Warren Alcock, Jeff Wilson and Darren Shand for speaking so freely and honestly. Several other prominent and influential figures were also generous with their time in helping me understand the story I was trying to write and allowed me to check facts against their knowledge. Their help was invaluable; thank you all.

I'd like to thank Eduan Roos, Winston Aldworth, Cameron McMillan, Steve Holloway and Miriyana Alexander at the *New Zealand Herald* for indulging me in my passion to write about the business of sport and develop the sort of understanding about the commercialisation of the All Blacks which made this book possible.

Of course, this book needed a champion and once again, I found one in Alex Hedley at HarperCollins, who was able to see that the arrival of giant US fund manager Silver Lake as an equity partner in New Zealand Rugby in 2022, would dramatically elevate the scale and speed of the commercialisation of the All Blacks. He and the rest of the team trusted me to bring a potentially complex and dry story to life and I'll forever be grateful that they gave me that opportunity. And specifically at HarperCollins, thank you to Chris Kunz and Julian Welch for making this a much better book.

And finally, thank you to my family, who endured hearing my endless phone calls on the topic of All Blacks commercialisation during the extended Auckland lockdown of 2021 and probably feel they know this story better than I do. And maybe they are right – I do shout when I'm on the phone, and I promise I'll try to fix that before I write another book.